TExES Reading Specialist
151 Teacher Certification Exam

By: Sharon Wynne, M.S.
Southern Connecticut State University

"And, while there's no reason yet to panic, I think it's only prudent that we make preparations to panic."

XAMonline, INC.
Boston

Copyright © 2007 XAMonline, Inc.
All rights reserved. No part of the material protected by this copyright notice may be reproduced or utilized in any form or by any means, electronic or mechanical, including photocopying, recording or by any information storage and retrievable system, without written permission from the copyright holder.

To obtain permission(s) to use the material from this work for any purpose including workshops or seminars, please submit a written request to:

XAMonline, Inc.
21 Orient Ave.
Melrose, MA 02176
Toll Free 1-800-509-4128
Email: info@xamonline.com
Web www.xamonline.com
Fax: 1-781-662-9268

Library of Congress Cataloging-in-Publication Data

Wynne, Sharon A.
    Reading Specialist 151: Teacher Certification / Sharon A. Wynne. -2nd ed.
    ISBN 978-1-58197-941-1
        1. Reading Specialist 151.   2. Study Guides.   3. TExES
        4. Teachers' Certification & Licensure.   5. Careers

Disclaimer:
The opinions expressed in this publication are the sole works of XAMonline and were created independently from the National Education Association, Educational Testing Service, or any State Department of Education, National Evaluation Systems or other testing affiliates.

Between the time of publication and printing, state specific standards as well as testing formats and website information may change that is not included in part or in whole within this product. Sample test questions are developed by XAMonline and reflect similar content as on real tests; however, they are not former tests. XAMonline assembles content that aligns with state standards but makes no claims nor guarantees teacher candidates a passing score. Numerical scores are determined by testing companies such as NES or ETS and then are compared with individual state standards. A passing score varies from state to state.

Printed in the United States of America   œ-1

TExES: Reading Specialist 151
ISBN: 978-1-58197-941-1

TABLE OF CONTENTS

DOMAIN I. **INSTRUCTION AND ASSESSMENT: COMPONENTS OF LITERACY**

Great Study and Testing Tips!

What to study in order to prepare for the subject assessments is the focus of this study guide but equally important is *how* you study.

You can increase your chances of truly mastering the information by taking some simple, but effective steps.

Study Tips:

1. Some foods aid the learning process. Foods such as milk, nuts, seeds, rice, and oats help your study efforts by releasing natural memory enhancers called CCKs (*cholecystokinin*) composed of *tryptophan*, *choline*, and *phenylalanine*. All of these chemicals enhance the neurotransmitters associated with memory. Before studying, try a light, protein-rich meal of eggs, turkey, and fish. All of these foods release the memory enhancing chemicals. The better the connections, the more you comprehend.

Likewise, before you take a test, stick to a light snack of energy boosting and relaxing foods. A glass of milk, a piece of fruit, or some peanuts all release various memory-boosting chemicals and help you to relax and focus on the subject at hand.

2. Learn to take great notes. A by-product of our modern culture is that we have grown accustomed to getting our information in short doses (i.e. TV news sound bites or USA Today style newspaper articles.)

Consequently, we've subconsciously trained ourselves to assimilate information better in neat little packages. If your notes are scrawled all over the paper, it fragments the flow of the information. Strive for clarity. Newspapers use a standard format to achieve clarity. Your notes can be much clearer through use of proper formatting. A very effective format is called the *"Cornell Method."*

Take a sheet of loose-leaf lined notebook paper and draw a line all the way down the paper about 1-2" from the left-hand edge.

Draw another line across the width of the paper about 1-2" up from the bottom. Repeat this process on the reverse side of the page.

Look at the highly effective result. You have ample room for notes, a left hand margin for special emphasis items or inserting supplementary data from the textbook, a large area at the bottom for a brief summary, and a little rectangular space for just about anything you want.

3. Get the concept then the details. Too often we focus on the details and don't gather an understanding of the concept. However, if you simply memorize only dates, places, or names, you may well miss the whole point of the subject.

A key way to understand things is to put them in your own words. If you are working from a textbook, automatically summarize each paragraph in your mind. If you are outlining text, don't simply copy the author's words.

Rephrase them in your own words. You remember your own thoughts and words much better than someone else's, and subconsciously tend to associate the important details to the core concepts.

4. Ask Why? Pull apart written material paragraph by paragraph and don't forget the captions under the illustrations.

Example: If the heading is "Stream Erosion", flip it around to read "Why do streams erode?" Then answer the questions.

If you train your mind to think in a series of questions and answers, not only will you learn more, but it also helps to lessen the test anxiety because you are used to answering questions.

5. Read for reinforcement and future needs. Even if you only have 10 minutes, put your notes or a book in your hand. Your mind is similar to a computer; you have to input data in order to have it processed. *By reading, you are creating the neural connections for future retrieval.* The more times you read something, the more you reinforce the learning of ideas.

Even if you don't fully understand something on the first pass, *your mind stores much of the material for later recall.*

6. Relax to learn so go into exile. Our bodies respond to an inner clock called biorhythms. Burning the midnight oil works well for some people, but not everyone.

If possible, set aside a particular place to study that is free of distractions. Shut off the television, cell phone, and pager and exile your friends and family during your study period.

If you really are bothered by silence, try background music. Light classical music at a low volume has been shown to aid in concentration over other types. Music that evokes pleasant emotions without lyrics is highly suggested. Try just about anything by Mozart. It relaxes you.

7. <u>Use arrows not highlighters</u>. At best, it's difficult to read a page full of yellow, pink, blue, and green streaks. Try staring at a neon sign for a while and you'll soon see that the horde of colors obscure the message.

A quick note, a brief dash of color, an underline, and an arrow pointing to a particular passage is much clearer than a horde of highlighted words.

8. <u>Budget your study time</u>. Although you shouldn't ignore any of the material, *allocate your available study time in the same ratio that topics may appear on the test.*

Testing Tips:

1. Get smart, play dumb. Don't read anything into the question. Don't make an assumption that the test writer is looking for something else than what is asked. Stick to the question as written and don't read extra things into it.

2. Read the question and all the choices *twice* before answering the question. You may miss something by not carefully reading, and then re-reading both the question and the answers.

If you really don't have a clue as to the right answer, leave it blank on the first time through. Go on to the other questions, as they may provide a clue as to how to answer the skipped questions.

If later on, you still can't answer the skipped ones . . . *Guess.* The only penalty for guessing is that you *might* get it wrong. Only one thing is certain; if you don't put anything down, you will get it wrong!

3. Turn the question into a statement. Look at the way the questions are worded. The syntax of the question usually provides a clue. Does it seem more familiar as a statement rather than as a question? Does it sound strange?

By turning a question into a statement, you may be able to spot if an answer sounds right, and it may also trigger memories of material you have read.

4. Look for hidden clues. It's actually very difficult to compose multiple-foil (choice) questions without giving away part of the answer in the options presented.

In most multiple-choice questions you can often readily eliminate one or two of the potential answers. This leaves you with only two real possibilities and automatically your odds go to Fifty-Fifty for very little work.

5. Trust your instincts. For every fact that you have read, you subconsciously retain something of that knowledge. On questions that you aren't really certain about, go with your basic instincts. **Your first impression on how to answer a question is usually correct.**

6. Mark your answers directly on the test booklet. Don't bother trying to fill in the optical scan sheet on the first pass through the test.

Just be very careful not to miss-mark your answers when you eventually transcribe them to the scan sheet.

7. Watch the clock! You have a set amount of time to answer the questions. Don't get bogged down trying to answer a single question at the expense of 10 questions you can more readily answer.

DOMAIN I.   **INSTRUCTION AND ASSESSMENT:
                                                   COMPONENTS OF LITERACY**

COMPETENCY 1.0 ORAL LANGUAGE

**Skill 1.1   Knows the basic linguistic patterns and structures of oral
              languages, such as continuous and stop sounds and
              coarticulation of sounds**

The theory of coarticulation was developed in the 1960's and 70's in order to
overcome a deficiency in the theory of classical phonetics. In classical phonetics,
the individual sounds are isolated and taught out of context. These sounds had
static descriptions and were often prescriptive, not paying any attention to the
dynamics of speech. However, through experimenting with speech sounds, it
became apparent that speech was continuous rather than being discrete sounds.

According to coarticulation theorists, speech is a string of discrete sounds that
run into each other. They even proposed that it involved muscular control to
produce individual sounds. The movement of the tongue is responsible for
producing specific sounds, and children learn to control the tongue as they start
to speak. The greater the speed of the speech, the more continuous the sounds
become.

Coarticulation is not specific to any one language, but it does seem to vary with
language and dialect. Speech requires ongoing decision making based on
modeling of sounds that children hear from adult and child models.

Phonology is the study of speech and sounds. How each person pronounces a
word in English depends to a great deal on where that person is from and the
specific dialect of the region. It also depends on the age of the person. Hearing
how words are pronounced has a definite effect on how the listener will
pronounce a word as well.

**Skill 1.2   Demonstrates knowledge of stages and milestones in
              acquiring oral language and of relationships between oral
              language development and the development of reading**

There are five major milestones in the acquisition of oral language:

- Birth to 6 months – prelinguistic stage
- 6 to 8 months is the first onset of language acquisition in the form of
  babbling
- First words emerge at about 10 to 12 months
- First manifestation of syntax emerges at about 20 to 24 months when
  children start to put words together
- Telegraphic speech develops at about 36 to 40 months

Parents do not teach children grammar when they first learn to speak. Rather children learn by hearing adults and those around them speaking. The words are not pronounced properly, and sentence structure evolves as children start to put words together.

While children do not need direct instruction to learn to speak, they do need direct instruction to read. Beginning readers need to learn phonological awareness – a knowledge of letters and their respective sounds. As children develop in oral language, they realize that print carries meaning. When children are read to, they develop this recognition and are able to read pictures first because they remember the stories associated with them. They can also make up their own stories based on the pictures because of background knowledge about pictures telling stories. This, of course, depends on the amount of exposure that young children have to books and reading.

The stages of progressing from speaking and listening to reading and writing involve learning the following:

- The letters of the alphabet

- The sounds of the language

- How to segment words into syllables

- Simple word recognition

- Phonemic blends

When children enter school in kindergarten, they have mastered most of the sounds of the English language and can communicate with other students and the teacher. Children do have difficulty realizing that every spoken word corresponds to a written word, mainly because of the spaces between the words on a page. When spoken, the words seem to be a continuous stream, and many children begin reading with little or no awareness of how speech is divided into units – words. Teachers can help students develop a sight vocabulary of the words in their oral vocabulary. When students see words they use on a regular basis in print, they can then easily transfer their oral language skills to reading.

Skill 1.3   **Knows how to plan, implement, and monitor age-appropriate instruction that is responsive to individual students' strengths, needs, and interests and is based on ongoing informal and formal assessment of individual student's oral language development**

In kindergarten, teachers must be aware of the students' oral language skills as this is central to them becoming fluent readers and writers in the later grades. In any grade, the instruction the teacher designs must include opportunities for the students to use oral language to make sense of their experiences and to engage in new learning. Just as there should be daily opportunities for reading, listening, writing, and viewing; there must be daily opportunities for speaking built into the lesson plans. What this looks like is different for each grade level. For primary grades, it will be how the students interact with each other at play; while in the higher grades, it could be the form of discussion the students engage in about the topics being taught in class.

Experimenting with correct and incorrect language is the way students make sense of the learning. By listening to the students' oral language and making anecdotal notes, the teacher can have an informal assessment that shows growth over time. In the primary grades, teachers will be concerned with the correct pronunciation of the words and children's willingness to speak in class. In the upper elementary and high school grades, the assessment will take the form of how well the students can use oral language to make a point, demonstrate how much they have learned, debate an issue, or present a point of view.

Formal assessment of oral language skills will also differ according to the age and grade level of the student. For younger students, it can take the form of having them retell a story in their own words. The teacher can assess how well they can communicate the idea of the story in words so that the meaning is clear to the listeners. The use of vocabulary and pronunciation of words will help the teacher determine what direction the next instruction has to take. For older students, formal assessment can take the form of evaluating student performances when speaking to an audience, such as in giving a report or in general discussion in a literature group.

Skill 1.4 **Applies knowledge of instructional progressions, methods and materials that build on and support students' oral language skills, reflect students' cultural and linguistic diversity and are based on a convergence of research evidence (e.g., reading aloud, dramatic play, classroom conversations, songs, rhymes, stories, games, language play, discussions, questioning, sharing information)**

<u>Choral speaking</u> is one of the most effective ways to help build oral language skills. Using the phrase "repeat after me" helps students develop the proper pronunciation of words. When teachers use this instructional method when pointing to words written on a chart, they not only build on the students' oral language skills, but they show how print carries meaning and how the spoken word is represented in print.

<u>Reading Aloud</u> to students is entertaining and helps to develop a love of reading in the students. However, it also provides them with a model of what good reading and speaking sounds like. By reading aloud to students on a daily basis, teachers help to increase their attention span and listening ability. It helps to expand the students' vocabulary, and demonstrates the connection between oral and written text. When reading aloud to the class, teachers should read the material silently beforehand to demonstrate good reading techniques. If the book is one teachers have not read before, then they should tell the students this. It is also good for the students to see how teachers can stumble over words and use strategies to help figure out how to pronounce a word. For early grades, the students should be able to follow along by seeing the words and pictures. In all cases, teachers should speak clearly and distinctly.

<u>Dramatic Play</u> allows students to explore the world of the classroom and engage in imaginative conversations. Quite often, teachers so not realize the importance of this aspect of oral-language development and dismiss it in favor of covering the curriculum. Through the use of observing dramatic play in the classroom, teachers can informally assess the students and determine the direction individual instruction needs to take. Through the use of this activity, students can control what is happening and make use of their prior knowledge to build new experiences with language.
In order to make dramatic play a part of the classroom routine, reading teachers should make the time for such activity available in the daily timetable. They also need to make the necessary materials available to the children, such as in the form of a dress-up box or a puppet stage.

<u>Classroom Conversations</u> provide an informal methods of finding out where students are in their oral language development. These conversations may be between teachers and students or among the students in a group. Students talk among themselves in all grades; and, in the higher grades, it can take the form of

class discussions, literature circles, debates, or dialogues between teachers and the students about what is happening in their lives.

Songs, Rhymes, Stories, Games – all of these contribute to oral language development. Children love to learn songs; and, by using rhyming books, they can associate the sounds of language with letters so that they can recognize other words and thus expand their vocabulary. Reading classrooms should have games that children can play at their age level, such as Scrabble, Charades, Pictionary, etc.

Questioning is a major part of all reading classrooms; teachers ask the students questions about what they have read or are reading. While teachers may be asking the questions to determine the students' comprehension, asking questions is also a way of determining oral language skills through monitoring the way that the students answer the questions. Students also ask questions of teachers, and by paying particular attention to the way the students phrase questions teachers can also determine instructional needs.

Skill 1.5   Knows how to provide systematic oral language instruction using language structures and pronunciations commonly associated with standard English

Children come to school with a considerable amount of oral language experience. Some of them, however, may not be able to pronounce their words correctly; and, depending on the home background of the child, they may not have an abundance of vocabulary or complex language structures. There may also be children in the classroom for whom English is not the native tongue. Regardless of the individual situations, teachers must model correct speech and language. They should also model language structures that are rich in vocabulary and that may be different from the structures (such as slang words) that students use outside of school.

Reading specialists and teachers must provide frequent opportunities in the classroom for students to use and develop their oral language skills. This includes frequent opportunities for discussion, conversation, and asking and answering questions.

Skill 1.6 **Demonstrates knowledge of delays or differences in students' oral language development and when such delays/differences warrant further assessment and additional intervention**

Not all children progress at the same rate in oral language development. For some children, delays and differences are recognizable right from the start; and, for others, they may not be identified until the children start school. Researchers estimate that between 5% and 10% of school age children do have developmental delays in speaking. A delay in oral language is defined as one that is characterized by a deficiency in comprehension or production of language. It can involve problems with phonology, syntax, semantics, pragmatics or form. Children with a deficiency in oral language development will likely experience problems with reading and writing. For this reason, it is important for the reading specialist to be able to identify these children and take steps to remedy the situation.

A language delay means that students need direct instruction to enable them to develop as they should. For some children, it may mean instruction in the correct pronunciation of words or instruction in how to put words together to form sentences. Age-appropriate vocabulary instruction will help children to expand their vocabulary; and, through continued help, students will eventually catch up with those of their age group.

At ages four to six, children should be easy to understand when they speak. They may still be experiencing difficulty with certain sounds, such as "sh," "ch," "z," "th," "j," and "r". Mistakes with consonant blends are relatively common in this age group. By the age of eight, students should be able to pronounce all consonant blends clearly.

Children with language disorders need more-specialized help. There are three categories of language disorders that reading specialists should be aware of:

1. Central Processing – these are language disorders related to the function of the brain. They are evident in children with Down's Syndrome, ADD, or brain injuries.

2. Peripheral Factors – children who are hearing or visually impaired may have disorders that affect the sensory and motor systems, resulting in an inability to progress normally in oral language development.

3. Environmental Factors – these are factors that reading specialists can work on, but they may need help in some circumstances. Children who do suffer a language delay or disorder due to environmental conditions may be the victims of neglect or abuse. Once reading specialists work with them with focused oral language instruction, they usually develop normally. However, there may be behavioral or emotional development issues that reading specialists are not equipped to handle.

Some children may need to be referred to a speech pathologist. This professional is trained in speech, language and communication disorders and has the skills necessary to help children (through focused instruction in oral skills) who do not seem to progress at a regular rate.

COMPETENCY 2.0 PHONOLOGICAL AND PHONEMIC AWARENESS

Skill 2.1   Demonstrates knowledge of expected stages and milestones in acquiring phonological and phonemic awareness and of relationships between phonological and phonemic awareness and reading acquisition

Phonological awareness means the ability of the reader to recognize the sounds or phonemes of spoken language. This recognition includes how these sounds can be blended together, segmented (divided up), and manipulated (switched around).   This awareness eventually leads to phonics, a method for decoding language by unlocking letter-sound or grapheme-phoneme relationships.

Development of phonological skills for most children begins during the pre-K years. Indeed by the age of 5, a child who has been exposed to fingerplays and poetry can recognize a rhyme. Such a child can demonstrate phonological awareness by filling in the missing rhyming word in a familiar rhyme or rhymed picture book. The procedure of filling in a missing word is called the cloze procedure. It can be used in oral or print literacy activities.

One teaches children phonological awareness by directly pointing out the sounds made by letters singly (as in /b/) or in combination (as in /bl/), and to recognize individual sounds in words.

Phonological awareness skills include but are not limited to the following:

I. Rhyming and syllabification
2. Blending sounds into words—such as pic-tur-bo-k
3. Identifying beginning or initial phonemes and ending or final phonemes in short, one-syllable words
4. Breaking words down into sounds- which is also called "segmenting" words
5. Removing initial sounds, and substituting others. An example is /bat/ minus the /b/ with an /m/ substituted becomes /mat/.

Phonemic awareness and the sounds of the letters are important factors in teaching children to read. Phonemic awareness is the ability to hear sounds (phonemes) and to manipulate them to produce words. Being able to recognize phonemes is the first step in beginning to read.

Based on convergent research, it is known that phonemic awareness can be taught and learned. It helps students learn to read and spell, but it is most effective when teachers use the letters of the alphabet when teaching phonemes rather than using phonemes alone. Additionally, teachers should concentrate on only one or two phonemes at a time rather than introducing too many at once. Using too many at once confuses the students and makes it more difficult for them. Small-group instruction has also proven to be more effective for this direct instruction rather than whole-class settings.

The stages of phonological development are discussed in Skill 1.2, and students should be able to detect phonemes and blend sounds together regularly by the time they are 7 or 8 years old.

Skill 2.2   **Knows how to plan, implement, and monitor age-appropriate instruction that is responsive to individual students' strengths, needs and interests and is based on ongoing informal and formal assessment of individual students' phonological and phonemic awareness**

The Role of Phonological Awareness in Reading Development

Instructional methods to teach phonological awareness may include any or all of the following:

1. Auditory games during which children recognize and manipulate the sounds of words, separate or segment the sounds of words, take out sounds, blend sounds, add in new sounds, or take apart sounds to recombine them in new formations.

2. Snap game- the teacher says two words. The children snap their fingers if the two words share a sound, which might be at the beginning, or end of the word. Children hear initial phonemes most easily, followed by final ones. Medial or middle sounds are most difficult for young children to discriminate. One sees this in their oral responses as well as in their invented spelling. Silence occurs if the words share no sounds. Children love this simple game and it also helps with classroom management.

3. Language games model for children identification of rhyming words. These games help inspire children to create their own rhymes.

4. Read books that rhyme such as *Sheep in A Jeep* by Nancy Shaw or *The Fox on a Box* by Barbara Gregorich.

5. Share books with children that use alliteration (words that begin with the same sound) such as *Avalanche, A to Z*.

Assessment of Phonological Awareness

These skills can be assessed by having the child listen to the teacher say two words. Then ask the child to decide if these two words are the same word repeated twice or two different words.

When making this assessment, when using two different words, make certain that they only differ by only one phoneme, such as /d/ and /g/.

Children can be assessed on words which are not real words that are familiar to them. Words used can be make-believe words.

The Role of Phonological Processing in the Development of Individual Students

Children who are raised in homes where English is not the first language and or where standard English is not spoken, may have difficulty with hearing the difference between similar sounding words like "send" and "sent." Any child who is not in a home, day care, or preschool environment where English phonology operates, may have difficulty perceiving and demonstrating the differences between English language phonemes. If children can not hear the difference between words that "sound the same" like "grow" and "glow," they will be confused when these words appear in a print context. This confusion will of course, sadly, impact their comprehension.

Considerations for teaching phonological processing to ELL children include recognition by the teacher that what works for the English language speaking child from an English language speaking family, does not necessarily work in other languages.

Research recommends that ELL children learn to read initially in their first language. It is critical for ELL learn to speak English before being taught to read English. Research supports that oral language development lays the foundation for phonological awareness.

All phonological instruction programs must be tailored to the children's learning backgrounds. Rhymes and alliteration introduced to ELL children should be read or shared with them in their first language, if at all possible.

Within the classroom setting, many opportunities will present themselves for students to speak and listen for various purposes, and often these may be spontaneous. Activities for speaking and listening should be integrated throughout the language arts program, but there should also be times when speaking and listening are the focus of the instruction. By incorporating speaking and listening into the language arts program, students will begin to see the connection between the two and, therefore, be able to improve their reading skills with more efficiency.

Some of the ways that speaking and listening can be integrated include:

- Conversations
- Small group discussions
- Brainstorming
- Interviewing
- Oral reading
- Readers' Theatre
- Choral speaking
- Storytelling
- Role playing
- Booktalks
- Oral reports
- Class debates
- Listening to guest speakers

Skill 2.3   Applies knowledge of instructional sequences, strategies, and materials that reflect cultural and linguistic diversity, are based on a convergence or research evidence, and promote students' phonological and phonemic awareness

Phonemic awareness is a specific skill within the broader category of phonological awareness. Probably developing fairly late, it is the knowledge that words are comprised of individual phonemes that can be blended.
Theorist Marilyn Jager Adams who researches early reading has outlined five basic types of phonemic awareness tasks.

Task 1- Ability to hear rhymes and alliteration.
For example, the children would listen to a poem, rhyming picture book or song and identify the rhyming words heard which the teacher might then record or list on chart.

Task 2- Ability to do oddity tasks (recognize the member of a set that is different [odd} among the group.
For example, the children would look at the pictures of grass, a garden and a rose, answering, Which one starts with a different sound?

Task 3 –The ability to orally blend words and split syllables.
For example, the children can say the first sound of a word and then the rest of the word and put it together as a single word.

Task 4 –The ability to orally segment words.
For example, the ability to count sounds. The child would be asked to count or clap the sounds in "hamburger."
Task 5- The ability to do phonics manipulation tasks.
For example, replace the "r" sound in rose with a "p" sound.

The Role of Phonemic Awareness in Reading Development

Children who have problems with phonics generally have not acquired or been exposed to phonemic awareness activities at home or in preschool-2. This includes extensive songs, rhymes and read–alouds.

Instructional Methods

Since the ability to distinguish between individual sounds, or phonemes, within words is a prerequisite to association of sounds with letters and manipulating sounds to blend words—a fancy way of saying "reading," the teaching of phonemic awareness is crucial to emergent literacy (early childhood K-2 reading instruction). Children need a strong background in phonemic awareness in order for phonics instruction (sound –spelling relationship-printed materials) to be effective.

Instructional methods that may be effective for teaching phonemic awareness can include:

- Clapping syllables in words

- Distinguishing between a word and a sound

- Using visual cues and movements to help children understand when the speaker goes from one sound to another

- Incorporating oral segmentation activities which focus on easily distinguished syllables rather than sounds

- Singing familiar songs (e.g. Happy Birthday, Knick Knack Paddy Wack) and replacing key words those of a different ending

- Dealing children a deck of picture cards and having them sound out the words for the pictures on their cards or calling for a picture by asking for its first and last sound.

Since phonemic awareness is a mostly auditory skill, it can often be completed with little to no materials necessary. It can also be integrated into almost any activity you are completing during the day in any subject. The other nice thing about phonemic awareness instruction is that it is best delivered in short segments several times throughout the day. Usually, it is best worked on in less than five-minute intervals a few times during the school day.

As stated before, phonemic awareness skills are auditory skills. Some of these skills later will be combined with print as the child transitions to phonics; but, in a true phonemic awareness activity, there is no print involved. Phonemic awareness skills include rhyming, beginning-sound identification, ending-sound identification, syllabification, insertion of sounds, deletion of sounds, and segmentation of sounds.

In order to promote phonemic awareness in students, a teacher can employ many different types of activities. One of the most powerful methods can be using texts that contain rhyming and alliteration patterns. Using nursery rhymes or songs is an excellent way to help children begin to hear the patterns of sounds in words. Books with repetitive language also help students begin to apply these patterns. Many students also enjoy tongue-twisters and the old-fashioned jump-rope songs.

As you progress to more complex levels of phonemic awareness, introducing pictures and game formats is a fun way for teachers to help the students to move on to the next level. Anytime teachers can add manipulatives to a normally auditory-only skill, the students have a better chance at obtaining the skill. An example of this might be to provide the students with blocks or cubes to represent the number of sounds when counting syllables or sounds in a word,. The game format allows the students to receive numerous repetitions in a friendly format that they enjoy and will want to continue.

Other activities can be integrated throughout the day as opportunities arise. While waiting in the hall for a special class or for students to finish at the bathroom, teachers could ask one or several students for words that rhyme with a certain word or for words that begin with a given sound. In math class, teachers could test a counting skill and a phonemic awareness skill by asking students to count out the same number of blocks as a given word has syllables. In science class, clues could be given for the key concept by using phonemic-awareness skills. For example, teachers could state that they are thinking of a word that rhymes with ant and begins like 'please.' The children would then respond with 'plant,' and a unit on plants has been introduced. These easy-to-implement, quick activities are indeed the most effective methods for teaching phonemic awareness.

Assessment of Phonemic Awareness

Teachers can maintain ongoing logs and rubrics for assessment throughout the year of phonemic awareness for individual children. Such assessments would identify particular stated reading behaviors or performance standards, the date of observation of the child's behavior (in this context-phonemic activity or exercise), and comments.

The rubric or legend for assessing these behaviors might include the following descriptors:
- demonstrates or exhibits reading behavior consistently,
- makes progress/strides toward this reading behavior, and
- has not yet demonstrated or exhibited this behavior.

Depending on the particular phonemic task the teacher models, the performance task might include:

- Saying rhyming words in response to an oral prompt
- Segmenting a word spoken by the teacher into its beginning, middle and ending sounds
- Counting correctly the number of syllables in a spoken word

Phonological awareness involves the recognition that spoken words are composed of a set of smaller units such as onsets and rimes, syllables, and sounds.

Phonemic awareness is a specific type of phonological awareness which focuses on the ability to distinguish, manipulate and blend specific sounds or phonemes within an individual word.

Think of phonological awareness as an umbrella and phonemic awareness as a specific spoke under this umbrella.

Phonics deals with printed words and the learning of sound-spelling correlations, while phonemic awareness activities are oral.

In reviewing reading research and theory, new distinctions and definitions appear often. The body of reading knowledge changes over time. The information and definitions in this guide are those accepted in the year of its publication and the time of its authoring and updating. As changes occur in accepted theories, they will be made in the guides and in the certification exams.

"If you believe that you learn to read by reading, you must learn to want to read. Reading to children, therefore models both the "how" and "why" of reading."
Helen Depree and Sandra Iversen-Early Literacy in the Classroom
"The long talk that parents have put off about the ways of the world might need to be an introduction to the facts about the English alphabet."
Terrence Moore-Ashbrook Center Fellow-Principal of Ridgeview Classical Schools in Fort Collins, Colorado

Skill 2.4   Knows how to provide systematic age-appropriate instruction and reinforcing activities to promote the development of students' phonological and phonemic awareness

Strategies for Promoting an Understanding of the Directionality of Print

In order to become proficient readers, young students need to develop a complete understanding that all print is read from left to right and top to bottom. Modeling is one of the most important strategies a teacher can use to develop this understanding in children. The use of big books, poems, and charts are strategies teachers can use in both large and small group instruction. Simple questions can engage the students to pay closer attention to these skills (i.e. "We are going to read this passage, where should I put my pointer to start reading?").

Directionality of print should also be taught during the writing process. In language experience stories, interactive writing, and Kidwriting©, the teacher can incorporate explicit modeling and instruction in these skills. Sometimes it may be necessary to provide children with a dot at the top left corner of the paper in order to provide a visual reminder of where to begin.

Techniques for Promoting the Ability to Track Print in Connected Texts

Model directionality and one-to-one word matching by pointing to words, while using a big book, pocket chart, or poem written out on a chart. As you repeatedly lead the children in this reading, they can follow along and eventually track the print and make one to one matches on the connected text independently. They can also practice by using a pointer (all children love to use the pointer because then pleasure becomes associated with the reading) or their fingers to follow the words. Children happily volunteer to be the point person. Even before Vanna White, the joy of "signifying letters" existed and has tremendous appeal for children.

Copy down a brief, familiar rhyme (perhaps from a favorite book or song) and post it in the room at child's eye level, so the children can independently walk around and read it.

Copy down a brief or familiar rhyme or poem on individual word cards. Then challenge the children in small groups or independently to reassemble and display them on a pocket chart. As children "play" with constructing and reconstructing this pocket chart, they will develop an awareness of directionality, one on one matching of print to spoken words, spacing, and punctuation.

Model interactive emergent writing with the class. While the teacher is noting down the weather, deliberately ask and have the children suggest where the first word in that report should go, top or bottom of the board? Will the first letter be upper case or lower case? What goes at the end of the sentence?

Create with the children sing-song repetitions/rules for using capitals, periods, commas, etc. Encourage the children to begin reciting these sing-songs as soon as they identify specific concepts of print in connected texts.

Model for children how, when pointing at words, they can start at the top and move from left to right. Tell the children that if there are more words to the sentence they are reading under the first line of print, they must go back to the left and under the previous line. Young children enjoy practicing this kinesthetic "return sweep." You might want to teach them to identify the need to do this by saying "Don't fall asleep at the page" or "Time to get to the "return sweep" stage!!" Post this saying and encourage them to singsong as they joyously take ownership of their reading.

Have even beginning readers "read" through the text to find letters they recognize in the story and then share some of the text that includes these specific letters to whet their appetite for reading.

Strategies for Promoting Letter Knowledge and Letter Formation

Engage the children in a Tale Trail game. Use a story they have already heard or read. Ask the children to circle certain letters and then reread the story, sharing the letters they have circled.

Give the children lots of opportunities to do letter sorts. Pass out word cards which have the targeted letter on them. Ask the children to come up and display their answers to questions like these about the letter, say *R*.

*R as the first letter--rose, rise, ran,
*R as the last letter--car, star, far,
*R with a t after it--start, heart, part, smart
*R, two r's in the middle of a word-- carry, sorry, starry

Play "What's in a Name?"- Select a student's name "William." Copy it down on a sentence strip. Have the children count the number of letters in the name and how many of them appear twice. Allow them to talk about which letter is upper case and which letters are lower case. Have the students chant the name. Then rewrite the name on another sentence strip. Have the strip cut into separate letters and see if some one from the class can put the name back correctly.
As you read a book with or to children, ask that they show you specific letters or lower case or upper case letters. Read the text first and encourage as many children to come up and identify the letters as possible. Use a big book and have felt and sandpaper letters available for display as well. If grade, age and developmentally appropriate, have children then write the letter they identified themselves or even more fun, construct it using pipe cleaners, play dough or coded colored markers (different colors for upper and lower case letters).

Play "letter leap" with the children and have them look carefully at the room to identify labeled items that begin with a specific letter by "leaping" over to them and placing a large lettered placard next to them. Children who are advanced in letter formation can then be challenged to "leap" through the classroom when called upon to literally "letter" unlabeled objects.

Recognition that Phonemes are Represented by Letters and Letter Pairs

As young children begin to learn to read, connections are made between the printed letters on the page and the sounds they have heard in language. Phonemic awareness activities are crucial for building this bridge. Students have engaged in many auditory activities. At this time, it is important the teacher use explicit and systematic methods to demonstrate to the students how these auditory sounds are represented on a page by letters or sometimes letter pairs. As this occurs, students can begin to decode text and move toward becoming proficient readers.

Use of Reading and Writing Strategies for Teaching Letter-sound Correspondence

Provide children with a sample of a single letter book (or create one from environmental sources, newspapers, coupons, circulars, magazines or your own text ideas). Make sure that your already published or created sample includes a printed version of the letter in both upper and lower case forms. Make certain that each page contains a picture of something that starts with that specific letter and also has the word for the picture. The book you select or create should be a predictable one in that when the picture is identified, the word can be read.

Once the children have been provided with your sample and have listened to it being read, challenge them to each make a one letter book. Often it is best to focus on familiar consonants for the single letter book or the first letter of the child's first name. Using the first letter of the child's first name, invites the child to develop a book which tells about him or her and the words that he or she finds. This is an excellent way to have the reading and writing workshop enhance the teaching of the alphabetic principle. Encourage children to be active writers and readers by finding words for their book on the classroom word wall, in alphabet books in the special alphabet book bin and in grade and age appropriate pictionaries, (dictionaries for younger children which are filled with pictures).

Of course, the richest resource within the reading and writing workshop classroom for teaching and fostering the alphabetic principle lies in the use of alphabet books as anchor books for inspiring students writing. While young children in grades K-1 will do better with the one letter book authoring activity, children in grades 2 and beyond can truly be inspired and motivated by alphabet books to enhance their own reading, writing and alphabetic skills. Furthermore, use of these books which have and are being produced in a variety of formats to enhance social studies, science and mathematical themes, provide an opportunity for even young children to create a meaningful product that authenticates their content study as it enhances alphabetic skills and, of course, print awareness

An annotated bibliography of selected alphabet books has been provided in the bibliography section of this guide. It was limited by space considerations, but the teacher can with no expense and with much pleasure catch up on the latest titles and identify those most appropriate for the grade taught, by visiting a bookstore. Hold the print book in hand and then consider selecting an alphabet book that has a particularly inviting concept, art style, or adaptable format within the children's capacity to use as a model.

For instance, Tina Hoban uses actual color photographs of letters in her *26 Letters and 99 Cents*. Children may want to make clay letters or create letter sculptures that develop their own alphabet book similar to Hoban's. If nutrition is the science topic, children might want to examine Ehlert's very accessible *Eating the Alphabet: Fruits and Vegetables from A to Z*. This, combined with an examination of the fruits and vegetables in a local store (perhaps a pleasant walk from the school and a quick break from the routine) can yield a wonderful alphabet book on fruits and vegetables which can also include those fruits and vegetables eaten in various cultures (i.e. mangos, plantains, pomegranates, etc).

The alphabet book can also offer the class a chance to work collaboratively using a template page created by the teacher. Completion of this collaborative work can be shared with peers in another class and parents and be kept in the classroom library as a model for the following year's class with their recognition and acceptance of the authors!

Assessment Throughout the Year of Graphophonemic Awareness

The teacher will want to maintain individual records of children's reading behaviors demonstrating alphabetic principle/graphophonemic awareness.

The following performance standards should be part of a record template form for each child in grades K-1 and beyond as needed (depending on ELL or special needs):

- Match all consonant and short vowel sounds.
- Read one's own name.
- Read one syllable words and high frequency words.
- Demonstrate ability to read and understand that as letters in words change, so do the sounds.
- Generate the sounds from all letters including consonant blends and long vowel patterns. Blend those different sounds into recognizable words.
- Read common sight words.
- Read common word families.
- Recognize and use knowledge of spelling patterns when reading: run/running, hop/hopping.

Any record kept of an individual child's progress should include each date of observation and some legend or rubric detailing the level of performance, standard acquisition, or mastery.

The following template can be used by teachers to record student progress for each child in grades K-1 and beyond as needed (depending on ELL or special needs):

Reading Progress

Skill Area	Mastered	Making Progress	Not Yet	Comments
Matches all consonant and short vowel sounds				
Reads one's own name				
Reads one syllable words and high frequency words				
Demonstrates ability to read and understand that as letters in words change, so do the sounds				
Generates the sounds from all letters including consonant blends and long vowel patterns. Blend those different sounds into recognizable words				
Reads common sight words				
Reads common word families				
Recognizes and uses knowledge of spelling patterns when reading: run/running, hop/hopping				

Any record kept of an individual child's progress should include each date of observation and some legend or rubric detailing the level of performance, standard acquisition, or mastery.

Skill 2.5   Demonstrates knowledge of delays or differences in students' phonological and phonemic awareness and when such delays/differences warrant further assessment and additional intervention

While children develop phonemic awareness at an early age, if there is an absence of strong oral-language skills in the home, or if the students are not exposed to print at an early age, they may have difficulties in developing in phonological awareness at a normal rate. Another problem may develop from the dialect of the parents differing from that of the teacher. Usually, with instruction, problems with students' phonological development dissipate over time. However, students with certain problems (ADD, for example) may have more trouble and may have to be referred to other professionals.

Another problem that can cause children to have phonological development problems is their inability to hear the enunciation of the sounds. This does not mean they are hearing impaired. It can be the result of many ear infections or of having tubes in their ears. If children are having difficulty enunciating sounds, the first thing to do is have parents consult with a physician to rule out any medical problems. If none are evident, then children should be referred to a speech pathologist for further consultation. Under normal circumstances, children should be able to enunciate all sounds by the age of 8 or 9.

COMPETENCY 3.0 CONCEPTS OF PRINT

Skill 3.1   Demonstrates an understanding of the development of concepts of print (e.g., left-right progression, spaces between words) and knows how to model and teach concepts of print

As we examine the concepts of print and learn how to teach them, it is important to understand how they represent the underlying principles of other aspects of reading development.

The concepts of print provide the foundation to all other reading skills. In order for students to develop phonemic awareness skills, they must understand the difference between a word and a letter. They must understand that words are made up of smaller parts of language: phonemes (sounds). Making the transition to the written word, students need to realize that letters or letter combinations represent those smaller sounds.

Once they realize that letters and words are different, they can then begin to see how putting letters together makes different sound combinations. From that start, they can see how putting sound combinations together makes words and how words make sentences. Without this basic level of understanding, children have almost no chance of attaining reading comprehension.

Since the English language is written in a left-to-right format, it is essential that this format be taught to students from the very beginning. If the format is not learned, the child will not understand how to interpret a page of print. Imagine students with advanced skills in phonemic awareness and phonics, but still unable to read a text because they did not understand left-to-right progression.

Another concept of print that would directly impact students' ability to progress is the idea of a return sweep. Children could begin to read and come to the end of the first line; and, without efficiently knowing to return back to the left and begin again, they would become confused by the words on the page.

Book-handling skills should begin at such a young age that they will seem almost automatic by the time children reach kindergarten. However, for some children, this is not the case. The inability to master these simple concepts of print will hinder any and all further reading progress. As fluent readers, we take for granted the ease with which these skills were obtained; but, for some students, they were quite a struggle. The key to mastery is quality time spent practicing these simple skills with text.

Development of Book Handling Skills

Understanding the value and importance of the concepts of print for beginning readers developed out of the work of Marie Clay in New Zealand. Assessment of these skills typically occurs in kindergarten and into first grade as necessary. The following skills are part of the assessment process:

- <u>Print carries a message</u> – The students can demonstrate this skill even if unable to read the text by pretending to read. This may be demonstrated even if the child does not demonstrate any of the other concepts.

- <u>Book organization</u> – Students demonstrate an understanding of the organization of books by being able to identify the title, cover, author, left to right progression, top to bottom order, and one to one correspondence. Students may learn these skills individually as they become more familiar with books.

- <u>Print Consistencies-</u> This is the understanding that text is made up of letters, which then form words, which then are combined to form sentences. As the beginning reader makes these connections, they will next develop the concept of capital letters at the beginning and basic punctuation marks.

- <u>Letter Identification-</u> The final stage of the concepts of print assessment involves the identification of both upper- and lower- case letters. More advanced students may begin to recognize some of the most common spelling patterns in beginning texts.

Have the children identify the front cover, back cover, and title page of a specific book.

Model storytelling with the book held so that the audience can see the illustrations shown to them. Then have children demonstrate the skills for their peers.

Have children search through the class libraries for special features on the fronts or backs of books as they help return the books to their bins. Have the children display and talk about the special symbols they have found.

Review with the children, in an age and grade appropriate format, additional parts of the book as appropriate during mini lessons and read alouds. These additional parts of the book can include: title pages, dedication page, table of contents, and copyright date and glossary.

Skill 3.2 **Demonstrates knowledge of the elements of the alphabetic principle, including graphophonemic knowledge, and the relationship of the letters in printed words to spoken languages**

The Alphabetic principle is sometimes called graphophonemic awareness. This term means that written words are composed of letter (graphemes) which represent the sounds (phonemes) of written words.

Development of the Understanding that Print Carries Meaning

This understanding is demonstrated every day in the elementary classroom as the teacher holds up a selected book to read aloud to the class. The teacher explicitly and deliberately talks aloud about how to hold the book, focuses the class on looking at its cover, points to where to start reading, and sweeps her hands in the direction to begin, left to right.

When writing the morning message on the board, the teacher reminds the children that the message begins in the upper left hand corner at the top of the board to be followed by additional activities and a schedule for the rest of the day.

When the teacher invites children to make posters of a single letter such as *b* and list items in the classroom, their home, or outside which start with that letter, the children are concretely demonstrating that print carries meaning.

Strategies for Promoting Awareness of the Relationship between Spoken and Written Language

- Writing down what the children say on a language chart.

- Highlighting the uses of print products found in the classroom such as labels, yellow sticky pad notes, labels on shelves and lockers, calendars, signs, and directions.

- Reading together big-print and oversized books to teach print conventions such as directionality.
- Practicing how to handle a book: How to turn pages, to find the top and bottom of pages, and how to tell the difference between the front and back covers.

- Discussing and comparing with children the length, appearance and boundaries of specific words. For example, children can see that
- the names Dan and Dora share certain letters and a similar shape.

- Having children match oral words to printed words by forming an echo chorus as the teacher reads poetry or rhymes aloud and they echo the reading.

- Having the children combine, manipulate, switch and move letters to change words.

- Working with letter cards to create messages and respond to the messages that they create.

The Role of Environmental Print in Developing Print Awareness

An environmental print book can be created by the children, which contains collaged symbols of their favorite lunch or breakfast foods. The children cut and clip symbols from the packaging of these foods and then place them in alphabetical order in their class-made book. Magazines and catalogues are another source of environmental print that is accessible with ads for child centered products. Supermarket circulars and coupons from the newspaper are also excellent for engaging children in using environmental print as reading, especially when combined with dramatic play centers or prop boxes. What is particularly effective in using environmental print is that it immediately invites the child from ELL background into print awareness, through the familiarity of commercial logos and packaging symbols used.

What is particularly effective in using environmental print is that it immediately invites the child from ELL background into print awareness, through the familiarity of commercial logos and packaging symbols used.

Skill 3.3 **Demonstrates knowledge of expected stages and patterns in students' developing understanding of the alphabetic principle and implications of individual variations in the development of this understanding**

In the alphabetic phase, students start to associate phonemes with graphemes. Graphemes are the letters of the alphabet, and phonemes are the sounds associated with the letters. It takes time for students to realize that one sound can be associated with several letters, such as /f/, /ph/ and /gh/. The development of this association paves the way for decoding words and reading.

The first stage of the alphabetic principle is a non-alphabetic process in which students memorize words associated with pictures and in which they do not make a connection between sounds and letters. This phase is often called the pre-alphabetic phase: children associate a word with its shape (such as two humps in the letter m) and use the shape to help them decode a word. In this stage, words are actually visual pictures to which they have attached a name.

The next stage of the alphabetic principle is called the logographic stage of development. In this stage, the children (in addition to noticing what the words look like) start to notice the context in which they see the words. For example, children will recognize the letter M when it appears in a MacDonald's sign, but they are unable to recognize it in other contexts. Size, shape, color, and location become the main ways in which children can identify letters. Although children are not actually reading in this stage, they will develop a sight vocabulary of a limited number of words.

The alphabetic stage of reading begins with a partial development in which the students can identify only some of the sounds associated with letters. As the teacher models the sounds on a daily basis, students reach the full alphabetic stage in which they can recognize all the sounds associated with the letters of the alphabet. At first, children will focus on the individual letters in a word when attempting to decode. Eventually, they will connect the graphemes and phonemes in the words.

Children progress from the alphabetic principle to being beginning readers. In this stage, the phonetic cues become more important than the visual cues. It is important to remember that not all students progress through these stages at the same rate and do not operate in any one manner at the same time.

Development of Alphabetic Knowledge in Individual Students

Researchers Laura M. Justice and Helen K. Ezell (2002) evaluated alphabetic knowledge and print awareness in pre-school children from low income households. In their post-tests, children who had participated in shared reading sessions that emphasized a print focus outperformed their control group peers (other Head Start children) on three measures of print awareness: words in print, print recognition, and alphabetic knowledge.

Other researchers including Chaney (1994) have demonstrated a statistically significant and inverse relationship between household income and children's performance on measures of print awareness and the alphabetic principle. Lonigan (l999) found that substantial group differences existed on a variety of pre literacy tasks administered to 85 preschool children from lower and middle income households. The researchers looked at environmental print, print and book reading conventions, and alphabet knowledge. Results showed that preschool children from middle income households showed significantly higher levels of skill across all print awareness tasks in comparison with preschoolers from low income households.

Obviously this data highlights the importance of extensive alphabetic knowledge activities and print awareness opportunities for some children from low income households in grades K-1 and even beyond if necessary.

Two other studies undertaken by Ezell and Justice (in the year 2000) suggested that structuring adult-child shared book reading interactions to include an explicit print awareness and alphabetic principle focus resulted in a substantial increase in children's verbal interactions with print.

This work highlights the importance of not only classroom and preschool emphasis on print awareness and alphabetic principle routines, but also the need for teachers to reach out to parents and to model for them these shared reading experiences so that family life can parallel the classroom experiences. Many schools currently have parent volunteers and reading buddy programs. Training of these volunteers, particularly in high need, low economic income status communities is certainly warranted.

David J. Chard and Jean Osborn (l999) have reflected on the guidelines necessary for teachers to use in selecting supplemental phonics and word-recognition materials for addressing students with learning disabilities. They note that an important way to help children with reading disabilities figure out the system underlying the printed word is leading them to understand the alphabetic principle. Children with learning disabilities (LD) in particular, benefit from organized instruction that centers on letters, sounds, and the relations between sounds and letters. They also benefit from word-recognition patterns instruction that offers practice with word families that share similar letter patterns.

Children who are LD also benefit from opportunities to apply what they are learning to the reading and re-reading of stories and other texts. Such texts contain a high portion of words which reflect the letters, sounds, and spelling patterns the children are learning.

For special needs children, a beginning reading program should include the following elements of alphabetic knowledge instruction:

1. A variety of alphabetic knowledge activities in which the children learn to identify and name both upper and lower case letters.
2. Games, songs, and other activities that help children to learn to name the letters quickly.
3. Writing activities that encourage children to practice the letters which they are writing.
4. A sensible sequence of letter introduction that can be adjusted to the needs of the children.

Sequence of Phonics Skills

- Letter Naming
    - Lower Case Letters
    - Upper Case Letters
- Letter Sounds
    - Continuous Sounds
    - Stop Sounds
    - Both Consonant and Vowel Sounds
- Short Vowels in CVC Words
- Short Vowels with Digraphs and –tch Trigraph
- Short Vowels and Consonant Blends
- Long Vowels
- Variant Vowels and Diphthongs
- R- and L- Controlled Vowels
- Multisyllabic Words

Explicit and Implicit Strategies for Teaching Phonics

Uta Frith has identified three phases which describe the progression of children's phonic learning from ages four through eight. These are:

<u>Logographic Phase</u>
Children recognize whole words that have significance for them such as their own names or the names of stores they frequent or products that their parents buy. Examples are McDonald's, SuperValu, and the like. Strategies which nurture development in this phase include explicit labeling of class room objects, components, furniture and materials and showing the children's names in print as often as possible. Toward the end of this phase children start to notice initial letters in words and the sounds that they represent.

<u>Analytic Phase</u>
During this phase the children begin to make associations between the spelling patterns in the words they know and new words-they encounter. Children in this phase of reading development are able to generalize that hat and cat are going to be read in a similar manner because they recognize that the /at/ portions of the words are the same. This is helpful with word families and can be transferred to encoding words through many activities. Some teachers find it helpful to add word families or family houses to their word walls around the room. In this way, students can begin to make these generalizations more rapidly. As the students find more complex words that fall into the family/house, they add them.

<u>Orthographic Phase</u>
In this phase, children recognize words almost automatically. They can rapidly identify an increasing number of words. Students are able to apply many different strategies in a seamless manner to help them decode unknown words. This may include: phonics, structural analysis, syntax, semantics, and contextual clues. Students at this level are fluent readers with good prosody. They are reading to make the shift from learning to read to reading to learn. It is a critical shift for children.

To best support these phases and the development of emergent and early readers, teachers should focus on elements of phonics learning which help children analyze words for their letters, spelling patterns, and structural components. The children need to be involved in activities in which they use what they know about words to learn new ones.

The teacher needs to build on what the children know to introduce new spelling patterns, vowel combinations, and short and long vowel investigations. The teacher must do this and be aware that these will be reintroduced again and again as needed.

Keep in mind that children's learning of phonics and other key components of reading is not linear, but rather falls back to review and then flows forward to build new understandings.

Among suggested activities to support phonics instruction to address the needs of these three phases of phonics learning are:

(These activities have specifically been provided in detail so that the educator can study them and use them in the sample constructed response questions which have been provided at the end of the guide. Since the role of phonics in promoting reading development is so crucial, it is highly likely that a constructed response question on the certification test will focus on the use of such strategies. Therefore it is a good idea for the certification candidate to study them closely. As a bonus, the detail with which these strategies are set forth also makes them readily useful with classes the teacher is currently teaching).

Sorting Words

This activity allows children to focus closely on the specific features of words and to begin to understand the basic elements of letter sound relationships. Start with one syllable (monosyllabic) words. Have the children group them by their length, common letters, sound, and/or spelling pattern.

Prepare for the activity by writing ten to fifteen words on oaktag strips and place them randomly on the sentence strip holder. These words should come from a book previously shared in the classroom or a language experience chart.

Next begin to sort out the words with the children, perhaps by where a particular letter appears in a word. While the children sort the place of a particular letter in a given word, they should also be coached (or facilitated) by the teacher to recognize that sometimes a letter in the middle of the word can still be the last sound that we hear and that some letters at the end of a word are silent (such as "e").

Children should be encouraged to make their own categories for word sorts and to share their own discoveries as they do the word sorts. The children's discoveries should be recorded and posted in the rooms with their names so they have ownership of their phonics learning.

Spelling Pattern Word Wall

One of the understandings emergent readers come to about a word is that if they know how to read, write, and spell one word, they can write, read, and spell many other words as well.

Create in your classroom a spelling pattern word wall. The spelling word wall can be created by stapling a piece of 3" x 5" butcher block paper to the bulletin board. Then attach spelling pattern cards around the border with thumbtacks, so that the cards can be easily removed to use at the meeting area.

Once you decide on a spelling pattern for instruction, remove the corresponding card from the word wall. Then take a 1"x 3" piece of a contrasting color of butcher block paper and tape the card to the top end of a sheet the children will use for their investigation.

After the pattern is identified the children can try to come up with other words that have the same spelling pattern. The teacher can write these on the spelling pattern sheet, using a different color marker to highlight the spelling pattern within the word. The children have to add to the list until the sheet is full, which might take two days or more.

After the sheet is full, the completed spelling pattern is attached to the wall.

Letter Holder Making Words

Use a 2" x 3" piece of foam board to make a letter holder. On the front of the board, attach 16 library pockets —one for each letter from A to P. Use the back of the board to attach another 10 pockets for the rest of the alphabet.

Write the letter name on each pocket and use clear bookbinding tape to secure each row of cards with clear tape. Make twelve cards for each letter. On the front of each 2"x 6" strip, make a capital letter and on its back write that letter in lower case. Write consonants in, say, black marker and vowels in red marker.

Through use of this letter holder, children can experience how letters can be rearranged, added, or removed to make new words. They can use these cards also to focus as needed on letter sequences and to support them in recognizing spelling patterns in words.

The words you choose to use for this activity can be selected from Patricia Cunningham and Dorothy P. Hall's, *Making Words* (1994). Select a word that is called the "secret word." Build up toward the creation of that word through a focus on the smaller words within it. Words should be chosen which reflect the spelling patterns being studied by the class.

You can create letter holders for the children by folding up the bottom third of a used manila file folder and taping the ends to form a shallow pocket. Give them letter cards which are made of 2"x 6" oaktag. So, for example, if the secret word is bicycle, the children would be given the separate letter cards which would make up that word. The children keep the letters on the floor in front of them and only place them in the holder when they are actually making a word.

Making words should begin with making two letter words and then progress as the individual child is ready to make larger words. The teacher provides the instruction of which two letters the child is to use to make a word. After the instruction is given the children select the correct letters and make the word in their folder. The teacher then writes the word down and the children check their letter holder word against it. The teacher goes around checking through and reviewing the letter holders to see which children are "getting it" and then continues to build up words with more letters if the children are ready.

Word Splits

Splitting compound words. Through working with compound words, children can actually experience bigger words that are often made up of smaller words. By working with five to ten compound words on oaktag cards, children can analyze letter-sound relationships and meaning.

Before children meet in a group, write five to ten words on oaktag cards and arrange them on the sentence strip holder. After the words have been read, cut each of the words into its two smaller words and randomly arrange them on the sentence strip holder. Allow the children to randomly take turns arranging the small words back into the original compound words. Also, encourage them to form new compound words. For example, if one of two original compound words is "rainbow" and the other is "dropping," the children should be able to come with "raindrop." The new words the children come up with should be written on blank oaktag cards with the names of the children who came up with them attached. In this way the children can add to their growing bank of new words and have ownership in the words that they have added.

Role of Phonics in Developing Rapid, Automatic Word Recognition, Decoding, and Reading Comprehension

To decode means to change communication signals into messages. Reading comprehension requires that the reader learn the code within which a message is written and be able to decode it to get the message.

Although effective reading comprehension requires identifying words automatically (Adams, 1990, Perfetti, 1985), children do not have to be able to identify every single word or know the exact meaning of the every word in a text to understand it. Indeed, Nagy (1988) says that, children can read a work with a high level of comprehension even if they do not fully know as many as 15 percent of the words within a given text.

Children develop the ability to decode and recognize words automatically. They then can extend their ability to decode to multi-syllabic words.
J. David Cooper (2004) and other advocates of the Balanced Literacy Approach, feel that children become literate, effective communicators and able to comprehend, by learning phonics and other aspects of word identification through the use of engaging reading texts. Engaging text, as defined by the balanced literacy group, are those texts which contain highly predictable elements of rhyme, sound patterns, and plot. Researchers, such as Chall (1983) and Flesch (1981), support a phonics-centered foundation before the use of engaging reading texts. This is at the crux of the phonics versus whole language/ balanced literacy/ integrated language arts, teaching of reading controversy.

It is important for the new teacher to be informed about both sides of this controversy, as well as the work of theorists who attempt to reconcile these two perspectives, such as Kenneth Goodman (1994). There are powerful arguments on both sides of this controversy, and each approach works wonderfully with some students and does not succeed with others.

As far as the examinations go, all that is asked of you is the ability to demonstrate that you are familiar with these varied perspectives. If asked on a constructed response question, you need to be able to show that you can talk about teaching some aspect of reading using strategies from one or the other or a combination of both approaches.

This guide is designed to provide you with numerous strategies representing both approaches.

The working teacher can, depending on the perspective of his /her school administration and the needs of the particular children he or she serves, choose from the strategies and approaches which work best for the children concerned.

Blending Letter Sounds

Prompts for Graphophonic Cues

You said (the child's incorrect attempt). Does that match the letters you see?
If it were the word you just said, (the child's incorrect attempt), what would it have to start with?

If it were the word you just said (the child's incorrect attempt), what would it have to end with?

Look at the first letter/s . . . look at the middle letter/s
. . . the last letter. . What could it be?

If you were writing (the child's incorrect attempt) what letter would you write first?
What letters would go in the middle?
What letters would go last?

A good strategy to use in working with individual children is to have them explain how they finally correctly identified a word that was troubling them. If prompted and habituated through one on one teacher/tutoring conversations, they can be quite clear about what they did to "get" the word.

If the children are already writing their own stories, the teacher might say to them: "You know when you write your own stories, you would never write any story which did not make sense. You wouldn't and probably this writer didn't either. If you read something that does make sense, but doesn't match the letters, then it's probably not what the author wrote. This is the author's story, not yours right now, so go back to the word and see if you can find out the author's story. Later on, you might write your own story."

Letter Sound Correspondence and Beginning Decoding

Use this procedure for letter-sound investigations that support beginning decoding. First, focus on a particular letter/s which you want the child to investigate. It is good to choose one from a shared text which the children are familiar with. Make certain that the teachers' directions to the children are clear and either focuses them on looking for a specific letter or listening for sounds.

Next, begin a list of words that meet the task given to the children. Use chart paper to list the words that the children identify. This list can be continued into the next week as long as the children's focus is maintained on the list. This can be easily done by challenging the children with identifying a specific number of letters or sounds and "daring" them as a class team to go beyond those words or sounds.

Third, continue to add to the list. Focus the children at the beginning of the day on the goal of their individually adding to the list. Give them an adhesive note (sticky pad sheet) on which they can individually write down the words they find. Then they can attach their newly found words with their names on them to the chart. This provides the children with a sense of ownership and pride in their letter-sounding abilities. During shared reading, discuss the children's proposed additions and have the group decide if these meet the directed category. If all the children agree that they do meet the category, include the words on the chart.

Fourth, do a word sort from all the words generated and have the children put the words into categories that demonstrate similarities and differences. They can be prompted to see if the letter appeared at the beginning of the word, or in the end of the word. They might also be prompted to see that one sound could have two different letter representations. The children can then "box" the word differences and similarities by drawing colors established in a chart key.

Finally, before the children go off to read, ask them to look for new words in the texts which they can now recognize because of the letter sound relationships on their chart. During shared reading, make certain that they have time to share these words they were able to decode because of their explorations.

Strategies for Helping Students Decode Single Syllable Words that Follow Common Patterns and Multi-syllable Words

(This activity is presented in detail so it can actually be implemented with children in an intermediate classroom and also to provide detail for a potential constructed response question on a certification examination.)

The CVC phonics card game developed by Jackie Montierth, a computer teacher in South San Diego for use with 5th and 6th grade students, is a good one to adapt to the needs of any group with appropriate modifications for age, grade level and language needs.

The children use the vehicle of the card game to practice and enhance their use of consonants and vowels. Their fluency in this will increase their ability to decode words. Potential uses beyond whole classroom instruction include use as part of the small group word work component of the reading workshop and as part of cooperative team learning. This particular strategy also is particularly helpful for grade four and beyond English Language learners who are in a regular English Language classroom setting.

The card game works well because the practice of the content is implicit for transfer as the children continue to improve their reading skills. In addition, the card game format allows "instructional punctuation" using a student centered high interest exploration.

Card Design: The teacher can use the computer or use 5"x 8" index cards or actual card deck sized oaktag cards to create a deck. For repeated use and durability, it is recommended that the deck be laminated.

The deck should consist of the following:
44 consonant cards (including the blends)
15 vowel cards (including 3 of each vowel)
5 wild cards (which can be used as any vowel)
6 final e cards

The design of this project can also focus on particular CVC words that are part of a particular book, topic or genre format. In advance of playing the game, children can also be directed to review the words on the word wall or other words on a word map.

Procedure:

The game is best introduced first as part of a mini lesson with the teacher reading the rules, and a pair of children demonstrating step by step, when the game is played before the class for the first time. Have the children divide into pairs or small groups of no more than 4 per group. Each group needs one deck of C-V-C cards.

Have each group choose a dealer. The dealer shuffles the cards and deals 5 cards to each player. The remaining cards are placed face down for drawing during the play. One card is turned over to form the discard pile. Players may not show their cards to the other players. The first player to the left of the dealer looks at his/her cards and if possible, puts down three cards which make a consonant-vowel-consonant word. For more points, four cards forming a consonant-vowel-consonant word can be placed down. The player must then say the word and draw the number of cards he or she laid down. If he or she is unable to form a word, he/she draws either a card from either the draw or discard pile. The player then discards one card. All players must have 5 cards at all times. Play moves to the left.

The game continues until one or more of the following happens:
1. There are no more cards in the draw pile
2. All players run out of cards.
3. All players cannot form a word

The winner is the player who has laid down the most cards during the game.

Players may only lay down words at the beginning of their turn.
Proper names may not be counted as words.

The game can be played with teams of individuals in a small group of four or fewer competing against one another (Excellent for special needs or resource room students). It can also be done as a whole class activity where all the students are divided into cooperative teams or small groups who compete against one another. This second approach will work well with a heterogeneous classroom that includes special needs and/or ELL children.

Teachers of ELL learners can do this game in the native language first and then transition it into English, facilitating native language reading skills and second language acquisition. They can develop their own appropriate decks to meet the vocabulary needs of their children and to complement the curricula.

Using Phonics to Decode Words in Connected Text

Identifying New Words

Some strategies to share with children during conferences or as part of shared reading include the following prompts:

- Look at the beginning letter/s... What sound do you hear?

- Stop to think about the text or story. What word with this beginning letter would make sense here?

- Look at the book's illustrations. Do they provide you with help in figuring out the new word?

- Think of what word would make sense, sound right, and match the letters that you see. Start the sentence over, making your mouth ready to say that word.

- Skip the word, read to the end of the sentence, and then come back to the word. How does what you've read help you with the word?

- Listen to whether what you are reading makes sense and matches the letters (asking the child to self-monitor). If it doesn't make sense, see if you can correct it on your own.

- Look for spelling patterns you know from the spelling pattern wall.

- Look for smaller words you might know within the larger word.

- Read on a little, and then return to the part that confused you.

Skill 3.4   **Knows how to plan, implement and monitor instruction that is responsive to individual students' strengths, needs and interests and is based on ongoing formal and informal assessment of individual students' understanding and application of the alphabetic principle**

The reading development of young children depends on how well they understand the alphabetic principle – the connection between letters and their sounds. Once children learn the predictable patterns between letters and sounds, they can apply these patterns to familiar and unfamiliar words and begin to become fluent readers.

Instruction in phonics is intended to help children learn and be able to use the alphabetic principle. Through phonics, students learn the connections between the spoken and written words. In order to teach children to become fluent readers, teachers should teach the letters and the sounds together. They should also provide ample opportunities during the day for students to practice the relationships between the letters and the sounds. In addition to providing practice time for the new learning, they also need to be constantly reviewing the previously-taught material.

There is no one correct way or rate by which teachers should introduce the alphabetic principle. Through continuous assessment, teachers can determine how fast or slowly they need to proceed with the students. Some students may need more instruction and practice than others, so it is possible to have several groups of students learning and practicing different letters and sounds. The main point is to help students to start reading words as soon as possible.

Some guidelines to follow when instructing students in the alphabetic principle include:

- Not all children learn the letter-sound relationships at the same rate

- The introduction of letters and sounds should be at a reasonable rate, such as two-to-four per week

- Teach the letters that are used most in the English language first

- Do not confuse students by introducing letters than have similar sounds at the same time

- Consonants and vowels should be introduced at a rate that will allow students to read words fairly quickly

Blends and clusters should be introduced separately.

Skill 3.5 **Applies knowledge of instructional strategies and materials that reflect cultural diversity, are based on a convergence of research evidence, and promote students' understanding and application of the alphabetic principle**

See Skill 2.4

Skill 3.6 **Knows how to provide systematic instruction and reinforcing activities to promote students' understanding and application of concepts of print and the alphabetic principle**

The students' discovery that a letter has the same sound at the beginning of different words is an example of the alphabetic principle at work. The Alphabet Song and all kinds of alphabet books are excellent resources to use to reinforce this concept in the classroom. Big books are excellent to use because all of the students can see the print as teachers point to the letters and the words. All alphabet books are not the same; many of them help promote cultural diversity in the classroom by teaching the students about different cultures at the same time that they teach letters and letter sounds. Examples include:

- It Begins With A (Calmenson)
- Jambo Means Hello: Swahili Alphabet Book
- B is for Bluegrass (a Kentucky alphabet book)
- B is for Buckaroo (a cowboy's alphabet book)
- D is for Democracy

There are also many games that reading specialists can play with children to help them develop graphophonic awareness. While singing the alphabet song, teachers can point to each letter and vary the speed to develop fluency in reciting the alphabet.

- Use one-letter books that focus on words beginning with only one letter
- At the activity center, children can trace letters or make letters from a variety of materials
- Encourage children to find specific letters in their names
- Use letters to have children make words. For example, they can use the letters N and O to make "on" and "no"
- A collection of alphabet books should be displayed in the classroom for the children to read at their leisure.
- Have students brainstorm a list of words beginning with a specific letter
- Use Picture dictionaries in the classroom
-

When students see and hear their own words in print, they realize that what they say can be written. By immersing the students in a world of print, they can see and hear the sounds as they listen to others read and as they attempt to read themselves.

Skill 3.7 **Demonstrates knowledge of delays or differences in students' understanding of and ability to apply concepts of print and the alphabetic principle and when such delays/differences warrant further assessment and additional intervention**

Students build upon their oral language skills as they begin to recognize how letters work to form words. Sound awareness of the letters usually starts with rhyme in the early years. Teachers will recognize that some students will have difficulty with sounds because of a delay in their development of the alphabetic principle and graphophonic awareness.

Some of these students need more time than others to learn about letters and sounds. Through direct instruction and modeling, teachers can bring these students along to the level at which they should be for their age.
When students do not seem to progress at a regular rate, or if they do not seem to progress at all, then teachers should consult with other professionals. There is a wide variety of services available for students who need help with reading in the early grades. The first step that teachers should take is to make a referral to have the child tested to determine whether or not there is a medical reason for the delay or difference.

Through both formal and informal assessments, teachers can determine whether or not specific students need extra help or specific interventions to make sure they succeed in reading. This may mean extra planning for individual students and working one-on-one with these children. They should make use of the specialists within the school to determine other resources to help them with this process.

See also Skill 3.2

COMPETENCY 4.0 WORD IDENTIFICATION

Skill 4.1   Demonstrates knowledge of word identification strategies and strategies for reading words (e.g., application of the alphabetic principle, phonics, structural analysis, syllabication, identification of high-frequency sight words, use of context clues)

Development of Word Analysis Skills and Strategies, Including Structural Analysis

Structural analysis is a process of examining the words in the text for meaningful word units (affixes, base words, inflected endings). There are six types of word types which are formed and therefore can be analyzed using structural analysis strategies. They include:

1. Common prefixes or suffixes added to a known word ending with a consonant
2. Adding the suffix –ed to words that end with consonants
3. Compound words
4. Adding endings to words that end with the letter e
5. Adding endings to words that end with the letter y
6. Adding affixes to multisyllabic words

When teaching and using structural analysis procedures in the primary grades, teachers should remember to make sound decisions on which to introduce and teach. Keeping in mind the number of primary words in which each affix appears and how similar they are will help the teacher make the instructional process smoother and more valuable to the students.

Adding affixes to words can be started when students are able to read a list of one-syllable words by sight at a rate of approximately twenty words correct per minute. At the primary level, there is a recommended sequence for introducing affixes. The steps in this process are:

- Start by introducing the affix in the letter-sound correspondence format
- Practice the affix in isolation for a few days
- Provide words for practice which contain the affix (word lists, flash cards, etc.)
- Move from word lists to including passage reading, which include words with the affix (and some from the word lists/flash cards).

1. Word Study Group

This involves the teacher taking time to meet with children from grades 3-6 in a small group of no more than 6 children for a word study session. Taberski (2000) suggests that this meeting take place next to the Word Wall. The children selected for this group are those who need to focus more on the relationship between spelling patterns and consonant sounds.

It is important that this not be a formalized traditional reading group that meets at a set time each week or biweekly. Rather the group should be spontaneously formed by the teacher based on the teacher's quick inventory of the selected children's needs at the start of the week. Taberski has templates in her book of *Guided Reading Planning Sheets.* These sheets are essentially targeted word and other skills sheets with her written dated observations of children who are in need of support to develop a given skill.

The teacher should try to meet with this group for at least two consecutive twenty minute periods daily. Over those two meetings, the teacher can model a Making Words Activity. Once the teacher has modeled making words the first day, the children would then make their own words. On the second day, the children would "sort" their words.

Other topics for a word study group within the framework of the Balanced Literacy Approach that Taberski advocates are: inflectional endings, prefixes and suffixes, and/or common spelling patterns. These are covered later in this chapter. It should be noted that this activity would be classified by theorists as a structural analysis activity because the structural components (i.e. prefixes, suffixes, and spelling patterns) of the words are being studied.

2. Discussion Circles

Cooper (2004) believes that children should not be "taught" vocabulary and structural analysis skills. Flesch and E.D. Hirsch , who are key theorists of the phonics approach and advocates of Cultural Literacy (a term coined and associated with E. D. Hirsch), believe that specific vocabulary words at various grade and age levels need to be mastered and must be explicitly taught in schools. As far as J. David Cooper is concerned, all the necessary and meaningful (for the child and ultimately adult reader) vocabulary can't possibly be taught in schools (no apologies to Hirsch). To Cooper it is far more important that the children be made aware of and become interested in learning words by themselves. Cooper feels that through the child's reading and writing, he or she develops a love for and a sense of "ownership" of words. All of Cooper's suggested structural analysis word strategies are therefore designed to foster the child's love of words and a desire to "own" more of them through reading and writing.

Discussion Circles is an activity which fits nicely into the balanced literacy lesson format. After the children conclude a particular text, Cooper suggests that respond to the book in discussion circles. Among the prompts, the teacher-coach might suggest that the children focus on words of interest they encountered in the text. These can also be words that they heard if the text was read aloud. Children can be asked to share something funny or upsetting or unusual about the words they have read. Through this focus on children's response to words as the center of the discussion circle, peers become more interested in word study.

3. Banking, Booking, and Filing It: Making Words My Own

Children can literally realize the goal of making words their own and exploring word structures through creating concrete objects or displays that demonstrate the words they own. Children can create and maintain their own files of words they have learned or are interested in learning.

The files can be categorized by the children according to their own interests. They should be encouraged to develop files using science, history, physical education, fine arts, dance, and technology content. Newspapers and web resources, which the teacher has approved, are excellent sources for such words. In addition, this provides the teacher with the opportunity to instruct the child in appropriate age and grade-level research skills. Even children in grades 2 and 3 can begin simplified bibliographies and webliographies for their "found" words. Children can learn how to annotate and note the page of a newspaper, book, or URL for a particular word.

They can also copy down the word as it appears in the text (print or electronic). If appropriate, the child can place the particular words found for a given topic or content in an actual bank of the child's own making. The words can be printed on cards. This allows for differentiated word study and appeals to those children who are kinesthetic and spatial learners. Of course, children can also choose to create their own word books which include their specialized vocabulary and descriptions of how they identified or hunted down their words. Richard Scarry, watch out! Scarry books can be anchor books to inspire this structural analysis activity.

ELL learners can share their accounts in their native language first and then translate (with the help of the teacher) these accounts into English with both the native language and the English language versions of the word exploration posted.

4. Write out your Words, Write with your words

Ownership of words can be demonstrated by having the children use them as part of their writings. The children can author a procedural narrative (a step by step description) of how they went about their word searches to compile the words they found for any of the activities. If the children are in grades K-1, or if the children are struggling readers and writers, their procedural narratives can be dictated. Then they can be posted by the teacher.

ELL students can share their accounts in their native language first and then translate (with the help of the teacher) these accounts into English with both the native language and the English language versions of the word exploration posted.

Children with special needs may model a word box on a specific holiday theme, genre or science/social studies topic with the teacher. Initially this can be done as a whole class. As the children become more confident, they can work with peers or with a paraprofessional to create their own individual or small team/pair word boxes.

Special needs children can create a storyboard with the support of a paraprofessional, their teacher or a resource specialist. They can also narrate their story of how they all found the words, using a tape recorder.

5.- Word Study Museum Within the Classroom

This strategy has been presented in detail so it can be used by the teachers within their own classrooms. In addition, the way the activity is described and the mention at the end of the description of how the activity can address family literacy, ELL, and special needs children's talents, provides an example of other audiences a teacher should consider in curriculum design.
Almost every general education teacher and reading specialist will have to differentiate instruction to address the needs of special education and ELL learners. Family or shared literacy is a major component of all literacy instruction.

Children can create either a single or multiple exhibits, museum style, within their classrooms celebrating their word study. They can build actual representations of the type of study they have done including word trees (made out of cardboard or foam board), elaborate word boxes and games, word history timelines or murals, and word study maps. They can develop online animations, Kids Spiration graphic organizers, quick movies, digital photo essays, and PowerPoint presentations to share the word they have identified. The classroom or the gym or cafeteria can be transformed into a gallery space. Children can author brochure descriptions for their individual, team or class exhibits. Some children can volunteer to be tour guides or docents for the experience. Other children can work to create a banner for the Museum. The children can name the Museum themselves and send out invitations to its opening. Invitations can be sent to parents, community, staff members and peer or younger classes.

Depending on their age and grade level, children can also develop interactive games and quizzes focused on particular exhibits. An artist or a team of class artists can design a poster for the exhibit, while other children choose to build the exhibits. Another small group can work on signage and a catalogue or register of objects within the exhibit. Greeters who will welcome parents and peers to the exhibit can be trained and can develop their own scripts.

If the children are in grades 4-6, they can also develop their own visitor feedback forms and design word-themed souvenirs. The whole museum within the school or classroom can be captured digitally or with a regular camera. The record of this event can be hung near the word walls. Of course, the children can use many of their newly recognized and owned words to describe the event.

The Word Study Museum activity can be used with either a phonics-based or a balanced literacy approach. It promotes additional writing, researching, discussing, and reading about words.

It is also an excellent family literacy strategy in that families can develop their own Word Exhibits at home. This activity can also support and celebrate learners with disabilities. It can be presented in dual languages by children who are ELL learners and fluent in more than a single language.)

Skill 4.2   Demonstrates knowledge of skills and strategies for confirming word pronunciation and/or meaning when reading words in context (e.g., use of context clues and resource materials)

Relationship Between Word Analysis Skills and Reading Comprehension

The explicit teaching of word analysis requires that the teacher pre-select words from a given text for vocabulary learning. These words should be chosen based on the storyline and main ideas of the text. The educator may even want to create a story map for a narrative text or develop a graphic organizer for an expository text. Once the story mapping and/or graphic organizing have been done, the educator can compile a list of words which relate to the storyline and/or main ideas.

The number of words that require explicit teaching should only be two or three. If the number is higher than that, the children need guided reading and the text needs to be broken down into smaller sections for teaching. When broken down into smaller sections, each text section should only have two to three words which need explicit teaching.

Some researchers, including Tierney and Cunningham, believe that a few words should be taught as a means of improving comprehension.

It is up to the educator whether the vocabulary selected for teaching needs review before reading, during reading, or after reading.

Introduce vocabulary BEFORE READING if. . .

- Children are having difficulty constructing meaning on their own. Children themselves have previewed the text and indicated words they want to know.

- The teacher has seen that there are words within the text which are definitely keys necessary for reading comprehension

- The text, itself, in the judgment of the teacher, contains difficult concepts for the children to grasp.

Introduce vocabulary DURING READING if . . .

- Children are already doing guided reading.

- The text has words which are crucial to its comprehension and the children will have trouble comprehending it, if they are not helped with the text.

Introduce vocabulary AFTER READING if. . .

- The children themselves have shared words which they found difficult or interesting

- The children need to expand their vocabulary

- The text itself is one that is particularly suited for vocabulary building.

Strategies, to support word analysis and enhance reading comprehension, include:

- Use of a graphic organizer such as a word map
- Semantic mapping
- Semantic feature analysis
- Hierarchical and linear arrays
- Preview in context
- Contextual redefinition
- Vocabulary self-collection
- (Note that these terms are in the Glossary.)

Skill 4.3   Demonstrates knowledge of expected stages and patterns of development in the use of word identification strategies, implications of individual variations in development in this area

Identification of Common Morphemes, Prefixes, and Suffixes

This aspect of vocabulary development is to help children look for structural elements within words which they can use independently to help them determine meaning.

Some teachers choose to directly teach structural analysis. In particular, those who teach by following the phonics-centered approach for reading do this. Other teachers, who follow the balanced literacy approach, introduce the structural components as part of mini lessons that are focused on the students' reading and writing.

Structural analysis of words as defined by J. David Cooper (2004) involves the study of significant word parts. This analysis can help the child with pronunciation and constructing meaning.

The term list below is generally recognized as the key structural analysis components.

Root Words

This is a word from which another word is developed. The second word can be said to have its "root" in the first, such as *vis, to see,* in visor or vision. This structural component can be illustrated by a tree with roots to display the meaning for children. Children may also want to literally construct root words using cardboard trees to create word family models.

ELL learners can construct these models for their native language root word families, as well for the English language words they are learning. ELL learners in the 5th and 6th grade may even appreciate analyzing the different root structures for contrasts and similarities between their native language and English.

Learners with special needs can focus in small groups or individually with a paraprofessional on building root word models.

Base Words

These are stand-alone linguistic units which cannot be deconstructed or broken down into smaller words. For example, in the word *re-tell*, the base word is "tell."

Contractions

These are shortened forms of two words in which a letter or letters have been deleted. These deleted letters have been replaced by an apostrophe.

Prefixes

These are beginning units of meaning which can be added (the vocabulary word for this type of structural adding is "affixed") to a base word or root word. They can not stand alone. They are also sometimes known as "bound morphemes" meaning that they can not stand alone as a base word. Examples are *re-, un-,* and *mis-.*

Suffixes

These are ending units of meaning which can be "affixed" or added on to the ends of root or base words. Suffixes transform the original meanings of base and root words. Like prefixes, they are also known as "bound morphemes," because they can not stand alone as words. Examples are *-less, -ful*, and *-tion*.

Compound Words

These occur when two or more base words are connected to form a new word. The meaning of the new word is in some way connected with that of the base word. Examples are *firefighter, newspaper*, and *pigtail*.

Inflectional Endings

These are types of suffixes that impart a new meaning to the base or root word. These endings in particular change the gender, number, tense, or form of the base or root words. Just like other suffixes, these are also termed "bound morphemes." Examples are *–s* or *-ed*.

Comments

Definitions are included because the structural analysis components are explicitly taught in schools which advocate the phonics-centered approach and are also incorporated into the word work component of the schools which advocate the balanced literacy approach for instruction.

Definition questions, that is multiple choice questions which have only a single right answer, test whether the teacher candidate has memorized the appropriate terminology. They constitute for no less than 15% of the multiple choice question on the test. Therefore by taking the time to memorize these easy definitions, scores are likely to improve.

Some of these activities are presented in detail to help answer the constructed response questions of the test.

Knowleddge of Greek and Latin Roots That Form English Words

Knowledge of Greek and Latin roots which comprise English words can measurably enhance children's reading skills and can also enrich their writing.

Word Webs

Sharon Taberski (2000) does not advocate teaching Greek and Latin derivatives in the abstract to young children. However, when she comes across (as is common and natural) specific Greek and Latin roots while reading to children, she uses that opportunity to introduce children to these rich resources.

For example, during readings on rodents (a favorite of first and second graders), Taberski draws her class's attention to the fact that beavers, gnaw at things with their teeth. She then connects the "dent" root or derivative to the children's lives, other words they are familiar with or experiences. The children then volunteer *"dentist," "dental," "denture."* Taberski begins to place these in a graphic organizer, or word web.

When she has tapped the extent of the children's prior knowledge of "dent" words, she shares with them the fact that *dens/dentis* is the Latin word for teeth. Then she introduces the word "indent," which she has already previewed with them as part of their conventions of print study. She helps them to see that the "indenting" of the first line of a paragraph can even be related to the "teeth" Latin root in that it looks like a "print" bite was taken out of the paragraph.

Taberski displays the word web in the Word Wall Chart section of her room. The class is encouraged throughout, say, a week's time to look for other words to add to the web. Taberski stresses that for her, as an elementary teacher of reading and writing, the key element of the Greek and Latin word root web activity is the children's coming to understand that if they know what a Greek or Latin word root means, they can use that knowledge to figure out what other words mean.

She feels the key concept is to model and demonstrate for children how fun and fascinating Greek and Latin root study can be.

Greek and Latin Roots Word Webs With an Assist From the World Wide Web

Older children in grades 3-6 can build on this initial print activity by searching online for additional words with a particular Greek or Latin root which has been introduced in class.

They can easily do this in a way that authentically ties in with their own interests and experiences by reading reviews for a book which has been a read-aloud online or by just reading the summaries of the day's news and printing out those words which appear in the stories online that share the root discussed.

The children can be encouraged to circle these instances of their Latin or Greek root and also to document the exact date and URL for the citation. These can be posted as part of their own online web in the word wall section study area. If the school or class has a website or webpage, the children can post this data there as a special Greek and Latin root word page.

Expanding the concept of the Greek and Latin word web from the printed page to the world wide web, nicely inculcates the child in the habits of lifelong reading and researching online. This beginning expository research will serve them well in intermediate level content area work and beyond.

Use of Syllabification as a Word Identification Strategy

Strategy: Clap Hands, Count those Syllables as They Come!! (Taberski, 2000)

The objective of this activity is for children to understand that there are every syllable in a polysyllabic word can be studied for its spelling patterns in the same way that monosyllabic words are studied for their spelling patterns.

The easiest way for the K-3 teacher to introduce this activity to the children is to share a familiar poem from the poetry chart (or to write out a familiar poem on a large experiential chart).

First the teacher reads the poem with the children. As they are reading it aloud, the children clap the beats of the poem and the teacher uses a colored marker to place a tic (/) above each syllable.

Next, the teacher takes letter cards and selects one of the polysyllabic words from the poem which the children have already "clapped" out.

The children use letter cards to spell that word on the sentence strip holder or it can be placed on a felt board or up against a window on display. Together the children and teacher divide the letters into syllables and place blank letter cards between the syllables. The children identify spelling patterns they know.

Finally and as part of continued small group syllabification study, the children identify other polysyllabic words they clapped out from the poem. They make up the letter combinations of these words. Then they separate them into syllables with blank letter cards between the syllables.

Children who require special support in syllabification can be encouraged to use many letter cards to create a large butcher paper syllabic (in letter cards with spaces) representation of the poem or at least a few lines of the poem. They can be told that this is for use as a teaching tool for others. In this way, they authenticate their study of syllabification with a real product that can actually be referenced by peers.

Techniques for Identifying Compound Words

The teaching of compound words should utilize structural analysis techniques. (See above section on structural analysis).
Here are some other strategies for helping students to identify and read compound words.
Use songs and actions to help children understand the concept that compound words are two smaller words joined together to make one bigger word
Use games like concentration, memory and go fish for students to practice reading compound words
Use word sorts to have students distinguish between compound words and non-examples of compound words

Identification of Homographs

Homographs are words that are spelled the same but have different meanings. A subgroup within this area includes words that are spelled the same, have different meanings, and are pronounced differently. Some examples of homographs include:
Lie
Tear
Bow
Fair
Bass

Teaching homographs can be interesting and fun for the students. Incorporating them into passages where the students can use the context clues to decipher the different meanings of the homographs.   Games are also a good strategy for using to help students understand multiple meaning words. Jokes and riddles are usually based on homographs, and students love to make collections or books of these.

Semantic Feature Analysis: This technique for enhancing vocabulary skills by using semantic cues is based on the research of Johnson and Pearson (1984) and Anders and Bos (1986). It involves young children in setting up a feature analysis grid of various subject content words which is an outgrowth of their discussion about these words.

For instance, Cooper (2004) includes a sample of a Semantic Features Analysis Grid for Vegetables. .

Vegetables	Green	Have Peels	Eat Raw	Seeds
Carrots	-	+	+	-
Cabbage	+	-	+	-

Note: that the use of the + for yes, - for no, and possible use for + and - if a vegetable like squash could be both green and yellow.

Teachers of children in grade one and beyond can design their own semantic analysis grids to meet their students' needs and to align with the topics the kids are learning. Select a category or class of words (could be planets, rodent family members, winter words, weather words).

Use the left side of the grid to list at least three if not more items that fit this category. The number of actual items listed will depend on the age and grade level of the children with three or four items fine for K-1 and up to 10-15 for grades 5 and 6. Brainstorm with the children or if better suited to the class, the teacher may list on his/her own features that the items have in common. As can be noted from the example excerpted from *Cooper's Literacy -Helping Children Construct Meaning* (2004), these common features such as vegetables' green color, peels, and seeds are usually fairly easy to identify.

Show the children how to insert the notations +, -, and even ?, (If they are not certain) on the grid. The teacher might also explore with the children the possibility that an item could get both a + and a -. For example, a vegetable like broccoli might be eaten cooked or raw depending on taste and squash can be green or yellow.

Whatever the length of the grid when first presented to the children (perhaps as a semantic cue lesson in and of itself tied in to a text being read in class), make certain that the grid as presented and fillied out is not the end of the activity.

Children can use it as a model for developing their own semantic features grids and share them with the whole class. Child-developed grids can become part of a Word Work center in the classroom or even be published in a Word Study Games book by the class as a whole. Such a publication can be shared with parents during open school week and evening visits and with peer classes.

Contextual Redefinition

This strategy encourages children to use the context more effectively by presenting them with sufficient context BEFORE they begin reading. It models for the children the use of contextual clues to make informed guesses about word meanings.

To apply this strategy, the teacher should first select unfamiliar words for teaching. No more than two or three words should be selected for direct teaching. The teacher should then write a sentence in which there are sufficient clues supplied for the child to successfully figure out the meaning. Among the types of context clues the teacher can use are: compare/contrast, synonyms, and direct definition Then the teacher should present the words only on the experiential chart or as letter cards. Have the children pronounce the words. As they pronounce them, challenge them to come up with a definition for each word. After more than one definition is offered, encourage the children to decide as a whole group what the definition is. Write down their agreed upon definition with no comment as to its accurate meaning.

Then share with the children the contexts (sentences the teacher wrote with the words and explicit context clues). Ask that the children to read the sentences aloud. Then have them come up with a definition for each word. Make certain that as they present their definitions, the teacher does not comment. Ask that they justify their definitions by making specific references to the context clues in the sentences. As the discussion continues, direct the children's attention to their previously agreed upon definition of the word. Facilitate their discussing the differences between their guesses about the word when they saw only the word itself and their guesses about the word when they read it in context. Finally have the children check their use of context skills to correctly define the word by using a dictionary.

Development of Word Analysis Skills by Individual Students

This type of direct teaching of word definitions is useful when the children have dictionary skills and the teacher is aware of the fact that there are not sufficient clues about the words in the context to help the students define it. In addition, struggling readers and students from ELL backgrounds may benefit tremendously from being walked through this process that highly proficient and successful readers apply automatically

By using this strategy, the teacher can also "kid watch" and note the students' prior knowledge as they guess the word in isolation. The teacher can also actually witness and hear how various students use context skills.

Through their involvement in this strategy, struggling readers gain a feeling of community as they experience the ways in which their struggles and guesses resonate with other peers' responses to the text.

In its earliest stages, word identification strategies include teacher modeling during shared reading experiences with the students. During the reading, teachers should focus on the patterns of language, such as rhyme and repetition. Sentence patterns are also important in this pre-word- recognition stage. Time should be allowed for students to focus on interesting words so that the teacher can provide direct instruction on decoding skills.

The use of authentic literature provides opportunities for students to practice word-identification skills. Guided reading, cooperative reading and, finally, independent reading allow students time to practice reading words they know and help them to decode unfamiliar words. Once students reach the independent stage of word recognition, teachers need to focus on fluency in reading through texts that contain words students automatically recognize and do not have to spend time trying to decode.

Skill 4.4   **Knows how to plan, implement and monitor age-appropriate instruction that is responsive to individual students' strengths, needs and interests and is based on ongoing informal and formal assessment of individual students' word identification skills**

See Skills 4.1 and 4.2

Skill 4.5   **Applies knowledge of instructional strategies and materials that reflect cultural diversity, are based on a convergence of research evidence, and promote students; understanding and application of word identification skills**

See Skills 4.1 and 4.2

Skill 4.6   **Knows how to provide systematic instruction and reinforcing activities to promote students' word identification skills, including the use of increasingly complex, connected text**

See Skills 4.1 and 4.2

Skill 4.7   Demonstrates knowledge of delays or differences in students' development of word identification skills and strategies and when such delays/differences warrant assessment and additional intervention

When students develop word-recognition skills, they have a wide repertoire of words that they can recognize as soon as they see them in a text. When they cannot automatically recognize words without having to think about decoding them, reading becomes a laborious process. This causes greater difficulty as students move into more challenging texts. Instant word recognition helps to increase reading fluency and reading comprehension.

Words for recognition are sorted into grade levels; and, having mastered words from an earlier grade level does not necessarily mean that students are developing new word knowledge. They must learn how to decode more words, and this is important when encountering more challenging text.

Quite often, the key to helping students develop word-recognition skills is to find reading materials that they are interested in. In the early grades, students should recognize words that teachers have modeled frequently. There will be students in the class who are not progressing as rapidly as the others. Some of these students will have problems in reading if their delays or differences are not identified. Teachers may have to work with these students in small groups or even on an individual basis to help them progress.

If there are students in the class for whom direct instruction and other intervention strategies in word-recognition skills are not working, then it is time for teachers to look at other methods of helping those students. Assessments related to recognizing words will confirm or deny that the students are having problems and will point the way to what teachers should do next. By sharing the results of the assessment with parents/guardians and other professionals in the school setting, information may come to light about medical issues. An intervention plan needs to be developed so that parents know how to help children at home and are aware of the strategies that teachers are using in the classroom. Reading specialists may need to set aside blocks of time for working with these students on a one-to-one basis or may need to review phonological awareness skills that the students have not yet grasped.

Teachers will want to maintain individual records of children's reading behaviors that demonstrate the alphabetic principle and graphophonemic awareness. The following performance standards should be part of a record template form for each child in grades K-1 and beyond as needed (depending on ELL or special needs):

- Match all consonant and short vowel sounds.
- Read one's own name.
- Read one-syllable words and high-frequency words.
- Demonstrate ability to read and understand that as letters in words change, so do the sounds.
- Generate the sounds from all letters including consonant blends and long vowel patterns. Blend those different sounds into recognizable words.
- Read common sight words.
- Read common word families.
- Recognize and use knowledge of spelling patterns when reading--run/running, hop/hopping.
- Decode (sound out) regular words with more than one syllable (vacation, graduation).
- Recognize regular abbreviations (Feb., Mr., PS).

Any record kept of an individual child's progress should include each date of observation and some legend or rubric detailing the level of performance, standard acquisition, or mastery. Some teachers use 'Y' for 'exhibits the reading behavior consistently,' 'M' for 'making progress toward the standard,' and 'N' for 'has not yet exhibited the behavior.' Beyond this objective legend for the assessment, the teacher should include any other comments which detail the child's progress in reading.

COMPETENCY 5.0 FLUENCY

Skill 5.1 **Recognizes the components of reading fluency (e.g., rate, accuracy, and prosody), and demonstrates knowledge of the relationship between fluency and reading comprehension**

Fluency is the ability to read a text quickly and with comprehension. It is an important connection between word recognition and reading. Children that can read fluently do not have to spend large chunks of time trying to decode words and thus lose the meaning of the text. The rate at which students read is affected by how automatically they recognize words. Fluency and automaticity are not the same thing. Students many be able to automatically identify words in a list, but still not be fluent readers able to read sentences quickly with prosody.

There are three components to being able to read fluently. The rate at which the students read should be at the same rate of speech. Many students can read rapidly, but they do not have accuracy or prosody. Accuracy is the number of words they read correctly and prosody is reading with expression, putting in the correct intonation depending on the punctuation and the meaning of the text. When students have all three of these present when reading a passage, they are fluent readers at their grade level.

In the early stages of reading, students may read slowly because they are focusing on the words. The rate at which they read changes according to the text, their familiarity with the topic, and the amount of interest that they have in reading. Thus, students may read a familiar rhyme fluently, but have trouble with the same words in a story. They also need time to practice the reading.

In the instruction of reading, fluent reading has often been an overlooked, under-taught skill in schools. It was with the research review from the work of the National Reading Panel that fluency came to the forefront. The research has indicated that there is a correlation that a child who reads fluently will be more likely to comprehend the text than a child who does not demonstrate fluent reading. Since the end result of all reading is comprehension, this body of research cannot be ignored.

Reading fluency is a broad term that is used to describe reading that has a high degree of accuracy, appropriate phrasing, smoothness, and an appropriate pace. In order to achieve all of these goals, children must be able to decode words in a very automatic and rapid way.

Reading is a complex task requiring many cognitive processes to occur simultaneously. Efficient and automatic decoding of text allows students to free up some of their mental energy to better address other areas, particularly comprehension. Children who struggle with decoding spend so much mental energy attempting to decode words that there is not enough of a reserve to address the comprehension issues.

Fluency develops over time and with much repetition and practice. The analogy is often drawn to learning to drive a car. When individuals first learn to drive a car, they must concentrate on every little aspect involved - which foot goes on the accelerator, how much pressure should be place on the pedal, and how to keep the car within the lane, etc. Often, distractions such as pedestrians or radio noise cause large over-corrections or require additional time for the newer drivers to respond correctly. However, as the drivers become more skilled, they spend less energy on those more rote tasks previously described. They now have more time to devote to anticipating events. In some cases, they can use their mental energy to think about things unrelated to driving completely. How many times have you driven somewhere and not remembered how you got there? This is because, for you, driving has become automatic and freed you up for other more complex cognitions.

This automatic capacity in reading is essential as the amount of information in texts grows and students are required to comprehend more and more information in order to be successful. Imagine trying to proceed through a college level course or text if you had to spend time decoding every word presented. You would gain nothing from the work and time you devoted; thus it is vital that students develop automaticity with decoding.

Skill 5.2   Demonstrates knowledge of expected patterns of development in reading fluency (including the developmental benchmarks), implications of individual variations in the development of fluency

Fluency is the ability to read a text quickly and accurately. When reading silently, fluent readers can recognize words automatically, and they fully comprehend what they read. If comprehension is not immediate, these readers can use context clues to grasp the meaning of the sentence or paragraph. When reading aloud, fluent readers display confidence, and they read effortlessly and with expression (prosody). This is in contrast to readers who are not fluent – they read so slowly, often one word at a time, that meaning is lost.

Fluency is an important skill when learning to read because it helps readers to develop from the word-recognition stage to one where they can understand what they read. When readers don't have to spend time focusing on reading individual words, they can group words together to form ideas, which leads to comprehension. Not only can they grasp the main idea of the text, but they can make connections between the text and their prior knowledge and events in their own lives.

Fluency is a skill that readers have to develop over time with repeated practice and exposure to literature and opportunities to read for various purposes. Early readers read words rather than phrases and sentences, and the act of reading often appears to be laborious rather than enjoyable. In order to become fluent, readers have to decode the letters and words. Eventually this leads to comprehension of ideas.

Even when readers do have a repertoire of words that they recognize easily, they may not be fluent readers. This is because the expression is missing from the reading. Reading fluently with expression means that the reader must be able to chunk the text into meaningful segments – phrases and clauses. Fluency changes over time as readers are exposed to more difficult texts. The most fluent readers at one level may read slowly when they are first introduced to a more difficult text because they need time for comprehension.

Some techniques to use when teaching students to read fluently include:

- repeated reading of the same text
- oral reading practice using audiotapes
- provide models of what fluent reading looks and sounds like
- read to students
- choral reading
- partner reading
- Readers' Theatre

Automaticity

Automaticity is not the same as fluency. This is the fast and effortless recognition of words that only comes through repeated practice. Automaticity refers to accurate reading of words. It does not refer to reading with expression or reading with comprehension. It deals with word recognition only. It is necessary for fluency, but it is not the only factor that determines whether or not a student can read fluently.

Decoding and Reading Comprehension

To decode means to change communication signals into messages. Reading comprehension requires that the reader learn the code within which a message is written and be able to decode it to get the message.

Although effective reading comprehension requires identifying words automatically (Adams, 1990, Perfetti, 1985), children do not have to be able to identify every single word or know the exact meaning of the every word in a text to understand it. Indeed, Nagy (1988) says that, children can read a work with a high level of comprehension even if they do not fully know as many as 15 percent of the words within a given text.

Children develop the ability to decode and recognize words automatically. They then can extend their ability to decode to multi-syllabic words.

J. David Cooper (2004) and other advocates of the Balanced Literacy Approach feel that children become literate, effective communicators and able to comprehend by learning phonics and other aspects of word identification through the use of engaging reading texts. Engaging text, as defined by the balanced literacy group, are those texts containing highly predictable elements of rhyme, sound patterns, and plot. Researchers such as Chall (1983) and Flesch (1981) support a phonics-centered foundation before the use of engaging reading texts. This is at the crux of the Phonics versus Whole Language /Balanced Literacy/ Integrated Language Arts teaching-of-reading controversy.

It is important for the new teacher, educator, and/or for the teacher candidate to be informed about both sides of this controversy and the work of theorists who attempt to reconcile these two perspectives, such as Kenneth Goodman (1994). Take it from a veteran teacher and educator that there are powerful arguments on both sides of this controversy, and each approach works wonderfully with some students and does not succeed with others.

As far as the examinations go, all that is asked of you is the ability to demonstrate that you are familiar with these varied perspectives. If asked on a constructed-response question, you need to be able to show that you can talk about teaching some aspect of reading using strategies from one or the other or a combination of these approaches.

Working teachers can, depending on the perspective of their school administration and the needs of the particular children they serve, choose from the strategies and approaches.

Skill 5.3   Knows how to plan, implement, and monitor age-appropriate instruction that is responsive to individual students' strengths, needs and interests and is based on ongoing informal and formal assessment of individual students' reading fluency

Age-appropriate instruction for reading fluency involves immersing the students in print and modeling reading fluency for them. Students need ample time to practice the skills that teachers provide instruction on in the classroom.

Repeated readings – reading the same passages over and over again is one way that students can develop fluency and automaticity in reading. However, this practice does not work well if teachers expect students to read and reread passages that they do not enjoy. It is not a good idea to reread a text several times in the same class period. Instead, this should be done by introducing a story or rhyme one day and them rereading it for the next several days. Encourage students to supply words by stopping at places in the text where the students know the word that comes next and having them say it. Having students read along with the teacher after the first few rereading is also another strategy to use in repeated readings. The text should also be available in the classroom for students to read on their own or to take home for reading with parents.

Books on tape also help encourage fluency in reading as students read along with the tape. The students should have a book to follow along with as they listen to the reader on the tape. Then they can reread the text by reading along with the tape. This helps them to have a model to read along with as they practice fluency.

Partner Reading – Paired students take turns reading aloud to each other. Teachers can pair a fluent readers with those who need practice so that there is a model provided. The stronger reader of the pair reads part of the text out loud, and then the weaker reader takes a turn reading the same passage.

Teachers can also pair two readers of the same skill level to reread a story on which they have already received instruction for word identification. It then becomes a matter of practice for them to develop fluency in reading.
In **choral reading** the students can read along with the teacher as a group, but they do need to be able to see the text as they are reading. This could be from a big book or from their own books. Patterned or predictable books are the best choice for this method as students will be able to predict what lines or words are coming next after repeated readings.

As teachers listen to students read either independently or along with a model, they can assess how well the students are progressing with fluency. By making notes on how well the students are doing, teachers can adjust the rate of instruction to meet the needs of those who are progressing well and for those who need extra help.

In order to determine how well students are progressing with reading fluently, teachers can do a timed assessment of a student reading a passage. In this assessment, the teacher chooses a grade-level passage and counts the number of words in the passage. Allow the student to read for one minute, and then count the number of words the student has read. Also, count the number of errors the student made, and subtract them from the total words read in the time allotted. Compare the results with norms that have been published at the grade level to determine how fluently the student is reading.

Skill 5.4   Applies knowledge of instructional strategies and materials that reflect cultural diversity, are based on a convergence of research evidence, and promote students' reading fluency

Although students need models to follow to become fluent readers, they also need texts that are on their reading level. When students are not adept at recognizing all the words in the text and spend large amounts of time trying to decode the words, then they are not reading fluently. Teachers can tell when students need fluency instruction when they:

- Make more than 10% errors when reading an unfamiliar text

- Cannot read with expression

- Have poor comprehension of the text

The books that teachers have in the classroom for the students should be at their grade level. If there are some students who are above and below grade level, there should be reading materials provided for them as well.

See also Skill 5.3

Skill 5.5   Knows how to provide systematic instruction and reinforcing activities to promote students' reading fluency

See Skill 5.3

Skill 5.6   Demonstrates knowledge of delays or differences in students' reading fluency and when such delays/ differences warrant further assessment and additional intervention

Through formal and informal assessment, teachers can determine when students need help with developing as fluent readers. Students who cannot fluently read a story that has been modeled over-and-over by the teacher may need to be tested further to determine where the problem lies.

Adjustment of Reading Instruction Based on Ongoing Assessment

The running records taken of children help teachers learn about the cueing systems that children use. It is important for teachers to adjust reading instruction based on the pattern of miscues gathered from several successive reading records. When teachers carefully review a given student's substitutions and self corrections, certain patterns begin to surface.

Children may use visual cues as they read and add meaning to self correct. To the alert teacher, the reliance on visual cues indicates that readers aren't making sense of what they are reading. This means that teachers need to check to see what cueing system children use when they are reading "just right" books.

Children who use visual and structural cues when they are reading without paying heed to meaning need to use meaning more consistently for cues. Children who use meaning but not visual/graphophonic cues need to understand the importance of getting and reconstructing the author's message. They have to be able to share the author's story, not their own.

Not only can and should teachers use the material in the children's ongoing assessment notebook to adjust the child's current instruction, but also teachers should teach children to use the document to monitor their growth as successful readers over time.

In addition, if the same concerns surface over the use of a particular cueing system or high-frequency word, the teacher can adjust the class wall chart and even devote a whole class lesson to the particular element.

COMPETENCY 6.0 COMPREHENSION55

Skill 6.1   Knows a variety of comprehension theories/models (transactional, interactive, metacognitive, socio-psycholinguistic, constructivist) and their impact on instructional strategies

Transactional Theory

The transactional theory of reading comprehension suggests that there is an interaction between readers and texts. This theory places a great deal of responsibility on teachers in helping the students to make meaning of texts. Students should be encouraged to respond to their reading and reflect upon what they read. The classroom atmosphere must be one of cooperation where all student responses are accepted. Before reading, students should be asked to predict what they think the text is about, look for clues during reading, and confirm or deny their predictions after the reading.

Teachers make clear to the students that their responses are invited, and these ideas become the starting points for classroom discussions. Teachers may need to provide background information for those students who do not have any prior knowledge about the topic of the text. Students also need time to develop their ideas and need to be taught to respect other students' points of view. They should also be directed to connect their reading to other points in their lives – e.g., other books they have read, things they have seen, or places they have visited.

Interactive Theory

In this theory, reading is seen as the interaction between what readers bring to the text and what they read. Readers use both top-down and bottom-up skills. The top-down model starts with what the students know. They start with a hypothesis and prediction and then attempt to verify what they believe to be true. According to Goodman (1986), there are five processes that students employ when reading:

- Recognition-initiation

- Prediction

- Confirmation

- Correction

- Termination

It makes readers active participants in the reading process.

The bottom-up approach suggests that students decode the words by sounding them out, and this is what the students are doing when they are reading.

In the interactive theory, students need to use both of these approaches to make meaning of the text. There should not be an over-reliance of either approach; rather, each one should balance the other. Word substitutions are suitable if they make sense in the sentence and do not change the meaning. According to Stanovich (1980), the top-down approach makes reading easy for readers who have prior knowledge, but who have poor word recognition skills; and the use of the bottom-up approach makes reading easy for those who are skilled at word recognition, but who do not bring any prior knowledge of the topic to the text.

Metacognitive Theory

The metacognitive theory focuses on six strategies that students use when reading in order to make sense of the text. These are:

- Setting a purpose for reading

- Activating prior knowledge

- Paying attention to important ideas in the text

- Evaluating for consistency and compatibility with prior knowledge

- Self-monitoring for understanding

- Making inferences and confirming or denying them

In this theory readers learn that the text they are reading is an organization of concepts rather than words in isolation or isolated facts. They work to understand what the words and sentences mean, are able to retell the text in their own words, and make inferences.

Socio-psycholinguistic Theory

The socio-psycholinguistic theory of reading stems from the work of Kenneth Goodman and incorporates the linguistic nature of reading and the influence that social settings have on language. He states that rules for language differ according to the situation and region, and this is something that reading specialists and teachers should pay attention to.

According to this theory, students start reading by recognizing what they are reading and going through a series of experiments through letters and words to make meaning of the text. The way they read has a lot to do with what they expect to find in the text. This refers to the words they use to substitute for those they don't know. They will make informed inferences about the words as they use cueing systems to decode the words. They are able to recognize when words don't make sense with the meaning of the text and, therefore, will go back and make the necessary connections.

Within this theory, reading is cyclical rather than linear. Readers constantly use visual, perceptual, syntactic, and semantic cues. Reading is goal-oriented, with the overall meaning being the goal. Students use prediction and inference to help them move toward their goals.

<u>Constructivist Theory</u>
The constructivist theory is based on the work of Jerome Bruner and suggests that readers, while relying on a cognitive structure, construct new knowledge from the text based on their prior knowledge. Teachers using this theory will encourage the students to discover things about reading on their own. This means there is active dialogue in the classroom, and that the instruction should be organized in a spiral manner so that readers build on what they have learned before.

The instruction teachers provide must be consistent with the willingness of the students to learn. It must be easy for the students to grasp and designed to facilitate the acquisition of new knowledge or to fill in any gaps in the learning.

Decoding

In the late I960's and the I970's, many reading specialists, most prominently Fries (1962), believed that successful decoding resulted in reading comprehension. This meant that if children could sound out the words, they would then automatically be able to comprehend the words. Many teachers of reading and many reading texts still subscribe to this theory.

Asking questions

Another theory or approach to the teaching of reading that gained currency in the late sixties and the early seventies was the importance of asking inferential and critical thinking questions of the reader which would challenge and engage the children in the text. This approach to reading went beyond the literal level of what was stated in the text to an inferential level of using text clues to make predictions and to a critical level of involving the child in evaluating the text. While asking engaging and thought-provoking questions is still viewed as part of the teaching of reading, it is only viewed currently as a component of the teaching of reading.

Comprehension "Skills"

As various reading theories, practices, and approaches percolated during the 1970's and 1980's, many educators and researchers in the field came to believe that the teacher of reading had to teach a set of discrete "Comprehension Skills" (Otto et al, 1977). Therefore the reading teacher became the teacher of each individual comprehension skill. Children in such classrooms came away with: main idea, sequence, cause and effect, and other concepts that were supposed to make them better comprehenders. However, did it make them lifelong readers?

Bottom-up, Top-down, Interactional Theories of Reading

Bottom-up theories of reading assume that children learn from part-to-whole starting with the smallest segments possible. Instruction begins with a strong phonics approach, learning letter-sound relationships and often using basal readers or *decodable books*. Decodable books are vocabulary-controlled using language from word families with high predictability. Thus we get sentences like "Nan has a tan fan." Reading is seen as skills-based, and the skills are taught one at a time.

Top-down theories of reading suggest that reading begins with the reader's knowledge, not the print. Children are seen as having a drive to construct meaning. This stance views reading as moving from the whole to the parts. An early top-down theory was the *whole word* approach. Children memorized high-frequency words to assist them in reading the Dick and Jane books of the 30s. Then teachers helped children discover letter-sound correpondences in what they read. A more recent top-down theory is the *whole language* approach. This approach was influenced by research on how young children learned language. It was thought that children could learn to read as naturally as they learned to talk. Children were surrounded by print in their classrooms, using quality literature often printed in Big Books and were viewed as writers from the start. Hence journals kept by kindergarten children. Advocates of whole language viewed the "skill'em-drill'em-and kill'em" approach based on bottom-up theories as a deadly dull introduction to the world of reading.

Interactive theories of reading combine the strengths of both bottom-up and top-down approaches. Teachers need to be able to teach decoding, vocabulary, and comprehension skills to support children's drive for meaning and desire for a stimulating exchange with high-quality literary texts from their earliest days in school. Strategies include shared, guided, and independent reading, Big Books, reading and writing workshops, and the like. Today this approach is called the *balanced literacy approach.* It is considered to be a synthesis of the best from bottom-up and top-down methods.

Literacy and Literacy Learning

To be literate in the 21ˢᵗ century world means more than being able to read and write. To live well and happily in today's society an individual has to be able to read, not only newspapers and books, but emails, blogs, directions for how to use one's cell phone, and the like. There has evolved a "disconnect" between the isolated reading comprehension skills the schools were teaching and the literacy skills including listening and speaking that are crucial for employment and personal and academic success. Thornburg (1992, 2003) has also noted that technology capacities and the ability to communicate online are now integral parts of our sense of literacy.

Cooper (2004) views literacy as reading, writing, thinking, listening, viewing, and discussing. These are not viewed as separate activities or components of instruction, but rather as developing and being nurtured simultaneously and interactively. Children learn these abilities by engaging in authentic explorations, readings, projects and experiences.

Just as in learning how to ride a bike, the learner goes through various approximations before learning how to actually ride the bike, so too does the reader with the scaffold (support) of the teacher go through various approximations before developing his/her own independent literacy skills and capacities.

Emergent Literacy: the concept that young children are emerging into reading and writing with no real beginning or ending point. Children are introduced into the word of print as soon as their parents read board books to them at the age of one or two. When children scribble write or use invented spelling during the preschool years, they reveal themselves as detectives of the written word, having watched parents and teachers make lists, write thank-you notes, or leave messages. This view of the reader assumes that all children have a drive to make meaning in print and will begin doing it almost on their own if surrounded by a print-rich environment.

Reading Readiness: an approach which is antithetical to emergent literacy in that it assumes that all children must have mastered a sequence of reading skills before they can begin to read. This approach stands in contrast to emergent literacy.

Language Acquisition: continuous and never-ending. From the perspective of this theory and research, all children come to school with a language base which the school must build on. As a consequence of the connection between oral language and reading, it is important that schools build literacy experiences around the language the child brings to the school.

Prior Knowledge, Schemata, Background, and Comprehension

Schemata are structures which represent generic concepts stored in our memory (Rumelhart, 1980). Young children develop their schemata through experiences. Prior knowledge and the lack of experiences in some cases influence comprehension. The more closely the reader's experiences and schemata approximate those of the writer, the more likely the reader is to comprehend the text. It is obvious that for many children from non-native English language speaking backgrounds and perhaps for those from struggling socio-economic family structures schemata deficits indicate the need for intense teacher support as these children become emergent and early readers.

Often the teacher will have to model and scaffold for the child the steps to form a schemata from the information provided in a text.

Comprehension

Cooper defines comprehension as: "a strategic process by which readers construct or assign meaning to a text by using the clues in the text and their own prior knowledge. " We view comprehension as a process where the reader transacts with the text to construct or assign meaning. Reading and writing are both interconnected and mutually supportive. Comprehension is a strategic process in which readers adjust their reading to suit their reading purpose and the type or genre of text they are reading. Narrative and expository texts require different reading approaches because of their different text structures.

Strategic readers also call into play their metacognitive capacities as they analyze texts so that they are self aware of the skills needed to construct meaning from the text structure.

The Role of Literature in Developing Literacy

The balanced literacy approach advocates the use of "real literature"— recognized works of the best of children's fiction and non-fiction trade books and winners of such awards as the Newberry and Caldecott medals for helping children develop literacy.

Balanced literacy advocates argue that:

- Real literature engages young readers and assures that they will become lifelong readers.

- Real literature also offers readers a language base that can help them expand their expressiveness as readers and as writers.

- Real literature is easier to read and understand than grade-leveled texts

There are districts in the United States where the phonics-only approach is heavily embedded. However, the majority of school districts would describe their approach to reading as the balanced literacy approach which includes phonics work as well as the use of real literature texts. To contrast the phonics and balanced literacy approaches as opposite is inaccurate, since a balanced approach includes both.

It is important to go online and to visit the key resources of the NCTE, National Council of Teachers of English, and the IRA, International Reading Association, to keep abreast of the latest research in the field.

Skill 6.2　Identifies student factors that affect reading comprehension (e.g., schema, past reading instruction, oral language, interests, attitudes, word recognition skills, vocabulary, fluency, ability to monitor understanding)

Some of the factors that affect students' reading comprehension include:

- Schema (Background knowledge). In order for students to have comprehension of what they read, they do need to have some background knowledge of the subject matter. Sometimes they do have some knowledge, but do not know how to bring it to a conscious level. Through such prereading activities as brainstorming, using graphic organizers, questioning, and writing activities, teachers can assess how much prior knowledge the students have and what background information they need to provide to them. Once they do determine what background knowledge is needed, teachers will know how much time they need to allot to the instruction and what activities they need to use to help reinforce the learning.
- Lack of vocabulary knowledge – when students do not have the necessary vocabulary knowledge, they will not be able to understand what the words mean.
- Fluency difficulties – students who read slowly because they have to spend time decoding will lose the meaning as they focus on the individual words. They may not put expression into their reading; and, thus, they lose the meaning that is conveyed through punctuation and phrasing.
- Lack of word-recognition skills – if students do not have a sight vocabulary at their grade level, they will have difficulty understanding what they read. They will spend most of the time trying to decode the words, and this will hamper the understanding they get from the text.
- Metacognition – students are aware of their own thinking while they attempt to understand the material.
- Student motivation – when students are not motivated by the material teachers ask them to read, they will not be able to comprehend the material because they don't have the same amount of interest in it as they would if it were a topic they liked.

- Syntax and sentence structure- students need instruction on how connecting words in the text can affect their understanding of the text
- Text structure – students in the early grades are familiar with narrative writing, but may have difficulty with comprehension when they are introduced to expository writing
- Strategies – students need instruction in strategies to help them with comprehension, such as inferencing, summarizing, predicting, formulating questions, and visualizing the text.
- Integration of background knowledge with the information in the text
- Past reading instruction – as students progress through the grades, they go through different teachers and therefore different methods of instruction. Reading specialists have to take this into consideration, especially if they are dealing with students who are learning English.

Skill 6.3   Applies knowledge of textual factors that affect reading comprehension (e.g., readability, vocabulary, visual representations, text organization, author's schema, genre, syntactical and conceptual density)

<u>Readability</u>
The text must be, first of all, on the students' reading level. It refers to the ease with which students can read a passage. If it is too hard, then students will have difficulty reading and understanding the material. When material is presented at the students' reading level, they will recognize 90% of the words and will be able to read fluently without having to stop to decode the words.

Some of the factors that can affect the readability include:

- Technical material beyond the scope of the students' understanding

- Use of vocabulary with which the students are not familiar

- The length of the text

<u>Text Organization</u>
Traditionally, the aspects of expository-text reading comprehension have been taught in a dry format using reference books from the school or public library (the Atlas, Almanac, dusty, large geography volumes, etc.) to teach these necessary and meaningful skills.

Although these worthy library (and perhaps classroom library) books can still be used, it is much easier to take a simple newspaper to introduce and provide children with daily, ongoing, authentic experiences in learning these necessary skills while they also keep up with real world events that positively and negatively affect their daily lives.

They can go on a chronological hunt through the daily newspaper and discover the many formats of schedules contained therein. For instance, some newspapers include a calendar of the week with literary, sports, social, movie, and other public events. Children can also go on scavenger hunts through various sections of the newspaper and on certain days find full blown timelines detailing famous individuals' careers, business histories, milestones in the political history of a nation, or even key movies made by famous movie directors up for an Oscar.

The nature of newspaper reportage and the public's need to know the why and wherefore behind natural disasters, company takeovers, and political upheavals lead newspapers to represent events graphically and to use cause /effect diagramming and comparison/contrast wording. If teachers specifically wants to make certain that the students come away with this material, they can pre-clip "teaching" stories from the news for the children and post them in a special NEWS center.

After children have been walked through these comparison/contrast news writings and cause/effect diagramming as it has appeared in the newspaper, they can be challenged to find additional examples of these text structures in the news or challenged to reframe or rewrite familiar stories using these text structures. They can even use desktop publishing to re-author the stories using the same text structures.
If a class participates in a local Newspapers in Education program, where the children receive a newspaper for free two to three times a week within the classroom, the teacher can teach index skills using the index of the newspaper and having children race to find various features.

Map and chart skills take on much more relevance and excitement when the children work on these skills using sports charts detailing the batting averages and pass completions of their favorite players or perhaps the box scores of their older siblings' football and baseball games. Maps dealing with holiday weather become meaningful to children as they anticipate a holiday vacation.

Visual Representations
Students often refer to pictures when they are reading to help them infer or predict what will come next in the passage they are reading. They use the pictures to help them understand the story. Often teachers have students draw pictures about what they read to help assess whether or not students are comprehending what they read.

Genre

The genre of the text also affects how well the students can understand the material. Stories are the easiest for early readers to comprehend, and they have more difficulty understanding non-fiction than they do understanding fiction.

Authors use various ways to tell a story while employing various literary techniques. If teachers want students to understand the techniques, they need to teach them the characteristics of each narrative genre. It may be necessary to draw the students' attention to the elements and structure of narratives as well as the strategies they can use for reading each of the genres. Before students actually read a selection, the teacher can address the literary techniques, forms, and vocabulary in mini-lessons to provide the students with knowledge about what they will be reading about. This helps them to become more engaged with the text and to have an idea of what they should think about as they are reading.

Narrative genres:

Prose fiction - this is literature about imaginary people, places and events. The purpose of this narrative genre is to stimulate the students' imaginations and to present the author's view of the world. This genre includes novels, short stories and plays; each of which has its own distinctive characteristics. They all have a setting, conflict, plot, climax and resolution in varying degrees.

- Short story - this narrative usually has only one focus and a smaller world view. The students do have to determine whether the person telling the story is an outside narrator or is a character within the story. They do have to take note of the central conflict and determine why the characters act as they do. As a response to the story, they can decide how they feel about the characters and their actions and ask questions about the message that the author is trying to convey in the story.
- Novel - a novel is a longer version of the short story, often with sub-plots. During the reading, the students have to be able to keep the subplots separated and understand their relationship to the main plot of the novel. They must be aware of the motives of the various characters and of their own reactions to the characters' actions.

Prose non-fiction - this is literature that is about real events, times and places. It includes essays, journals, articles, letters, biographies and autobiographies. Much of the contemporary nonfiction reads like fiction; with suspense, expression and ingenuity of style. Because it is vivid and personal, it can provide the students with a model for their own writing. When students are reading for information, they need to keep this purpose in mind and may need time and instruction to help them summarize or restate the main ideas.

Poetry - this form of literature helps the author communicate ideas and feelings through an arrangement of words and sounds. Poetry can be used to capture a mood, tell a story, or explore different ideas. There are various literary techniques authors use in writing poetry, which the teacher can discuss with the class through mini-lessons.

Plays - these can be read for the purpose of performance or for literary effect. Students pay attention to the literary devices that the author uses. When reading a play, students can work on putting expression into their reading so that they can bring the characters to life.

Students should be aware of the purpose for reading so that they know what thinking is expected of them. When reading any text, students need to employ certain strategies. Therefore teachers need to engage the students in the reading process and model the appropriate strategies of:

- connecting
- making meaning
- questioning
- predicting
- inferencing
- reflecting
- evaluating

The Relationship Between Oral and Written Vocabulary Development and Reading Comprehension

Biemiller's (2003) research documents that those children entering 4th grade with significant vocabulary deficits demonstrate increasing reading comprehension problems. Evidence shows that these children do not catch up, but rather continue to fall behind.

Strategy One: Word Map Strategy

This strategy is useful for children grades 3-6 and beyond. The target group of children for this strategy includes those who need to improve their independent vocabulary acquisition abilities. The strategy is essentially teacher-directed learning where children are "walked through" the process. They are helped by the teacher to identify the type of information that makes a definition. They are also assisted in using context clues and background understanding to construct meaning.

The word map graphic organizer is the tool teachers use to complete this strategy with children. Word map templates are available online from the Houghton Mifflin web site and from READWRITETHINK, the web site of the NCTE (see webliography section). The word map helps the children to visually represent the elements of a given concept.

The children's literal articulation of the concept can be prompted by three key questions: What is it?; What is it like? What are some examples?

For instance, the word "oatmeal" might yield a word map with "What?", and in a rectangular box a hot cereal you eat in the morning, "What is it like?"; hot, mushy, salty, "What are some examples?", instant oatmeal you make in a minute, apple-flavor oatmeal, Irish Oatmeal.

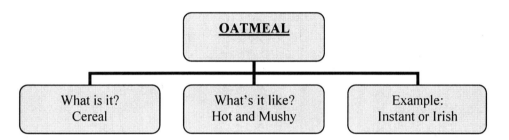

The procedure to be used in sharing this strategy with children is to select three concepts the children are familiar with. Then show them the template of a word map. Tell them that the three questions asked on the map and the boxes to fill in beneath them helps readers and writers to see what they need to know about a word. Next, help the children to complete at least two word maps for two of the three concepts that were pre-selected. Then have the children select a concept of their own to map either independently or in a small group. As the final task for this first part of the strategy, have the children, in teams or individually, write a definition for at least one of the concepts using the key things about it listed on the map. Have the children share these definitions aloud and talk about how they used the word maps to help them with the definitions.

For the next part of this strategy, the teacher should pick up an expository text or a textbook the children are already using to study mathematics, science or social studies. The teacher should either locate a short excerpt where a particular concept is defined or use the content to write model passages of definition on his/her own.

After the passages are selected or authored, the teacher should duplicate them. Then they should be distributed to the children along with blank word map templates. The children should be asked to read each passage and then to complete the word map for the concept in each passage. Finally, have the children share the word maps they have developed for each passage. Give them a chance to explain how they used the word in the passage to help them fill out their word map. End by telling them that the three components of the concept- class, description, example- are just three of the many components for any given concept.

This strategy has assessment potential because the teacher can literally see how the students understand specific concepts by looking at their maps and hearing their explanations. The maps the students develop on their own demonstrate whether they have really understood the concepts in the passages. This strategy serves to ready students for inferring word meanings on their own. By using the word map strategy, children develop concepts of what they need to know to begin to figure out an unknown word on their own. It assists the children in grades 3 and beyond to connect prior knowledge with new knowledge.

This word map strategy can be adapted by the teacher to suit the specific needs and goals of instruction. Illustrations of the concept and the comparisons to other concepts can be included in the word mapping for children grades 5 and beyond. This particular strategy is also one that can be used with a research theme in other content areas.

Strategy Two: Preview in Context

This is a direct teaching strategy which allows the teacher to guide the students as they examine words in context prior to reading a passage. Before beginning the strategy, the teacher selects only two or three key concept words. Then the teacher reads carefully to identify passages within the text that evidence strong context clues for the word.

Then the teacher presents the word and the context to the children. As the teacher reads aloud, the children follow along. Once the teacher has finished the read aloud, the children re-read the material silently. After the silent re-reading, the children will be coached by the teacher to a definition of one of the key words selected for study. This is done through a child-centered discussion. As part of the discussion, the teacher asks questions which get the children to activate their prior knowledge and to use the contextual clues to figure out the correct meaning of the selected key words. Make certain that the definition of the key concept word is finally made by the children.

Next, help the children to begin to expand the word's meaning. Do this by having them consider the following for the given key concept word: synonyms, antonyms, other contexts or other kinds of stories/texts where the word might appear. This is the time to have the children check their responses to the challenge of identifying word synonyms and antonyms by having them go to the thesaurus or the dictionary to confirm their responses. In addition, have the children place the synonyms or antonyms they find in their word boxes or word journals. The recording of their findings will guarantee them ownership of the words and deepen their capacity to use contextual clues.

The main point to remember in using this strategy is that it should only be used when the context is strong. It will not work with struggling readers who have less prior knowledge. Through listening to the children's responses as the teacher helps them to define the word and its potential synonyms and antonyms, the teacher can assess their ability to successfully use context clues. The key to this simple strategy is that it allows the teacher to draw the child out and to grasp through the child's responses the individual child's thinking process. The more talk from the child the better.

The Role of Systematic, Noncontextual Vocabulary Strategies

Strategy One: Hierarchical and Linear Arrays

The very complexity of the vocabulary used in this strategy description, may be unnerving for the teacher. Yet this strategy included in the Cooper (2004) literacy instruction is really very simple once it is outlined directly for children.

By using the term "hierarchical and linear" arrays, Cooper really is talking about how some words are grouped based on associative meanings. The words may have a "hierarchical" relationship to one another. For instance, an undergraduate or a first grader is lower in the school hierarchy than the graduate student and second grader. Within an elementary school, the fifth grader is at the top of the hierarchy and the pre K or kindergartener is at the bottom of the hierarchy. By the way, the term for this strategy obviously need not be explained in this detail to K-3 children, but might be shared with some grade and age appropriate modifications with children in grades 3 and beyond. It will enrich their vocabulary development and ownership of arrays they create.

Words can have a linear relationship to one another in that they run a spectrum from bad to good-for example from K-3 experiences, pleased-happy-overjoyed. These relationships can be displayed in horizontal boxes connected with dashes. Below is another way to display hierarchical relationships.

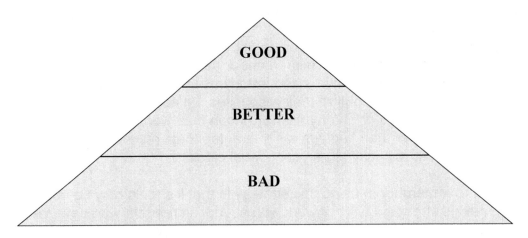

Once you get past the seemingly daunting vocabulary words, the arrays turn out to be another neat, graphic organizer tool which can help children "see" how words relate to one another.

To use this graphic organizer, the teacher should pre-select a group of words from a read aloud or from the children's writing. Show the children how the array will look using arrows for the linear array and just straight lines for the hierarchy. In fact invite some children up to draw the straight hierarchy lines as it is presented, so they have a role in developing even the first hierarchical model. Do one hierarchy array and one linear array with the pre selected word with the children. Talk them through filling out (or helping the teacher to fill out) the array. After the children have had their own successful experience with arrays, they can select the words from their independent texts or familiar, previously read favorites to study. They will also need to decide which type of array, hierarchical or linear, is appropriate. For 5th and 6th graders, this choice can and should be voiced using the now "owned" vocabulary words "hierarchical array" and "linear array."

This strategy is best used after reading, since it will help the children to expand their word banks.

Contextual Vocabulary Strategies

Vocabulary Self-Collection. This strategy is one in which children, even on the emergent level from grade 2 and up, take responsibility for their learning. It is also by definition, a student centered strategy, which demonstrates student ownership of their chosen vocabulary.

This strategy is one that can be introduced by the teacher early in the year, perhaps even the first day or week. The format for self-collection can then be started by the children. It may take the form of a journal with photocopied template pages. It can be continued throughout the year.

To start, ask the children to read a required text or story. Invite them to select one word for the class to study from this text or story. The children can work individually, in teams or in small groups. The teacher can also do the self-collecting so that this becomes the joint effort of the class community of literate readers. Tell the children that they should select words which particularly interest them or which are unique in some way.

After the children have had time to make their selections and to reflect on them, make certain that they have time to share them with their peers as a whole class. When each child shares the word which he or she has selected, have them provide a definition for the word. Each word that is given should be listed on a large experiential chart or even in a BIG BOOK format, if that is age and grade appropriate. The teacher should also share the word he or she selected and provide a definition. The teacher's definition and sharing should be somewhere in the middle of the children's recitations.

The dictionary should be used to verify the definitions. When all the definitions have been checked, a final list of child-selected (and single teacher-selected) words should be made.

Once this final list has been compiled, the children can record it in their word journals or they may opt to record only those words they find interesting in their individual journals. It is up to the teacher at the onset of the vocabulary self-collection activity to decide whether the children have to record all the words on the final list or can eliminate some. The decision made at the beginning by the teacher must be adhered to throughout the year.

To further enhance this strategy children, particularly those in grades 3 and beyond, can be encouraged to use their collected words as part of their writings or to record and clip the appearance of these words in newspaper stories or online. This type of additional recording demonstrates that the child has truly incorporated the word into his/her reading and writing. It also habituates children to be lifelong readers, writers, and researchers.

One of the nice things about this simple but versatile strategy is that it works equally well with either expository or narrative texts. It also provides children with an opportunity to use the dictionary.

Assessment is built into the strategy. As the children select the word for the list, they share how they used contextual clues and through the children's response to the definitions offered by their peers, their prior knowledge can be assessed.

What is most useful about this strategy is that it documents that children can learn to read and write by reading and writing. The children take ownership of the words in the self-collection journals and that can also be the beginning of writer observation journals as they include their own writings. They also use the word lists as a start for writers' commonplace books. These books are filled with newspaper, magazine, and functional document clippings using the journal words.

This activity is a good one for demonstrating the balanced literacy belief that vocabulary study works best when the words studied are chosen by the child.

The Relationship between Oral Vocabulary and the Process of Identifying and Understanding Written Words

One way to explore the relationship between oral vocabulary and the comprehension of written words is through the use of Oral Records (which are discussed at length in the appendix).

In *On Solid Ground: Strategies for Teaching Reading K-3*, Sharon Taberski (2000) discusses how oral reading records can be used by the K-3 teacher to assess how well children are using cueing systems. She notes that the running record format can also show visual depictions for the teacher of how the child "thinks" as the child reads. The notation of miscues in particular shows how a child "walks through" the reading process. They indicate if and in what ways the child may require "guided" support in understanding the words he or she reads aloud. Taberski notes that when children read they need to think about several things at once. First, they must consider whether what they are reading makes sense (semantic or meaning cues). Next, they must know whether their reading "sounds right" in terms of Standard English (syntactic and structural cues). Third, they have to weigh whether their oral language actually and accurately matches the letters the words represent (visual or graphophonic cues).

In taking the running record and having the opportunity first-hand to listen to the children talk about the text, the teacher can analyze the relationship between the child's oral language and word comprehension. Information from the running record provide the teacher with a road map for differentiated cueing system instruction.

For example, when a running record is taken, a child often makes a mistake but then self-corrects. The child may select from various cueing systems when he or she self-corrects. These include: "M" for meaning, "S" for syntax, and "V" for visual. The use of a visual cue means that the child is drawing on his or her knowledge of spelling patterns. Of course, Taberski cautions that any relationship between oral language and comprehension that the teacher draws from an examination of the oral-reading records, must be drawn using a series of three or more of the child's oral reading records, taken over time, not just one.

A teacher can review children's running records over time to note their pattern of miscues and which cues they have the greatest tendency to use in their self-corrections. Whichever cueing system the children use to the greatest extent, it is necessary for the teacher to offer support in also using the other cueing systems to construct correct meaning. Taberski suggests that while assessing running records to determine the relationship between oral language and meaning, the children read from "just right" books.

Skill 6.4 **Applies knowledge of contextual factors that affect students' reading comprehension (e.g., curriculum materials, time allotted for reading, grouping practices, environment, assigned task and purpose)**

Teachers need to look at flexible grouping within the classroom setting. Although students may be grouped for ability at different times, this should not be the standard. Some of the various instructional grouping strategies that teachers can use in the classroom are:

- Whole Class Instruction – used to introduce new materials and strategies to the whole class
- Small group Instruction – used for small groups of students who need more instruction on an objective
- Students working alone in teacher-directed activities – this enables the teacher to give one-on-one instruction or to assess how students are progressing
- Collaborative groups – students working together on a project
- Circle sharing – student discussion, such as author's chair
- Partner groups – paired reading, think par share, etc.

Strategies for Planning, Organizing, Managing, and Differentiating Reading Instruction to Support the Reading Development of All Students

The physical set up of your classroom is exceedingly important to support the effective development of all children.

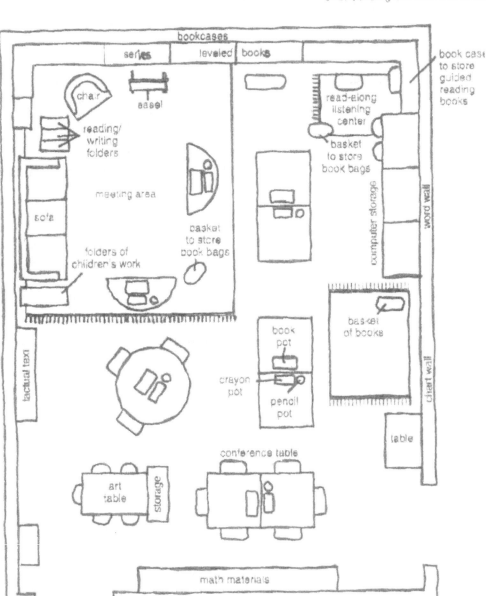

Understanding Our Role and Goals

The homey look of the classroom belies its deliberate design as a space where children can experience, practice, share and learn. Some teachers have done away with the large desk and use smaller tables instead. Sharon Taberski advocates for young children K-3 adjusting the height of the table legs so the children can use the tables as writing spaces and sit on the floor. Sharon gives each of her children a personal 12"x 9"x 2" tray on which they place their home possessions, books, homework, folder, etc. This is kept in a small storage unit near the coat closet during the day.

Children put their completed homework in a wire basket and notes from parents or the office in a second wire basket. Supplies such as pencils, markers, crayons, scissors, and erasers are not brought from home, but rather available for all in the class from "community" containers at the center of each of the children's tables.

All the children's reading, writing, and individual math folders are stored together in plastic bins in the meeting area. Every child has an individual book bag which is kept in one of two large wicker baskets set in different areas of the room.

This storing of materials away from children decreases their "fiddling with" their belongings during class, makes the room look much neater, and frees the children to focus on their learning experiences, rather than where their belongings are at any given time of day.

As you can see on the accompanying diagram the 10'x10' meeting area is the center of classroom learning. This is where the whole class is gathered at the beginning of the reading and the writing workshop and for sharing sessions. It is also the demonstration and modeling center for both the teacher and for children.

Generally, the presenter sits on the adult chair (in some balanced literacy classrooms, this is a rocking chair) near the easel with the chart. Generally, this chair and the easel are strategically positioned so that the teacher can see the door and any visitors or urgent messages from the office. Rearranging furniture during the day takes away from instruction time and is disruptive. Have a designated comfortable section of the room that can be a gathering place for a literacy community and then organize the rest of the classroom activities around that center.

The conference table which is at the back of the room (see diagram) is another key piece of classroom space furniture. It is the place where the four or five children and the teacher confer, wait and do their work. Having children come to a set conference table, rather than the teacher's going to them (although some teachers do advocate going to the children) saves time as far as Taberski is concerned. It serves to keep her and the children on task.

Taberski keeps two separate trays of supplies: a small magnetic board, letters, chalkboard, chalk, sentence strips, index cards, and blank books for her demonstrations during her conferences. She believes that teachers should store materials close to where they are used, so the teacher does not have to take time from the child to get up and get the materials.

The Classroom Library

On the tables, Taberski generally has book crates with books that are not leveled. Children choose from these books during the first independent reading session of her day which is from 8:40-9:00. During the second reading session from 9:30-10:20 the children select books from the leveled reading bins which are stored on the bookcase shelves.

Beyond the leveled books, which have already been discussed, Taberski also maintains a non-leveled, non fiction library which includes dictionaries, atlases, almanacs and informational books related to the themes, projects and investigations that the children will undertake throughout the year.

Beyond the leveled books and non-fiction books in the classroom, Taberski and other balanced literacy advocates generally include at least 10-15 big books which they routinely use to engage children with the text.

Since Guided Reading with groups of 6 children is a major part of the balanced literacy approach, Taberski and other disciplined and dedicated teacher educators "bundle" up six copies of selected books so that they can distribute them to their guided reading groups whenever they choose to do them. Taberski models the concept of a home library collection for the children by keeping books which she particularly likes in a bookcase behind her chair. She sometimes places "her" books on the easel so that they can be shared by the children and returned to her.

Wall Works

Much of creating a family atmosphere lies in the use of the room walls to document the children's learning experiences, skills work, and readings.

Generally at least one wall in a reading classroom is the Chart Wall. Charts with various spelling patterns discussed in class can be posted. If a child later has issues or concerns with that particular pattern, he or she should be directed to look at and to review the chart.

One of the centerpieces of the K-2 classroom is the High Frequency Word Chart. This is a growing list of commonly used words which the teacher tapes under the appropriate beginning letter according to the children's directions. At the end of each month, the newest high frequency words go into the children's folders and become part of their spelling words. Therefore reading, writing, and spelling are all intricately connected.

Supplies for children K-3 and beyond can include:

A red plastic double pocket reading folder
A blue plastic double pocket reading folder
A four sectioned pressed board spelling/poetry folder
A 4" x 6" assessment notebook for reading
A 4" x 6" assessment notebook for writing
A reading response notebook (loose-leaf- 60 pages)
A handwriting notebook

The Reading Folder contains the assessment notebooks, the reading response notebooks, a Weekly Reading Log, and the strategy sheets the child may be using that particular week.

The Assessment Notebook is a key evaluative tool and a recording document for the conscientious balanced literacy specialist. The teacher uses the notebook to record the child's running record, the retellings of stories shared by the child, and summarizing talks about leveled books read. Within the assessment books, the teacher also has notes about the child's progress, the strategies the child has learned to use well, the books he or she has read and those strategies the child still needs to practice. These assessment notebooks must be kept accessible so that the teacher can use them to confer with the child, parents, and administrator as needed.

The reading response notebook becomes a compilation of reading strategy sheets and children's writings and art in response to literature.

The Weekly Reading Log allows the child to maintain for himself or herself the titles of books they have read and written a bit about the narrative, style, and genre of that given book.

Book Bags: These are 10" x 12" heavy duty freezer bags which keep 3-10 books a child is "working on" during his/her free time. The teacher generally matches the children to the books and changes these books as needed by the children.

Writing Folders

Children keep several pieces of writing in their folders at a time. Within the writing folder is also a handwriting notebook and a beginning word book as well. The Spelling/Poetry Folder is one which helps children focus on the sequence of letters in words and learn more how words work.

The balanced literacy advocates have a definite schedule for the teaching of reading and writing workshop from which they generally do not deviate. A sample follows.

8:40-9:00- FIRST INDEPENDENT READING/WORD STUDY GROUP

9:00-9:30- MEETING-WHOLE GROUP SESSION in the meeting area
Read Aloud, Shared Reading, or Shared Writing

9:30-10:30- READING WORKSHOP
Reading Conferences or Guided Reading
Second Independent Reading
Reading Share 10:20-10:30

10:30-10:40- Writing Mini Lesson or Writing Share

10:40-11:20- Writing Workshop Writing Conferences, Guided Writing, Modeled Writing, Independent Writing

(11:10-11:20)-Writing Share

Adjustment of Reading Instruction Based on Ongoing Assessment

The running records taken of children help the teacher learn about the cueing systems that children use. It is important for the teacher to adjust reading instruction based on the pattern of miscues gathered from several successive reading records. When the teacher carefully reviews a given student's substitutions and self corrections, certain patterns begin to surface. A child may use visual cues as he or she reads and adds meaning to self correct. To the alert teacher, the reliance on visual miscues indicates that the reader doesn't make sense of what she is reading. This means that the teacher needs to check to see what cueing system the child uses when he or she is reading "just right" books. Children, who use meaning and structure but not visual/graphophonic cues, need to be reminded and facilitated to understand the importance of getting and reconstructing the author's message. They have to be able to share the author's story, not their own.

Not only can and should the teacher use the material in the children's ongoing assessment notebook to adjust the child's current instruction but the material also serves to document for the child his/her growth as a successful reader over time. In addition, if the same concerns surface over the use of a particular cueing system or high frequency word, the teacher can adjust the class wall chart and even devote a whole class lesson to the particular element.

Instructional Reading Strategies for Promoting the Development of Particular Reading Skills

Phonemic awareness can be developed through using leveled books that deal with rhyming words and segmenting phonemes into words. Children can also work with word or letter strips to continue the poems from the books and create their own "sequels" to the phoneme-filled story. They can also create an in-style rhyming story using some of the same phonemes from the leveled story they have heard.

Word Identification- Selective Cue Stage. Sometimes children have not yet experienced an awareness of the conventions of print and labeling in their own home environments. The teacher or an aide may have to go on a label adventure and support children in recognizing or affixing labels to parts of the classroom, halls and school building. A neighborhood walk with a digital or hand held camera may be required to help children identify uses and functions of print in society. A classroom photo essay or bulletin board could be the outgrowth of such an activity.

Sight Vocabulary- Beginning readers may enjoy outdoing Dolch (1936), who compiled the best known sight vocabulary word list. They can create their own class version of this list with illustrations and even some comments about why they have nominated certain words for the list.

Uses of Large Group, Small Group, and Individualized Reading Instruction

The framework for organizing the balanced literacy classroom is referred to as the one book-whole class mode. What this means is that everyone in the class has experiences with the same book. Everyone in the class discusses the literature. The teacher starts by activating prior knowledge and developing the context or background for the piece of literature. Some of the children within the class may have less prior knowledge or context with which to frame the book. The teacher will need to provide a preview of the book or develop key concepts to provide a stronger base for what the class will read together.

Some children will have to work with a paraprofessional or with a reading tutor before the class studies the book. Different modes of reading are accommodated within the class, by the books being read as a read-aloud, as part of shared reading or as guided reading. Student reader choices can also include: cooperative reading, reading with a partner, or independent reading.

Following the reading, the children respond to it which can be done through a literature circle and/or the whole class or in writing.

Strategies for Selecting and Using Meaningful Reading Materials at Appropriate Levels of Difficulty

Matching young children with "just right" books fosters their reading independently, no matter how young they are. The teacher needs to have an extensive classroom library of books. Books that emergent readers and early readers can be matched with should have fairly large print, appropriate spacing, so that the reader can easily see where word begins and ends, and few words on each page so that the young reader can focus on all important concerns of top-to bottom, left-to-right, directionality, and the one-to-one match of word to print.

Illustrations for young children should support the meaning of the text and language patterns and predictable text structures should make these texts appealing to young readers. Most important of all the content of the story should relate to the children's interests and experiences as the teacher knows them.

Only after all these considerations have been addressed, can the teacher select "just right" books from an already leveled bin or list. In a similar fashion, when the teacher is selecting books for transitional and fluent readers, the following ideas need to be taken into account:

The book should take at least two sittings to read, so children can get used to reading longer books. The fluent and transitional reader needs to deal with more complex characters and more intricate plotting. Look for books that set the stage for plot development with a compelling beginning. Age appropriateness of the concepts, plot and themes is important so that the child will sustain interest in the book. Look for book features such as a list of chapters to help children navigate through the book.

Series books are wonderful to introduce at this point in the children's development.

Creation of an Environment that Promotes Love of Reading

The aforementioned creation of the meeting area and the reading chair (sometimes a rocking chair) with throw pillows around it promotes a love of reading. Beyond that, some classrooms have adopted an author's hat, decorated with the pictures of famous authors and book characters which children wear when they read from their own works.

Many classrooms also have children's storyboards, artwork, story maps, pop-up books, and "in the style of" writing inspired by specific authors. Some teachers buy calendars for the daily schedule which celebrate children's authors or types of literature. Children are also encouraged to bring in public library books and special books from their home libraries. The teacher can model this habit of sharing beautiful books and inviting stories from his or her home library. In addition, news stories about children's authors, series books, television versions of books, theatrical film versions of books, stuffed toy book character decorations and other memorabilia related to books can be used to decorate the room.

Various chain book stores including Barnes and Nobles and Borders give out free book marks and promotional display materials related to children's books which can be available in the room for children to use as they read independently or in their guided groups. They might even use these artistic models to inspire their own book themed artifacts.

Strategies for Promoting Independent Reading in the Classroom and at Home

Pre-select books for the children that are just right for them. Provide the children with a quiet, relaxing space within the classroom where they can go to read these books. Don't get upset if they seem to take a break or wander around the room after fifteen minutes. Adults take breaks as well.

Make certain that the children who are reading independently fill in their weekly logs. Beyond telling what books they were reading and how many pages they have read, have the children respond to prompts such as "This week I was successful at ..." or, "Next week I plan to..." A response can also be an illustration or a sentence or two about the book.

Deliberately assign a child or a pair of children to read big books. These are a guaranteed success for the children because they have already been shared in class. Some children enjoy reading these independently using big rulers to point at words. This provides them with a sense of mastery over the words and ownership of their independent reading.

Some children enjoy working on their own strategy sheet such as a story map, character map, or storyboard panel, to demonstrate how they can apply a strategy to their own independent learning

Uses of Instructional Technology to Promote Reading Development

One of the most interesting ways in which the web complements the Reading and Writing Workshop involves the proliferation of author specific websites.   If used judiciously, these web resources allow authors to come into the classroom and allow children to write, question, discuss and share their literacy experiences with the authors themselves. Children can also readily become part of a distanced community of peers who are also reading works by a given author.

For instance, children who have been introduced to the work of Faith Ringgold, the author of *Tar Beach*, can easily visit her online site, www.faithringgold.com. Here they will not only find extensive biographic data on Ringgold, but they will also be able to learn a song inspired by her main character Cassie. They will be able to help illustrate a new story Ringgold has put up on the website, and also see if any of the questions they may have generated in their shared or independent reading of her books, has already been answered in the "frequently asked questions" section of her web resource. A few of the author websites respond online to individual children's questions.

There are even some reader response web resources such as the spaghetti review web site where young readers can post their response to different books they are reading. **http://www.book-club-review.com/view.php?cid=1**

Awareness of Strategies and Resources for Supporting Individual Students

Children who come from family backgrounds where English is not spoken lack a solid understanding of its syntactic structure. Therefore as they are being assessed using the oral running record, they may need additional support from their teacher in examining the structure and meaning of English. A child from a non-native English Language speaking background may often pronounce words that make no sense to him or her and just go on reading. They have to learn to stop to construct meaning. This child may have to be prompted to self-correct.

Children from non-native English Language speaking backgrounds can benefit from independent reading opportunities to listen to a familiar story on tape and read along. This also gives them practice in listening to standard English oral reading. Often these children can begin to internalize the language structures by listening to the book on tape several times.

Highly proficient readers can sometimes support early readers through a partner relationship. Some children, particularly the emergent and beginning early readers, benefit from reading books with partners. The partners sit side by side and each one takes turns reading the entire text.

Skill 6.5   Demonstrates knowledge of literal, inferential, critical, and evaluative comprehension skills and knows how to provide instruction to promote students' literal, inferential, critical and evaluative comprehension

There are five key strategies for child reading of informational/expository texts.

1.   Inferencing is a process that involves the reader making a reasonable judgment based on the information given and engages children to literally construct meaning. In order to develop and enhance this key skill in children, they might have a mini lesson where the teacher demonstrates this by reading an expository book aloud (i.e. one on skyscrapers for young children) and then demonstrates for them the following reading habits: looking for clues, reflecting on what the reader already knows about the topic, and using the clues to figure out what the author means/intends.

2.   Identifying main ideas in an expository text can be improved when the children have an explicit strategy for identifying important information. They can make this strategy part of their everyday reading style, "walking" through the following exercises during guided reading sessions. The child should read the passage so that the topic is readily identifiable to him or her. It will be what most of the information is about.

Next the child should be asked to be on the lookout for a sentence within the expository passage that summarizes the key information in the paragraph. Then the child should read the rest of the passage or excerpt in light of this information and also note which information in the paragraph is less important. The important information the child has identified in the paragraph can be used to formulate the author's main idea. The child reader may even want to use some of the author's own language in stating that idea.

3.   Monitoring means self-clarifying: As one reads, the reader often realizes that what he or she is reading is not making sense. The reader then has to have a plan for making sensible meaning out of the excerpt. Cooper and other balanced literacy advocates have a stop and think strategy which they use with children. The child reflects, "Does this make sense to me?" When the child concludes that it does not, the child then either re-reads, reads ahead in the text, looks up unknown words or asks for help from the teacher.

What is important about monitoring is that some readers ask these questions and try these approaches without ever being explicitly taught them in school by a teacher. However, these strategies need to be explicitly modeled and practiced under the guidance of the teacher by most, if not all child readers.

4.   Summarizing engages the reader in pulling together into a cohesive whole the essential bits of information within a longer passage or excerpt of text. Children can be taught to summarize informational or expository text by following these guidelines. First they should look at the topic sentence of the paragraph or the text and ignore the trivia. Then they should search for information which has been mentioned more than once and make sure it is included only once in their summary. Find related ideas or items and group them under a unifying heading. Search for and identify a main idea sentence. Finally, put the summary together using all these guidelines.

Generating questions can motivate and enhance children's comprehension of reading in that they are actively involved. The following guidelines will help children generate meaningful questions that will trigger constructive reading of expository texts. First children should preview the text by reading the titles and subheadings. Then they should also look at the illustrations and the pictures. Finally they should read the first paragraph. These first previews should yield an impressive batch of specific questions.

Next, children should get into a Dr. Seuss mode and ask themselves a "THINK" question. Make certain that the children write down the question. Then have them read to find important information to answer their "think" question. Ask that they write down the answer they found and copy the sentence or sentences where they found the answer. Also have them consider whether, in light of their further reading through the text, their original question was a good one or not.

Ask them to be prepared to explain why their original question was a good one or not. Once the children have answered their original "think" question, have them generate additional ones and then find their answers and judge whether these questions were "good" ones in light of the text.

Skill 6.6 **Demonstrates knowledge of characteristics of specific texts and genres and strategies for reading a variety of texts and genres(e.g., expository and narrative texts, including electronic media and other visual representations)**

In every classroom across the country, there are students at different reading levels. There is no such thing as one reading program to meet the needs of all students. Therefore, reading specialists within schools must adapt and develop reading programs so that children will experience success and develop further in reading skills. For some students, the reading material in the program is beyond their level, while for others it may be too easy.

One way to assure that all students are reading at their individual levels is to implement a guided-reading program. The Fountas and Pinnel method of guided reading is one that has been accepted everywhere, and one that is displaying major success with teaching children to read fluently and accurately. In this method, the students are assessed at the beginning of the year to see where they fit on the letter grade. Each letter in the guided reading system refers to the manner in which a book is written (eg. A – one word on a page, pictures to correspond to the word).

Once the students are assessed, the teacher gathers each group together on a regular basis to instruct them on a specific learning objective. The classroom must be rich in print, and the students must know exactly where to go to get the books they can read. Assessment takes place on a regular basis as well, and students move upwards as they grasp the strategies. The groups are constantly changing so that students will not get the idea they are in the slow group or the smart group.

Additionally, it is sometimes important to simply group the students by their interests. In this way, slower readers will be able to participate with better readers and gain valuable skills from working with their peers. Also, it provides motivation and excitement when students are engaged in something which attracts their interest.

Within the content areas, the reading material may have to be rewritten so that it is in words that the students can understand. The explanations may have to be more detailed, especially if the students do not have the appropriate background knowledge. Evaluations and tests may also have to be different for those students.

Finally, it is necessary to include works of literature which reflect all of society's diversity. In this way, students from those cultures can make more personal connections, and students not from those cultures can begin to understand relationships and issues which affect others.

If we have learned anything in education over the last few decades, it is that students do not all learn in the same way. Furthermore, we have learned that a steady diet of lecture and textbook reading is an extremely ineffective method of instruction. While students definitely should be exposed to lecture and textbooks, they will greatly benefit with the creativity and ingenuity of teachers who find outside resources to assist in the presentation of new knowledge.

Let's first discuss some possibilities: textual and media references, hands-on materials, and technology. Lately, some people have referred to the concept of "multiple texts" as a method of bringing into the classroom multiple types of texts. For example, a social studies teacher might ask students to read an historical novel to complement a unit of study.

In addition to texts, appropriately selected video or audio recordings may be useful. For example, a science teacher may wish to show a short clip of a video that demonstrates how to conduct a particular experiment before students do it on their own. Or, a language arts teacher may bring in an audio recording of a book to present a uniquely-dramatized reading of the book.

Hands-on materials are very important to student learning. For example, math teachers may introduce geometric principles with quilt blocks. The very idea of a science experiment is that hands-on materials and activities more quickly convey scientific ideas to students than do lectures and textbooks.

Finally, technologies such as personal computers are very important for student learning. First, it is extremely important that students learn new technologies so that they can easily adapt to the myriad of uses found in business and industry. Second, technology can provide knowledge resources that go beyond what a school library may be able to offer. Students will need, increasingly, to learn how to search for, evaluate, and utilize appropriate information in the Internet. Third, using technology is highly motivating for students and can provide that necessary incentive to encourage reading for students who are struggling.

Choosing an appropriate reference, text, material, or technology depends on many factors. First, realize that whatever is brought into the class should be done so based on the knowledge that the item will assist students in learning academic standards. There is no reason for teachers to show a movie to their students that is not for the explicit purpose of helping them reach specific academic objectives tied to the curriculum. Second, consider the developmental level of the students you are working with. You would not want to introduce complex experiments to second graders; likewise, you would not want to assume that twelfth graders have no knowledge of the Internet.

In choosing materials, teachers should also keep in mind that not only do students learn at different rates, but also they bring a variety of cognitive styles to the learning process. Prior experiences influence their cognitive styles, or methods of accepting, processing, and retaining information. According to Marshall Rosenberg, students can be categorized as:

    a) rigid-inhibited
    b) undisciplined
    c) acceptance-anxious
    d) creative

"The creative learner is an independent thinker, one who maximizes his/her abilities, can work by his/herself, enjoys learning, and is self-critical." This last category constitutes the ideal, but teachers should make every effort to use materials that will stimulate and hold the attention of learners of all types. commercially-produced tapes. Textbook publishers often provide films, recordings, and software to accompany the text, as well as maps, graphics, and colorful posters to help students visualize what is being taught. Teachers can usually scan the educational publishers' brochures that arrive at their principal's or department head's office on a frequent basis. Another way to stay current in the field is by attending workshops or conferences. Teachers will be enthusiastically welcomed on those occasions when educational publishers are asked to display their latest productions and revised editions of materials.

In addition, yesterday's libraries are today's media centers. Teachers can usually have opaque projectors delivered to the classroom to project print or pictorial images (including student work) onto a screen for classroom viewing. Some teachers have chosen to replace chalkboards with projectors that reproduce the print or images present on the plastic sheets known as transparencies which the teacher can write on during a presentation or have machine-printed in advance. In either case, the transparency can easily be stored for later use. In an art or photography class, or any class in which it is helpful to display visual materials, slides can easily be projected onto a wall or a screen.

Cameras are inexpensive enough to enable students to photograph and display their own work and to keep a record of their achievements in teacher files or student portfolios.

Studies have shown that students learn best when what is taught in lecture and textbook reading is presented more than once in various formats. This also allows for different learning styles or modalities to be explored and tapped. In some instances, students themselves may be asked to reinforce what they have learned by completing some original production—for example, by drawing pictures to explain some scientific process, by writing a monologue or dialogue to express what some historical figure might have said on some occasion, by devising a board game to challenge the players' mathematical skills, or by acting out (and perhaps filming) episodes from a classroom reading selection. Students usually enjoy having their work displayed or presented to an audience of peers. Thus, their productions may supplement and personalize the learning experiences that the teacher has planned for them.

There are many different types of reading materials available for use in classrooms. From trade books to basal readers, reading specialists need to understand the characteristics, benefits, and limitations of the materials available. Trade books are commercially-published materials. They are books, and have comprehensive information in them. They can be found to teach almost any subject or skill necessary for students. However, it takes a lot of time and effort on the part of the teacher to find and prepare lessons based on trade books. Students enjoy these because they are real books, and they feel proud to be able to read books that look like those that adults read. Sometimes it is difficult for teachers to locate the correct number of books for students to have their own copies. It is also difficult to focus on a sequential base of skills as the books are written to convey information rather than to teach skills.

Phonics readers are books available from specialized publishers. These books follow a specific, sequential order of phonics skills. The skills typically build upon each other so that students can practice previously introduced and learned skills in future reading. The text in phonics' readers usually seems contrived and unlike spoken language. Comprehension is also difficult to draw from these types of texts.

Basal programs themselves vary in design and structure. There are skill-based basal programs which are similar in characteristics to the phonics readers previously discussed. There are also literature-based basal programs, which are closer to the trade books discussed in the above passage. Both types of basal programs offer a school a continuity of reading instruction. Students progressing from one grade level to another are known to have been given the same exposure and skills. This makes deciding on what to teach easier. Also, the teachers have a scope and sequence which they can follow. The limitations include predetermined stories which may or may not be of interest to your students, less flexibility in addressing individual student needs, and, sometimes, overwhelming resources and supports provided by the company.

It does not matter which materials one uses, all have benefits and drawbacks. Sometimes reading specialists will use a combination approach in order to deliver what they feel is the most appropriate program to all of the students.

For expository and narrative text, see Skill 6.3

Skill 6.7 **Knows how to plan, implement, and monitor age-appropriate instruction that is responsive to individual students' strengths, needs, and interests and is based on ongoing informal and formal assessment of individual students; reading comprehension strategies**

Knowledge of Reading as a Process to Construct Meaning

If there were two words synonymous with reading comprehension as far as the balanced literacy approach is concerned, they would be "constructing meaning."

Cooper, Taberski, Strickland, and other key theorists and classroom teachers conceptualize the reader as interacting with the text and bringing his/her prior knowledge and experience to it. Writing is interlaced with reading and is a mutually integrative and supportive parallel process. Hence the division of literacy learning by the balanced literacy folks into reading workshop and writing workshop, with the same anchor "readings" or books being used for both.

Consider the sentence, "The test booklet was white with black print, but very scary looking."

According to the idea of constructing meaning as the reader read this sentence, the schemata (generic information stored in the mind) of tests the reader had experienced was activated by the author's notion that tests are scary. Therefore the ultimate meaning that the reader derives from the page is from the reader's own responses and experiences coupled with the ideas the author presents. The reader constructs a meaning that reflects the author's intent and also the reader's response to that intent.

It is also to be remembered that generally readings are fairly lengthy passages, composed of paragraphs which in turn are composed of more than one sentence. With each successive sentence, and every new paragraph, the reader refocuses. The schemata are reconsidered, and a new meaning is constructed.

Knowledge of levels of reading comprehension and strategies for promoting comprehension of imaginative literary texts at all levels

Sharon Taberski (2000) recommends that initially strategies for promoting comprehension of imaginative literary texts be done with the whole class.

Here are Taberski's four main strategies for promoting comprehension of imaginative literary texts. She feels that if repeated sufficiently during the K-3 years and even if introduced as late as grade 4, these strategies will even serve the adult lifelong reader in good stead.

Strategy One: "Stopping to Think" –reflecting on the text as a whole. x
As part of this strategy, the reader is challenged to come up with the answer to these three questions: "What do I think is going to happen?" (Inferential), "Why do I think this is going to happen?" (Evaluative and inferential), and "How can I prove that I am right by going back to the story?" (inferential).

Taberski recommends that teachers introduce these key strategies with books that can be read in one sitting and recommends the use of picture books for these instructive strategies.

Taberski also suggests that books which are read aloud and used for this strategy also contain a strong storyline, some degree of predictability, a text that invites discussion and a narrative with obvious stopping points.

Strategy Two: story mapping, for promoting comprehension of imaginative/literary texts.

For stories to suit this strategy, they should have distinct episodes, few characters and clear-cut problems to solve. In particular, Taberski tries to use a story where a single, central problem or issue is introduced at the beginning of the story and then resolved or at least followed through by the close of the story. To make a story map of a particular story, Taberski divides the class into groups and asks one group of children to illustrate the "Characters" in the book. Another group of children are asked to draw the "Setting," while a third and fourth group of children tackle "Problem " and "Resolution." The story map may also help children hold together their ideas for writing in the writing workshop as they take their reading of an author's story to a new level.

Strategy Three: The Character Mapping strategy also used by Taberski focuses the children as readers on the ways in which the main character's personal traits can determine what will happen in the story. Character mapping works best when the character is a non-stereotypical individual, has been featured perhaps in other books by the same author, has a personality that is somewhat predictable, and is capable of changing behavior as a consequence of what happens.

Skill 6.8 **Applies knowledge of instructional strategies and materials that reflect cultural and linguistic diversity, are based on a convergence or research evidence, and promote students' reading comprehension skills**

Teachers who employ a balanced literacy curriculum in their classroom make choices on a daily basis in planning lessons that will benefit the students. This approach to teaching reading integrates all components of language arts and uses multiple strategies to help students develop as fluent readers. The main purpose is to integrate reading, writing, listening, speaking, and viewing so that each is not a separate part of learning to read.

Reading aloud to students is a main part of balanced literacy. However, the focus is on modeling the skills and strategies and then allowing the students time to practice them on their own. The components of a balanced literacy curriculum are:

- Shared reading
- Guided reading
- Independent reading
- Shared writing
- Guided writing
- Independent writing

Having students read and write in a shared setting provides models of the correct methods to the students. In small-group settings, guided reading and writing teaches them the strategies they need to develop as independent readers and writers. Word Study is one such example of small-group work that can take place. This involves teachers taking time to meet with children from grades 3-6 in a small group of no more than 6 children for a word-study session. Taberski suggests that this meeting take place next to the Word Wall. The children selected for this group are those who need to focus more on the relationship between spelling patterns and their consonant sounds.

It is important that this not be a formalized, traditional reading group that meets at a set time each week or biweekly. Rather, the group should be spontaneously formed by the teachers based on a quick inventory of the selected children's needs at the start of the week. Taberski has templates in her book of *Guided Reading Planning Sheets.* These sheets are essentially targeted-word and other skills sheets with her written, dated observations of children who are in need of support in developing a given skill (kid watching-see Dictionary).

Teachers should try to meet with such groups for at least two, consecutive-day, twenty-minute per periods. Over those two meetings, teachers can model a Making Words Activity. Once teachers have modeled making words the first day, the children would then make their own words. On the second day, the children would "sort" their words.

Other topics for a word-study group within the framework of the Balanced Literacy Approach that Taberski advocates are inflectional endings, prefixes and suffixes, and common spelling patterns. It should be noted that this activity would be classified by theorists as a structural-analysis activity because the structural components (i.e. prefixes, suffixes, and spelling patterns) of the words are being studied.

Discussion Circles and Literature Circles are other ways of having students involved in reading and writing in a balanced literacy framework. Cooper believes that children should not be "taught" vocabulary and structural-analysis skills. Flesch and E.D. Hirsch , who are key theorist of the Phonics approach and advocates of Cultural Literacy (a term coined and associated with E. D. Hirsch), believe that specific vocabulary words at various grade and age levels need to be mastered and MUST be explicitly taught in schools. As far as J. David Cooper is concerned, all the necessary and meaningful (for the child and, ultimately, adult reader) vocabulary can't possibly be taught in schools (no apologies to Hirsch). To Cooper it is far more important that the children be made aware of and become interested in learning words by themselves. Cooper feels that, through reading and writing, children develop a love for and a sense of "ownership" of words. All of Cooper's suggested Structural Analysis word strategies are therefore designed to foster children's love of words and a desire to "own" more of them through reading and writing.

Discussion Circle is an activity which fits nicely into the Balanced-Literacy Lesson Format as part of a SHARE. (See Dictionary of Terms). After the children (and this activity works well from grades 3-6 and beyond) conclude a particular text, Cooper suggests that they get together in discussion circles to respond to the book. Among the prompts, the teacher-coach might suggest that the children focus on words-of-interest that they encountered in the text. These can also be words that they heard if the text was read aloud. Children can be asked to share something funny or upsetting or unusual about the words they have read. Through this focus on children's response to words as the center of the discussion circle, peers become more interested in word study.

Skill 6.9 **Knows how to promote students' comprehension skills by providing them with multiple opportunities to listen to, read, and respond in various ways to a wide variety of fiction and nonfiction texts**

Strategic reading occurs when students are reading for information. The purpose for reading is simply to learn. Typically then, strategic reading occurs in nonfiction or expository texts. The students are generally given some guidance on what information they are to find.

In strategic reading, however, it is not a simple recall of facts. This is not literal comprehension. The students are required to read a great deal of information about a topic. Then they need to then take all of that information and build their own foundation of knowledge. Constructing knowledge is what makes strategic reading different than simple literal recall. It is through this process that information is connected to prior knowledge.

These connections are key factors in the success of comprehension. Strategic reading requires the reader to be able to tie new and old learning together to compound it into useful information. This process of thinking about reading and manipulating all that was learned is known as metacognition.

It presents complex set of variables for the reader. The reader needs to be aware of the reading process and be able to recognize when information does not make sense to them. At this point, they need to adjust the things they are doing in order to clarify and make the necessary connections. Throughout this process, the reader must continue to integrate the new and old.
Strategic readers call into play their metacognitive capacities as they analyze texts so that they are aware of the skills needed to construct meaning from the text structure.

When reading strategically, students need to keep in mind several factors.

Self-Monitoring- When students self-monitor, they are able to keep track of all the factors involved in the process. In this way, they are able to process the information in the manner that is best for them.

Setting the Purpose for Reading- In strategic reading, children have a specific reason for reading the text. There is information they wish to gain, and teachers should make that clear to the students. If it is unclear, the students will not be successful.

Rereading- Rereading is probably one of the most-used methods for taking in initially-overwhelming information. By revisiting the text more than once, the students are able to then take in smaller pieces of information that they missed in the first read through.

.Adjusting Reading Rates and Strategies-This is similar to self-monitoring; the students must be able to understand that sometimes it will be necessary to read slower than at other times. Sometimes they will need to make adjustments to the way they are reading in order to be successful at gaining the information they want to gain.

Text Factors-Understanding the arrangement of nonfiction text with section titles and other unique organizational devices can provide the students with important tools leading to success. Knowing the structure of the text can save valuable time and decrease the need for rereading.

Consideration for the planning of reading can be a complex task to undertake. It is important to base the information you are relaying to the students on the appropriate grade-level standards and grade-level curriculum for the students with whom you are working.

A dilemma comes into play when the students are not functioning at grade level or are not demonstrating grade-level skills. Reading specialists must find yet another balance in their planning and later in their instructional methodologies. Finding the right combination of skills to teach requires much planning. Since teachers will be working with students across grade levels or with the same skill at various grade levels, it is necessary to be familiar with the appropriate standards/curriculum at the various grade levels. In this manner, teachers can sit down and look at the standards, curriculum and needs of the students and find the correct approach.

However, it is important that all students, no matter how far behind, be exposed to grade-level standards/curriculum. The question for teachers, then, becomes how to deliver that piece of information. When planning instruction, reading specialists must think carefully about what strategies will allow the students to gain the most benefit.

From here, it is simply determining the techniques or modifications that will need to be made to deliver this instruction. Will the vocabulary work well if you introduce some synonyms that the students have already learned successfully? Would this story work better if taught in smaller chunks so that the students can better manage the information? Is there a piece of information which needs to be taught first in order for the students to be successful with the material?

In the end, it is these types of questions that must be thought of prior to the teaching in order for the information to be presented to the students. Sometimes this planning phase requires tremendous thought and effort in order to determine the appropriate method to help the students be successful.

General expectations for grade levels include phonemic awareness for kindergarten and grade one and phonics the emphasis through grade one and grade two. Fluency, comprehension, and vocabulary then become the focus as reading shifts from learning to read in the early primary grades to reading to learn from the late elementary grades through life. Keep in mind, however, that all general areas can certainly be worked on outside of these general guidelines.

Skill 6.10   Knows how to promote students' ability to apply strategies that facilitate comprehension before, after, and during reading, including metacognitive strategies

Use of comprehension skills before, after, and during reading

Cooper (2004) advocates that children ask themselves what a text is about before they read it and as they are in the process of reading the it. Further, he asserts that they should note what they think the text is going to be about. While children are reading the text, Cooper (2004) feels that they should be continually questioning themselves as to whether the text is confirming their predictions. Of course, after completing the text, the child can then review their predictions in summary fashion.

Again, within the framework set by Cooper in his work, Literacy-Helping Children Construct Meaning, children should be taught to look over the expository text subheads, illustrations, captions, and indices to get an idea about the book. Then children can decide where to look to find the target information.

During the reading, children are asking themselves, "Am I finding the answer to my question?"

After the reading, children make a note such as, "I have found the answer to my question" or "This book or electronic text is an excellent source of information for me about my question." If the book does not contain the needed information, the notes will take such forms as, "No, I have not found the answer to my question," "This book or electronic text is not a good source of information for me about my question," or "I will have to look for other resources."

Skill 6.11   Demonstrates knowledge of delays or differences in the development of students' comprehension skills/strategies and when such delays/differences warrant further assessment and additional intervention

Children who come from family backgrounds where English is not spoken lack a solid understanding of its syntactic and visual structure. Therefore, as they are being recorded for progress using the oral running record, they may need additional support from their teachers. Children from a non-native-English-speaking background may often pronounce words that make no sense to them and just go on reading. They have to learn to stop to construct meaning. Such children may have to be prompted to self-correct.

Children from non-native-English-speaking backgrounds can benefit from opportunities to listen to a familiar story on tape and read along. This also gives them practice in listening to standard English. Often these children can begin to internalize the language structures by listening to the book on tape several times.

Highly-proficient readers can sometimes support early readers through a partner relationship. Some children, particularly the emergent and beginning early readers, benefit from reading books with partners. The partners sit side-by-side, and each one takes a turn reading the entire text.

Use of talking books and author web resources provides special needs learners having visual or auditory handicapping conditions immediate contact with authors and with direct sharing in the wonders of stories. In addition to the accessibility of the keyboard, their responses to literature can be shared with a broad network of other readers, including close and distant peers. Technology literally enfranchises special needs learners into the circle of connected readers and writers.

In the classroom, there are numerous ways to determine which students are in need of additional assistance. The most effective methods are to examine the classroom performance and available assessment data and to work individually with the students.

Regular classroom teachers often have numerous concerns about the students that they are working with in the classroom. They will seek out help from reading specialists for additional strategies and support to help increase the reading skills. It is important that the specialists be able to determine what difficulties require additional assistance and in which specific areas of reading to provide that assistance.

As previously discussed, running records are of tremendous value in helping in this area. They provide a fast and efficient way to examine the errors the students are making and the number of errors they are making. Also, the levels at which the students are able to read can be a warning flag. If students are struggling with material several grade levels below their current grade, it is important to determine the cause(s).

Once a general warning flag appears, it may be necessary for the specialist to look in depth and administer additional skill-specific assessments or examine the data present more in depth. In general, it's good to keep in mind the five larger areas of reading as a method of narrowing down the problem. These include phonemic awareness, phonics, fluency, comprehension, and vocabulary.

Identifying which of these areas is causing the problems helps teachers and specialists to determine an appropriate plan of action to address the skill deficits. Many children will demonstrate deficits in more than one area, so it is critical to follow the appropriate skill sequence to move the students forward in the most efficient manner possible.

Even knowing the broad area of difficulty may not be enough in itself. Sometimes very skill-specific assessment or identification will need to occur before the instruction can begin. Other times, a more global approach would be prudent. An example of a time when using a global approach might be more beneficial would be with students who have all of the phonics skills in isolation, but have difficulty applying them in text. In this case, spending more time teaching the phonics skills will not benefit children, but rather spending the time helping them to use other cueing systems through many passages and texts would be a more suitable use of time.

One of the first things that teachers learn is how to obtain resources and help for their students. All schools have guidelines for receiving this assistance, especially since the implementation of the Americans with Disabilities Act. The first step in securing help is for the teacher to approach the school's administration or exceptional education department for direction. Many schools have a committee designated for addressing these needs, such as a Child Study Team or Core Team. These teams are made up of both regular and exceptional education teachers, school psychologists, guidance counselors, and administrators. The particular student's classroom teacher usually has to complete some initial paper work and will need to do some behavioral observations.

Teachers will take this information to the appropriate committee for discussion and consideration. The committee will recommend the next step to be taken. Often, subsequent steps include a complete psychological evaluation along with certain physical examinations such as vision and hearing screening and a complete medical examination by a doctor.

The referral of students for this process is usually relatively simple for classroom teachers and requires little more than some initial paper work and discussion. The services and resources that the students receive as a result of the process typically prove to be invaluable.

Collaborative teams play a crucial role in meeting the needs of all students, and they are an important step to identifying students with special needs. Under the Individuals with Disabilities Act (IDEA), which federally mandates special education services in every state, it is the responsibility of public schools to ensure consultative, evaluative, and, if necessary, prescriptive services to children with special needs. In most school districts, a collaborative group called the Child Study Team (CST) handles this responsibility. If teachers or parents suspect that children have academic, social, or emotional problems, they refer them to the CST. There, a team consisting of educational professionals (including teachers, specialists, the school psychologist, guidance, and other support staff) review the case and situation through meetings with teachers and/or parents/guardians. The CST will determine what evaluations or tests are necessary, if any, and will also assess the results. Based on these results, the CST will make suggestions.

One plan of action is an Academic Intervention Plan (AIP). An AIP consists of additional instructional services that are provided to students who have met certain criteria (such as scoring below the state reference point on standardized tests or performing more than two levels below grade-level) in order to help them achieve better academically.

Another plan of action is a 504 plan. A 504 plan is a legal document based on the provisions of the Rehabilitation Act of 1973 (which preceded IDEA). A 504 plan is a plan for instructional services to assist students with special needs in a regular-education classroom setting. When students' physical, emotional, or other impairments (such as Attention Deficit Disorder) impact their ability to learn in a regular education classroom setting, they can be referred for a 504 meeting. Typically, the CST and, perhaps, even the students' physician or therapist will participate in a 504 meeting to determine if a 504 plan is warranted.

Finally, children referred to CST may qualify for an Individualized Education Plan (IEP). An IEP is a legal document which delineates the specific, adapted services a student with disabilities will receive. An IEP differs from a 504 plan in that children must be identified for special education services to qualify for an IEP, and ALL students who receive special education services must have an IEP. Each IEP must contain statements pertaining to students' present performance level, annual goals, related services, supplementary aids, testing modifications, a projected date of services, and assessment methods for monitoring progress. Each year, the CST and guardians must meet to review and update students' IEP.

At times, teachers must go beyond the school system to meet the needs of some students. An awareness of special services and resources and how to obtain them is essential for all teachers and their students. When the school system is unable to address the needs of students, teachers often must take the initiative and contact agencies within the community. Frequently there is no special policy for finding resources.

It is simply up to individual teachers to be creative and resourceful in finding whatever helps the students. Meeting the needs of all students is certainly a team effort that is most often spearheaded by classroom teachers.

When considering students for whom English is not the primary language, it is critical to understand the natural development of second-language acquisition before applying the general knowledge of reading assessments to this subgroup of students.

In general, second-language students can take up to seven years to become proficient in the second language. This factors in the acculturation process with speaking, listening, reading and writing. Students who are fluent and able to read in their primary language before starting the second language are more likely to become fluent in the second language than those who are not fluent in the primary language.

This group of students attempting to learn in a second language generally tends to lag behind in vocabulary particularly. The connection between words and their meanings is essential for understanding what is being read. Students who can make the transition easily between the two languages have the advantage of seeing or hearing a word, translating it in their mind to the same or a similar word in their native language, and then making the connection and being able to access that information to help them understand the text. Though this is a slow and labor-intensive process, in the end the students are able to understand.

However, it is the students who are unable to complete these numerous steps who will require additional support, particularly in vocabulary development. Helping to build background knowledge through as concrete a process as possible is critical when introducing texts to these students. The more concrete examples teachers can provide, the better for the students.

Phonics and phonemic awareness skills can also pose problems. Students will sometimes substitute the sounds from their native language in the middle of the process or at other times. Additionally, they may have no reference within their native language because there may be no letters/combinations that make those sounds.

In the end, good reading assessment and instruction are essential when working with students acquiring a second language. However, they must be married well with the body of research into how children learn a second language. Remember that oral language will develop first (receptive before expressive), and that after oral language reaches a conversational level, one can begin the reading instruction.

There is no reason identified by scientists to explain why some children learn to read with no problems and others struggle to be successful. Doctors and researchers use MRI's and other brain-scanning techniques to pinpoint the parts of the brain being used when completing reading activities; and, in these scans, they can see definite differences between better and slower readers. However, the underlying cause still remains a mystery.

There are some identified factors which may contribute to reading difficulties:
- Language Development
- Birth Defects
- Genetic History
- Language Exposure
- Hearing Difficulties, including intermittent losses from infections
- Life experiences, especially as related to prior knowledge

This is not a complete list, but simply a few examples of identified reasons that reading problems may occur. No matter that the cause, children who experience problems need to have adaptations and/or modifications developed in order to help their skills develop.

Providing instruction to meet the individual needs of learners can be a daunting experience because no two readers are exactly the same. One student's own personal life experiences include unique and personal information another student does not have. Because of this, planning instruction can be a challenge. However, it is important for students to have instruction designed to meet their needs.

Reading specialists can tap into students with more prior knowledge to help support those with less. Those with stronger phonics skills can provide support to those who struggle. It is a complex balancing act for the teacher, but one that is essential.

Other strategies include:

- Providing texts on the students' reading level
- Using individual assessment data to complete plans
- Providing different assignments based on the same reading to help students develop the skills they are lacking
- Small-group or individual instruction
- Differentiated instruction

COMPETENCY 7.0 VOCABULARY

Skill 7.1   Recognizes the importance of teaching and modeling the use of a wide range of general, technical, and specialized vocabularies

Reading does not end when children leave the reading classroom; it, in fact is an inherent component of every subject area taught in schools today. Content-area reading (science, social studies, math, etc.) can sometimes be much more difficult for students. Typically, the information is nonfiction, and there is a great deal of knowledge contained in smaller amounts of text. Deciphering content-area reading requires a unique set of strategies in order to best acquire the necessary information.

Text Format. Teaching children that nonfiction texts are laid out significantly differently than fictional texts is an important skill. Often times the format of the text helps provide an automatic organizational tool to help chunk information. Key words or section headings can help provide students with catch phrases through which they can remember the information. They can also help students to scan a large amount of information to find the particular information that they require to answer comprehension questions. Indexes and table of content skills can provide additional support with this.

Summarizing. As stated before, content subjects generally attempt to convey a great deal of information in a small amount of text. This is where the idea of summarizing can be so valuable and productive. Teaching the students to be able to take larger amounts of information and break it down into four or five sentences allows them to manage more details and learning. It also helps them to make connections and compartmentalize the information.

Graphic Organizers. There are numerous different forms of graphic organizers. They can be defined as pictorial methods of organizing information to help the student remember it more efficiently. Graphic organizers can be complex or simple and provided to the student or drawn from memory. The key is that the method or organizing tool used will help the students classify the information to be learned into smaller pieces with common characteristics. They also help the students to begin to see relationships between the concepts. Graphic organizers work well as study aids to help students acquire more information. Some graphic organizers use pictures or other visual cues to help the students remember the items to be learned.

Graphic Aids - It is important to teach students how to interpret graphic aids commonly occuring in content area texts. This may involve teaching some other subject-area skills (e.g. reading a graph or chart), but it is necessary for students to understand these additions to the text. Graphic aids often help to clarify the text and provide another format to help with accurate interpretation.

Semantic Mapping. In this strategy of organizing information, the students will use a visual representation to show how words or concepts are interrelated. This is a form of graphic organizer. In semantic mapping, the new knowledge is directly linked to the prior information. Sometimes called concept mapping, semantic maps allow the learner to see relationships between words or concepts and tie them to their own background knowledge in a meaningful manner.

| Skill 7.2 | Identifies student factors that influence vocabulary development (e.g., experiential background, cultural and linguistic diversity, interest in words, reading experience) |

Content area vocabulary is the specific vocabulary related to the particular concepts of various academic disciplines (social science, science, math, art, etc.). While teachers tend to think of content area vocabulary as something that should just be focused on at the secondary level (middle and high school), even elementary school students studying various subjects will understand concepts better when the vocabulary used to describe them is explicitly explained. But it is true that in the secondary level (where students go to different teachers for the various subjects) content area vocabulary becomes more important. Often, educators believe that vocabulary should just be taught in the language arts classroom, not realizing that (a) there is not enough time for students to learn the enormous vocabulary in order to be successful with a standards-based education, and (b) that the teaching of vocabulary related to a particular subject is a very good way to help students understand the subject better.

A wide variety of texts is a necessity in any classroom, whether it is a kindergarten class or a high school class. Students need to have opportunities to read for many reasons – pleasure, to find information for a paper, or just to satisfy their curiosity. When students have ready access to literature and non-fiction texts, they have everything they need within easy reach to help them expand their knowledge. Most teachers allow students to read when they finish their work. When students have ample books in the classroom, teachers can also monitor their choices and supervise them as they make these choices to ensure success.

When there are many books in the classroom, teachers have a book at hand for every occasion. Students love to listen to stories, and this is the perfect way to introduce any lesson – no matter what the subject. Books teachers read should also be made accessible for students to read on their own.

There are various ways teachers can have books arranged in the classroom. In guided reading, there are usually bins of books arranged according to the letter of the reading level. In addition, there can be bins of books arranged according to the topics being studied and books that the students have expressed an interest in reading. Books by specific authors are another way for students to develop an interest in finding a favorite author.

Skill 7.3   **Knows how to plan, implement, and monitor age-appropriate instruction that is responsive to individual students' strengths, needs and interests and is based on ongoing informal and formal assessment of individual students' vocabulary knowledge**

Vocabulary is an integral part of all reading instruction. Comprehension is heavily reliant on understanding the vocabulary of the story. Vocabulary building can be done through word games, crossword puzzles, and board games like Scrabble and Scattergories.

Vocabulary in reading has two levels. First, there is reading vocabulary, which is simply recognizing and knowing the words in the text. In the lower grades, this is mostly made up of high-frequency and sight words.

Word Sorts. Sorting words helps children to begin to recognize patterns in words or similar sounds. Students are given one to three rules and a list of words which they must sort into groups according to the provided rules. For example, if the rules given would be words with the long e sound and words with the short e sound, the students would then read each word to determine which sound would be found in the word.

Classification. At the primary level, classifying words can be very similar to word sorts. Words could be classified by tense or in other similar ways. Students could use graphic organizers to classify words. In later grades, students may classify words by roots, suffixes, prefixes, or even by meaning. Second, there is definitional vocabulary. This includes words that the students need to know in order to better understand the story itself.

Word Banks. Word banks can be very helpful when completing vocabulary activities. They provide a limited choice of words for the students to draw from to complete various activities, including cloze activities. Cloze activities consist of reading passages where certain words have been replaced with a blank line. Word banks also provide a narrow list of terms for the students to master.

Semantic Mapping. As previously discussed, semantic mapping allows students to generate a visual representation of how words and concepts interrelate. In this case, it can be an indispensable tool for the students to make comparisons and to see the connections betweens words in their reading. Overall, vocabulary development can be facilitated using a variety of instructional activities across many grade levels. It is important to vary the activities and materials used to reach more of the students in the classroom. One approach is generally not successful for all students, and teachers have to use a varied approach to reach more students.

Skill 7.4 **Applies knowledge of age-appropriate instructional strategies and materials that reflect students' cultural diversity, are based on a convergence of research evidence, and promote and accelerate students' vocabulary knowledge**

When reading, often times students will come across words with which they are unfamiliar. In some cases, the students will be able to accurately decode the word, but will be unable to determine the meaning after a first read. At this point, students could turn to the dictionary and look up the meaning of the word before proceeding; but, though a valid method, it is not the most efficient means for gaining meaning. The students need to use the remainder of the sentence, paragraph, or even page to attempt to construct a rough meaning for the unknown word.

Word Analysis. Analyzing the word itself is one strategy students can use to successfully derive meaning from words. Looking at the word itself, students can begin to recognize prefixes and suffixes in words. Teachers should take time to teach the meanings of the most common prefixes and suffixes used in the English language so that students can better attack unknown words having those affixes. In addition, by teaching the meanings of Latin and Greek root words, teachers can help students simplify words that are unknown into smaller known parts. Finally, combining the known definitions of root words and combining them with known prefix and/or suffix meanings will provide the students with a solid foundation with which to assess unknown words for comprehension.

Use of Context. Teachers often talk about using context, or the other words in a sentence or passage, to figure out unknown words; but sometimes they do not take the time to specifically teach this skill. For many students, it becomes a naturally-developing skill. Many proficient readers are even unaware of how they reached the conclusion as to the meaning of a word which they learned through context clues. However, struggling readers lack this innate ability to use context. Students need to be taught very specifically methods for using contextual clues to determine meaning. The most effective strategy is to use a think-aloud approach. In this approach, the teacher models out loud her entire thinking process for the students. She walks them through each thought she would have about determining the meaning. Teachers need to provide key questions for the students that they can use later to reflect upon. Some examples of questions might include: "Do any of the other words in the sentence help me to understand what this word may mean?" "If I finish reading the paragraph, does that help me understand better?" "Can I tell if this word is a noun, verb, and adjective by its placement in the sentence?" and "Does the word have any endings that can tell me what tense it may be or if it means more than one?" By answering questions like these for students, teachers can lay the foundation for contextual understanding. Eventually, teachers then move into the background, and the students step in to complete the activities.

Skill 7.5   **Knows how to promote and extend students' vocabulary knowledge by providing systematic age-appropriate instruction and reinforcing activities (e.g., morphemic analysis, etymology, use of graphic organizers, contextual analysis, multiple exposures to a word in various contexts)**

See Competency 7.0 and Skill 4.3

Skill 7.6   **Knows which strategies to use before, during, and after reading to facilitate students' vocabulary development**

When students do not understand the vocabulary used in a text that they are about to read, they will have difficulty comprehending that text. Research has shown that there is little or no merit in having students memorize lists of vocabulary before they start reading, and it definitely has no effect on improving their repertoire of vocabulary. This is because the words are not used in context. There is a place for presenting pre-reading vocabulary to students, but it must be done by presenting the words in relation to the key concepts of the text.

Teachers also have to keep in mind the extent of the students' background knowledge on the subject and the potential that the words have for enhancing their vocabulary. For example, teachers have to consider how important understanding the vocabulary words selected will be to the overall understanding of the text and how much the students will be expected to use them after the reading.

Before reading
Oral reading of a text by teachers beforehand will help convey the meanings of unfamiliar words. Some other strategies for pre-reading include:

1. Activating students' prior knowledge about words. For example, teachers can choose "dismember" as a vocabulary word. By activating students' prior knowledge about the word "member" and how adding the prefix "dis" changes the meaning, students will be able to handle "dismember" when they encounter it in their reading.
2. Defining the word in multiple ways. When teachers show students how the same word can have different meanings depending on how it is used, students will look for multiple meanings as they read.
3. Looking for context clues. The meaning of a word depends on how it is used in the sentence, and the words around it can give students clues as to its meaning. Teach the context clue system by asking students to look at the words before and after the word to help determine its meaning in the sentence.
4. Use the dictionary to look up the meanings of words and then determine the meaning that best fits in the situation.

During reading

Teachers can read a text out loud to the students, ask them to read it silently, or have them read it aloud. If students are expected to read the selection aloud, they should be given practice time. Students need to be encouraged to interact with the text using strategies to help them recognize when they don't understand the text or when they need to consult a dictionary. Teachers need to set a clearly-defined purpose for the reading so that students know exactly what they are looking for as they read.

Strategies that students need to know while reading are:

- How to connect the text with their prior knowledge and background
- How to determine what the author is saying about the topic
- How to pay attention to any words and ideas they may not understand
- How to make and confirm predictions
- How to infer by reading between the lines
- How to respond to what they read

Teachers need to model all of these strategies for the students in order for them to make sense of the text.

After reading

When the students are finished reading, teachers should prompt them to respond and reflect on their reading. They can do this through questioning on various points of the text such as:

- Initial response – "What is your first impression of the text?"
- Extending initial understanding – "Whose point of view is expressed in the text? Do you agree with the author?"
- Making connections – "How is this like or unlike another text?"
- Extending understandings – "How does the author want you to feel about the topic?"

Students can express their responses in a variety of ways, such as in journals, discussions, response groups, literature circles, reading and thinking guides, summarizing key points, art and graphics.

Skill 7.7   Demonstrates knowledge of age-appropriate strategies to teach students effective use of resources for vocabulary development (e.g., dictionaries, glossaries, indexes, electronic media)

Even the youngest children can be taught to use a dictionary. Picture dictionaries are perfect for use in the early grades where the children can see the picture of the word, the word itself, and the meaning. In these dictionaries, there is usually only one meaning given. As students get older, they can use dictionaries that give all the meanings of a word and its part of speech. Teachers need to teach dictionary skills by teaching the method of looking up words using the guide words on the top of each page. They also need to teach students how to determine which meaning of the word fits the context. It is also helpful to have students use the word in a sentence of their own.

Students should also be encouraged to create their own dictionaries where they write a new word under the correct letter of the alphabet, write a meaning for the word, and use it in an original sentence. This could be for personal use as they expand their vocabulary or in connection with a theme or topic under study in the classroom. Dictionaries are useful for spelling, writing, and reading. It is very important to initially expose and habituate students to enjoy using the dictionary.

Cooper (2004) suggests that the following be kept in mind as teachers of grades K-6 introduce and then habituate children in what (it is to be hoped) will be a lifelong fascination with the dictionary and with vocabulary acquisition. Requesting or suggesting that children look up a word in the dictionary should be an invitation to a wonderful exploration, not a punishment or busy work that has no reference to their current reading assignment.

Model the correct way to use the dictionary for children even as late as the third – sixth grade. Many have never been taught proper dictionary skills. Teachers need to demonstrate to the children that as adult readers and writers, they routinely and happily use the dictionary to learn new information that makes them better at reading and writing. Do not routinely require children to look up every new spelling word in the dictionary (this is Cooper's view, and many other theorists would disagree with him).

Cooper believes in beginning dictionary study as early as kindergarten, and this is now very possible because of the proliferation of lush picture dictionaries which can be introduced at that grade level. He also suggests that children not only look at these picture dictionaries, but also begin to make dictionaries of their own filled with pictures and beginning words. As children join the circle of lexicographers, they will begin to see themselves as compilers and users of dictionaries. Of course, this will support their ongoing vocabulary development.

In early grade levels, use of the dictionary can nicely complement children's mastery of the alphabet. They should be given whole-class and small-group practice in locating words.

As the children progress with their phonetic skills, the dictionary can be used to show them phonetic re-spelling using the pronunciation key. Older children in grades 3 and beyond need explicit teacher demonstrations and practice in the use of guide words. They also need to begin to learn about the hierarchies of various word meanings. In the upper grades, children should also explore using special-content dictionaries and glossaries in the backs of their books.

Glossaries
When teachers introduce a book to students, whether it is a textbook or an information book, they should spend some time teaching the parts of the book. This includes having them use the glossary. By pointing out how words are defined in the glossary, students can refer to this section of the book when they want to know the meaning of a word rather than have to start looking through a dictionary. The benefit of using a glossary is that the meaning of the word will be exactly related to how it is used in the text. Teachers can also have the students create their own glossaries as part of their learning throughout a unit or theme.

Indexes
Being able to use the index of a book saves enormous amounts of time when looking for information. As students get older, this is one skill teachers should include as direct instruction, especially when students are involved in research.

Electronic Media
When students use a word processor to write their stories or other writing, they can use the spell check feature of the software to choose the correct spelling of a word. They can also avail themselves of the thesaurus to find synonyms and antonyms to use in their writing.

Skill 7.8	Knows how to promote students' vocabulary development and knowledge by providing them with multiple opportunities to listen to read and respond in various ways to a wide variety of fiction and nonfiction texts

See Skill 7.2

Skill 7.9 **Demonstrates knowledge of delays or differences in students' vocabulary development and when such delays/differences warrant further assessment and additional intervention**

The strategies necessary to develop vocabulary in students for whom English is not the primary language mirror the strategies that work for other students. There is no one set of approaches that works best for second-language students; it is only through a combination of strategies and approaches that students' success can be assured.

Keeping in mind (and as previously discussed) that students who are learning English as a second language require time in order to make the transition. For those students who have received education in their primary language, the time is shortened, typically five years. For students who have received no formal instruction in their primary language, it may take as long as seven years.

Vocabulary development, in any case, needs to be meaning-based instruction. With or without schooling in their primary language, these students do have a mental framework of what words mean and of concepts. It is by tying the new information to these existing structures that the students progress and gain more skills in English.

This transfer between languages is not an easy process and requires time and both meaning-based and explicit teaching strategies. A general list of vocabulary words to memorize along with their meanings will not be a useful strategy for these students. A more promising approach is to tie the vocabulary into the context of the reading or situation. It is through contextual situations that students will better be able to progress.

Since the English language has many roots derived from the Latin and Greek languages (as do many other languages), these parallels can be explicitly shown to students. Through this, they will be able to find the necessary 'hooks' in their own language with which to connect the English variation. Students whose primary language also has many Latin and Greek derivatives will make the transition to English more easily than those whose primary language is not of these roots.

In any group of students, diversity is going to be present and a key factor in the educational process. Using teaching methodologies of a variant nature will be the most successful approach for helping second-language students become fluent in English. Vocabulary instruction needs to be flexible, sometimes explicit, and, other times, context based.

COMPETENCY 8.0 WRITTEN LANGUAGE

Skill 8.1   Recognizes the reciprocal nature of reading and writing, the similarities and differences between spoken and written language, and the relationships among listening, speaking, reading and writing

Strategies for Promoting Awareness of the Relationship between Spoken and Written Language

- Writing down what the children say on a language chart.

- Highlighting the uses of print products found in the classroom such as labels, yellow sticky pad notes, labels on shelves and lockers, calendars, signs, and directions.

- Reading together big-print and oversized books to teach print conventions such as directionality.

- Practicing how to handle a book: How to turn pages, to find the top and bottom of pages, and how to tell the difference between the front and back covers.

- Discussing and comparing with children the length, appearance and boundaries of specific words. For example, children can see that
- the names Dan and Dora share certain letters and a similar shape.

- Having children match oral words to printed words by forming an echo chorus as the teacher reads poetry or rhymes aloud and they echo the reading.

- Having the children combine, manipulate, switch and move letters to change words.

Working with letter cards to create messages and respond to the messages that they create.

Search for activities in word awareness and close observation where children are challenged to identify and talk about the length, appearance, and boundaries of specific words.

Developing the writing of students is a complex process. As with any other aspect of teaching, it's important to provide as many realistic opportunities as possible. When students write for an authentic purpose, the writing becomes more important to them, and there is an increased interest in completing the task.

In writing, teachers often spend time having the students complete journals, write stories, or complete other assignments. While all of these types of writing provide skill development and can be important for students, it is when teachers find ways to incorporate authentic and relevant writing that students find interest in it.

Sometimes, these realistic reasons to write automatically present themselves in schools. There will be times when the students are dissatisfied with a rule or decision that has been made within the school. During such times, the students could practice their persuasive writing skills by attempting to change the rule with which they disagree.

In other cases, students may exchange pen-pal letters with kids in another state or country. This type of correspondence, even if accomplished via email, develops letter-writing skills in a more realistic setting than asking the students to write a fictitious letter. Similarly, students could write jokes to be used on the announcements. They could add their own books to the library or even write books to share with younger students. Writing contests would provide another chance for teachers to provide students a more realistic reason for writing.

In the end, it is not the type of writing to be completed or the reason for which it is completed that is important. It is the understanding that children gain from the process: writing has a purpose in society, and it is a relevant skill that needs to be developed.

Using these authentic methods, children will begin to see writing's relevance in their own lives. They will then be able to come up with their own ideas and reasons to write. This takes the skill to the next level, that of application. Bringing students to the application level is an important goal of education.

In order to take students from where they are in English language arts to the next level of reading and writing, teachers need to know the individual levels of the students. Both formal and informal assessment should be a regular part of the classroom. Assessment for learning will help to determine the direction that the instruction needs to take. All students will not be at the same level or need the same supports. By using the balanced-literacy model, teachers are better able to individualize their lessons to provide the instruction that each student needs.

A comprehensive English language arts program should contain the following components:

1   Skills mini-lessons
2   Reading based on the skills lessons
3   Independent reading
4   Work with words
5   Shared and independent writing
6   Read-alouds
7   Author and novel studies
8   Student projects
9   Language arts integration with the content areas
10 Student conferencing (with teacher and with peers)

Teachers should also be familiar with current research regarding integrating all the components of language arts. The Internet is a valuable source of information in this regard with respect to the International Reading Association and grade-specific best practices for teachers in language arts. Two sites of interest are www.teachersfirst.com and www.literacyuconn.edu.

Skill 8.2   Demonstrates knowledge of the developmental continuum of students' written language, including milestones in physical and/or cognitive processes (e.g., letter formation, spelling, sentence construction, paragraph development)

Children's first attempts at writing are mainly scribbles. They do have a story in their minds and can read back the writing to you. Children in kindergarten love to write, and as they develop in letter formation and sounds associated with the letters, they use invented spelling. They love to illustrate their writing with a picture and may have a few words to explain the picture. As they gradually develop a sense of word identification, they will spell some words correctly.

The stages on the developmental continuum of writing are:

Emergent Writer

-   Knows that words can be written
-   Wants to write
-   Writes in scribbles or strings of letters
-   Knows that writing conveys meaning
-   Uses pictures in writing
-   May not have spaces between words
-   Uses words from the environment

Developing Writer

- Begins to use variation in sentence structure
- Tends to have a sense of voice in writing
- Uses story language
- Uses more conventions of English language
- Starts to use conventional spelling
- Starts to organize ideas into paragraphs
- Is satisfied with the first draft

Independent Writer

- Has a strong sense of voice
- Uses correct grammar and spelling
- Uses varied sentence structure
- Has a well developed sense of paragraph structure
- Includes descriptive vocabulary in writing

Skill 8.3   Knows how to create an environment in which students are motivated to express their ideas through writing and how to use age-appropriate instructional strategies and sequences for developing students' writing throughout the writing process (e.g., prewriting, drafting, editing, revising)

There is no one exclusive method for teaching the writing process. Beginning teachers need to understand that this is a process that takes students a long time to master, and that they need to continually model the steps in the writing process for the students. The prewriting stage is one that students prefer to skip and, therefore, is one that teachers need to constantly remind the students about. At first, this part of the process will be teacher-guided using such methodologies as helping the students discover what they want to say about a specific topic. Some of the ways students can become used to using this step before they start their actual draft include:

- Brainstorming
- Discussing
- Webbing
- Interviewing
- Surveying
- Listening
- Reading
- Charting
- Mapping
- Outlining

Free-writing is another way students can get their ideas down on paper before they start to refine their thoughts.

When teaching the drafting process, teachers should encourage the students to skip lines. This allows them space for revising and editing when they get to those stages. Quite often, students will ask how to spell words when they are writing their first draft. Since spelling is not as important at this point as it will be in later stages, teachers often tell them to write the words the way they think they are spelled. There will be plenty of time to make corrections later.

Revising and editing are the hardest stages of the writing process to teach. Exemplars provide the students with examples of what good and poor writing looks like. When students have a chance to study the exemplars and discuss the merits of each, they have an idea of the improvements they need to make in their own writing. In revising, students should read the writing out loud, either to themselves or to another student, to pick up on what parts make sense and what parts need additions or deletions. Author's chair is a way of encouraging students to provide comments on writing, but they do need to be encouraged not to make disparaging remarks and to provide only constructive criticism.

Editing is a time-consuming task, and it would be unreasonable to expect students to pick up on all the mistakes in a piece of writing. Therefore, teachers should ask students to edit for specific purposes, such as correct spelling, capitalization, or punctuation. The easiest way to pick up on incorrect spelling is to read the writing backwards. This way the students are focusing on each word rather than the meaning of the piece. The use of a word processor helps students in finding words that are not spelled correctly.

Publication means getting the writing ready for others to read. For many students, it means illustrating the work, creating an attractive cover, or even using a word processor to produce the final draft.

The classroom environment should be one where the students feel comfortable in taking risks with writing. Print on the walls and the availability of dictionaries and books that the students can refer to are essential. Students should be permitted to work in groups for peer editing and revising; and, by using Author's Chair, students have a chance to read their writing to other students.
The writing classroom should be a place where the teacher is a facilitator working with individual students and groups of students at different times. Assessment is a part of the process as the teacher discovers what parts of the writing process students are struggling with and matching instruction to student needs. There will be times when the teacher is instructing the whole class, and there will be other times when the teacher is delivering instruction to only a small group of students on one issue.

Skill 8.4 **Applies knowledge of instructional strategies for developing students' meaningful writing for a variety of audiences, purposes, and settings**

To start students with writing, it is necessary to initiate their thinking about possible topics to write about. This can be done through:

- Brainstorming about people, places and events
- Talking and listening to others
- Looking at pictures
- Listening to music
- Looking through information books
- Listing ideas
- Looking through newspaper articles

After students have generated ideas for their writing, teachers can discuss the possible audience who would read the writing. Teachers should help students consider the point of view they want to take in their writing, the reason for the writing, and the format the writing will take. The use of outlines, webs, charts, and maps can help them organize the information they want to present.

Ask the students to consider who they are writing for and whether they want to entertain, inform, describe, persuade, or inquire in their writing. The setting of the writing will depend on the purpose, so teachers should activate their prior knowledge about the different kinds of texts they have read.

Exemplars of each kind of writing should be available so students know what they can choose from. Some of these examples include:

- Reports
- Journal entries
- Advertisements
- Book reviews
- Speeches
- Comic strips
- Directions
- Songs
- Stories
-

Students need numerous opportunities to write for various purposes. Writing should be a daily activity in all classrooms, and students should be instructed in the writing process. The components of the writing process are:

- Pre-writing – brainstorming, webbing, story maps- helps students generate ideas for their writing. For younger writers, a picture can be the stimulus for writing. They draw a picture and then write a few sentences about the picture. For older writers, teachers can provide the picture or a prompt to generate ideas for writing.
- Drafting – Students get their ideas down on paper. Teachers should not worry about proper spelling or conventions. The main idea is to get the students writing. Correcting the mistakes is part of the editing process.
- Revising – in this stage of the writing process, students reread the writing to determine where they can add ideas or delete some things. They can also change around parts of the writing so that it flows more smoothly.
- Editing – this section of the writing process sees the students correcting the writing for conventions of grammar and correct spelling
- Publishing – in this component, the students prepare the writing to be displayed on a bulletin board or to be published in some other way. It is important to note that not all writing needs to be brought to this stage.

When students are given a writing assignment, the first instinct is to start writing. They also want to finish the piece and pass it in without reading it over or editing it. It is a chore to rewrite a draft, so teachers need to model this for them and to teach them that it is what all writers do.

Prewriting activities set the stage for writing in the classroom. Students need guidance in terms of how to plan for their writing and instruction in how to brainstorm, use a web, a story map, or some other graphic organizer to help them organize their thoughts. Modeling by teachers helps students understand the steps they need to take to tackle different forms of writing. The instruction needs to be very explicit so that students can see and hear every action they should take with their own writing. The prewriting activities include planning the writing, considering the purpose, and (in the case of a research project) considering where they will get the information they will need.

During the drafting stage, students will be putting their ideas on paper. The quality of the text should not be a concern at this point as it is more important for the students to just write. Students may even used inventive spelling in this stage and not bother with capitalization or punctuation.

Revising and editing stages are the ones where teachers do have to spend the most time teaching the concepts. In revising, students have to look at the relationship of the sentences and decide whether or not the piece flows smoothly. They may have to read the text out loud as this is when they can really hear where the text does not make sense. Teachers can work with students to revise their work by asking them to add information to clarify a point or to look at sections where certain sentences do not fit together. Modelling is crucial here, and the use of exemplars can really demonstrate to the students that revising makes a big difference.

Editing for grammatical structure, correct spelling, punctuation, and capitalization is another issue in teaching the stages of writing. Here students need plenty of practice. Many teachers have mini-lessons as the need arises in student writing and provide practice in the form of worksheets. However, the students may get all the answers correct on the worksheets and still not edit their own work. For this reason, teachers should look for only specific things in a piece of writing so as not to confuse the students. Instead of marking the paper with red ink, ask the students to look for all the places where they should have used capital letters. On another occasion, ask the students to underline all the words they think may be spelled incorrectly. Do not overload them with too much editing all at once.

Peer editing also helps with revising and editing. Providing opportunities for students to work together in small groups or pairs to edit each other's work not only helps the writer, but also the other student gains experience in editing and revising.

Once the writing has been revised and edited to the students' satisfaction, they can decide how to publish the work or even whether or not to publish. The students can rewrite the piece in good handwriting or even use a word processor. Colored paper and the use of colorful illustrations give the students the opportunity to show pride in their work and to display it for others to see.

Skill 8.5 **Applies knowledge of instructional strategies for developing students' writing in connection with listening and speaking and in response to reading**

There are numerous methodologies for teaching integrated-language-arts skills. There is no one approach which will meet the needs of all students in a classroom or building. It is important to be aware of various methods to be able to utilize as many different strategies as possible to meet the needs of students within the classroom.

Reading: There are several main approaches to teaching reading in today's society. They include:

- Balanced Literacy – wherein the students will spend portions of each day reading to themselves, reading to teachers, listening to teachers read, and reading with teachers
- Phonics – wherein the majority of reading instruction is accomplished by using systematic, sequential phonics instruction
- Whole Language- wherein the instruction is managed through a reader's workshop, and learning is accomplished by reading authentic literature
- Combination Approach-wherein authentic literature is combined with phonics instruction

Writing: Teachers generally teach writing through a process of grammar and more holistic writing assignments. Generally, the process involves explicit grammar instruction and specific spelling instruction. The holistic writing can include specific writing assignments from the various forms of writing (persuasive, narrative, expository, letters, etc.) and journaling. Most teaching of writing includes the writing process with brainstorming, rough drafts, peer editing and teacher editing being a complete part of the process. Students sometimes write for publication as well.

Listening and Speaking: Listening and speaking are generally not subjects for which you will find specific lesson plans in a teacher's plans. They are usually incorporated through reading and presentation activities. Listening skills are assessed and developed through the shared reading or other activities. Speaking skills are assessed through classroom discussion and oral presentations required throughout the curriculum. If there are difficulties in these areas, students may require specific instruction from a speech pathologist in these areas. At this point, more intensive and specific skill development will occur.

Viewing: As technology has increased and become an integral part of the society, students are required more and more often to view information and respond in some format. Students can gain and gather more information than ever before using the Internet in addition to traditional movies, slides, and filmstrips. Using these media information tools, students may respond in a variety of formats (written response, graphic organizers, oral presentations, etc.).

Visual Representation: Students need to understand how to use the visual formats to represent thoughts and ideas. Mind mapping is a technique involving visually recording notes instead of a traditional outline. This allows more complex ideas to be recorded and specifically personalized to an individual student's experiences. Creation of charts and graphs is also a method used which bridges math and reading and can cross content areas. This mode of teaching should be combined with all of the above-referenced methods to help students process information because manipulating data or information to represent it in a different format requires a higher level of thinking.

Responding to literature is one of the most important parts of reading. By the responses that students give to what they have read, teachers can determine the level of comprehension. It takes practice for students to be able to respond critically to a text because they have the idea that all published authors are perfect and should not be criticized.

Some of the strategies that teachers can use to provide opportunities for students to give creative and personal responses to their reading include:

1   Reading conferences – ask students to read a section of the text and then tell why they chose that section. Teachers can also ask students why they are reading a certain book or ask about their favourite author.
2   Reading Surveys – Teachers can devise a list of questions to find out what students are reading, how they decide what books to read, and how students feel about the topics or language used in the book.
3   Daily reading time – This could be a set time when everyone in the class is reading, including teachers, or it could be a center activity for a small group of children.
4   Literature Circles – using the role sheets developed by Harvey Daniels in Voice and Choice in a Student-Centered Classroom, students take on different roles each day. They discuss the chapter or book, find new vocabulary words, illustrate a scene, or pose questions for the group.
5   Reader's Theatre – students adapt part of the book or story and make it into a choral reading with expression that shows how they felt about what they have read.

Responding to literature does not always take the form of written responses. In a Reader's Workshop, students can choose to respond to what they read in art, painting, song, dance, or any number of ways to show an interpretation of the reading. Interviewing the author or asking students to change a scene so that the result is different are other examples of how students can give personal responses to reading.

Students who have a hard time coming up with a response would benefit from a sheet listing ideas for ways they can respond. These usually take the form of open-ended sentences such as:

1 The character I liked the best was
2 The character that is most like me is
3 If I were _____, I would have

Skill 8.6 **Knows how to provide students with opportunities to self-assess their writing (e.g., voice, coherence, depth of ideas, focus sentence-to-sentence movement) and elicit critiques of their writing from others**

Teachers are not the only ones who should assess student writing. By teaching the students to self-assess, teachers are also instructing the students when and how to recognize mistakes in their writing. After each writing assignment, students need time to self-assess their own work. This can be by using exemplars of good, average, and poor writing samples that they can use for comparison to their writing. Teachers should also develop rubrics with the students before they start writing and then have them grade their work according to the rubric before they hand it in to be graded by the teacher. If teachers avoid assigning a mark to a piece of writing and hand it back for students to work on again to improve, the students will have an idea of where they went wrong.

Other strategies that teachers can use are questionnaires about student attitudes and experiences with writing and a writing checklist for them to complete once they finish a piece of writing.

During pre-writing, students are allowed to write without having to worry about correct spelling or conventions. The intention is to get the ideas on paper. During the editing and revising stages of the writing process, the students then shift their focus to specific sections of the piece to prepare it for publishing. All of the aspects of editing and revising need to be modeled for the students and taught directly through mini-lessons and through whole and small-group instruction.

Voice is what gives writing a personality. It tells readers how enthusiastic the writer is about the topic and it is what holds their attention. Although students may find it hard to put their own voice into the writing, the best advice for teachers to give them is to tell them to be themselves. The students do have to keep the audience in mind as they write because the way you tell the same thing to two different people may be quite different. For students who do not know exactly who the audience is, tell them to write as if they were talking to a friend.

The **depth of ideas** presented in a piece of writing depends on the topic and the audience. The ideas presented in an explanation are different from those presented in a story, but they still need to be in depth enough so that the reader gains complete understanding. Some ideas need to be more detailed than others, and this is often where students have problems. They have to decide which ideas are the most important ones and therefore need more details or descriptions.

Coherence is an important part of any writing. The **sentence-to-sentence movement** of the piece must be smooth so that the reader does not lose any of the meaning. Students often jump from one idea to another in the same paragraph or do not use transition words correctly. Transition words are important to help produce a cohesive piece of writing. They include such words as however, meanwhile, although, on the other hand, etc. Teachers could have a list of words posted in the classroom where the students could easily refer to them as they are writing. The use of transition words is something that students need instruction for. The teacher can model the use of the words in writing, demonstrate how they are used by other authors, and provide sample paragraphs for students to analyze to see where transition words should be placed.

During the writing process, students should elicit critiques of their writing from their peers and teachers. Since it is difficult for teachers to critique every piece of writing, time should be included within the writing block for peer editing. This gives students a chance to work together with one or two others to look at each other's writing and to offer suggestions for improvement. As students get older, they do not feel comfortable reading their work to a large group of students, which is the opposite of what young writers like to do. For this reason, Author's Chair is better suited for the primary grades. Here students will read their writing to the whole class and elicit comments on how they feel about the writing and what corrections or revisions should be made.

The teacher can also give critiques on student work in progress. A way of doing this so as not to be overloaded with assessing writing on a nightly basis is to set up a schedule for five students to pass in what they have done each day. The teacher can then read these over after school and make comments for a writing conference with the student on the following day.

By engaging in peer editing, students learn that writing is not just for the teacher. It lets them see what other students are writing about and gives them ideas for their own writing.

Skill 8.7 **Knows how to model the use of writing conventions and appropriate grammar and usage to communicate clearly and effectively in writing and to reinforce students' use of writing conventions and appropriate grammar and usage**

See Skill 4.3

Skill 8.8 **Demonstrates understanding of the role of spelling and graphophonemic knowledge in reading and writing, factors that affect students' spelling, the stages of spelling development (i.e., prephonetic, phonetic, transitional, and conventional) and how and when to support students' development from one stage to the next, and procedures for providing systematic spelling instruction**

Spelling is of utmost importance in the writing process. At first young children will use invented spelling in which they write the words according to letter sounds. There are several factors that influence the development of spelling, such as:

- Surrounding students with an environment rich in print
- Understanding the developmental stages of spelling
- Understanding that learning to spell is problem solving
- Teaching of the rules of spelling
- Promoting an awareness about spelling

Spelling should be taught within the context of meaningful language experiences. Giving a child a list of words to learn to spell and then testing the child on the words every Friday will not aid in the development of spelling. The child must be able to use the words in context, and they must have some meaning for the child. The assessment of how well a child can spell or where there are problems also has to be done within a meaningful environment. The main reasons for assessing spelling are:

- To find out what the child knows about spelling patterns and strategies
- To determine what the teacher needs to teach
- To develop spelling growth over a period of time

In order for spelling assessment to be authentic, it must have meaning for the child. Taking a list of words that a child misspells from a piece of writing is one example of a spelling list that teachers can use. If teachers keep a list of words the children ask to spell, this can also be the basis for a word list.

Since spelling is something that does happen over time, teachers may notice that children keep spelling the same words incorrectly again and again. Through explicit teaching of strategies and even tricks to help spell the words, eventually they will see success in spelling. Assessment is something that has to happen over the course of a grade. Correct spelling is not something that children learn and retain automatically. When assessing spelling, there are behaviors that teachers should look for:

- Knowledge of sounds and symbols
- Development of visual memory
- Development of morphemic knowledge
- Mastery of high frequency words at specific grade levels
- Location and knowledge of how to use spelling resources
- Attempts at spelling unknown words
- Risk-taking attempts in using invented spelling

Spelling Pattern Word Wall
One of the understandings emergent readers come to about a word is that if they know how to read, write, and spell one word, they can write, read, and spell many other words as well.

Create in your classroom a spelling-pattern word wall. Wylie and Durrell have identified spelling patterns and highlighted them in their classic thirty-seven "dependable" rimes. The spelling word wall can be created by stapling a piece of 3" x 5" butcher block paper to the bulletin board. Then attach spelling pattern cards around the border with thumbtacks so that the cards can be easily removed to use at the meeting area.

Once you decide on a spelling pattern for instruction, remove the corresponding card from the word wall. Then, take a 1"x 3" piece of a contrasting color of butcher block paper, and tape the card to the top end of a sheet the children will use for their investigation. Next, read one of Wylie and Durrell's short rimes with the children and have them identify the pattern.

After the pattern is identified, the children can try to come up with other words that have the same spelling pattern. Teachers can write these on the spelling pattern sheet, using a different color marker to highlight the spelling pattern within the word. The children have to add to the list until the sheet is full, which might take two days or more.

After the sheet is full, the completed spelling pattern is attached to the wall. Some of the techniques teachers use to determine the words students need to spell include:

- Lists of misspelled words from student writing
- Lists of theme words
- Lists of words from the content areas
- Word banks

It is important for beginning writers to know that spelling is an important part of the writing process. However, insisting on correct spelling right from the beginning may actually hamper the efforts of beginning writers. In early spelling development, children should be allowed to experiment with words and use invented spelling. Spelling development is something that occurs over time as a developmental process. It does develop in clearly-defined stages, which the teacher should take into consideration when planning lessons. Teachers should assess students' spelling knowledge and then plan mini-lessons for whole class and small groups as necessary. Some of the ways teachers can provide spelling instruction in the context of meaningful reading and writing activities include:

- Shared reading
- Guided reading
- Shared writing
- Shared reading
- Poetry reading using rhyming words with the same spelling patterns
- Reading chants
- Writing lists
- Writing daily news in the classroom
- Writing letters
- Writing invitations

By planning spelling instruction, teachers will help children recognize word patterns, help then discern spelling rules, and help them develop their own tricks for remembering how to spell words. Direct instruction is necessary for students to develop the knowledge they need regarding the morphological structure of words and thus the relationships between words. Students also need to be taught graphophonic relationships in order to know the relationship between letters and sounds, the probability of letter sequences, and the different letter patterns.

Developing visual methods of recognizing correct spelling is also an aid to helping students learn to spell. Tracing around the shape of a word helps them develop a visual memory as to whether or not the word looks as if it is spelled correctly. Memory aids (mnemonics) also aid in spelling development, such as in the word PAINT – Pat Added Ink Not Tar.

Along with direct teaching of spelling, teachers should model the process at all times. By talking about spelling and having students assist in class writing, they will help students develop the awareness that spelling is important. Some activities where teachers can use this approach include:

- Experience charts
- Writing notes to parents
- Writing class poems and stories
- Editing writing with students

Students also need to be encouraged to take risks with spelling. Rather than have students constantly asking how words are spelled, teachers can use "Have a Go Sheets. These sheets consist of three columns in which students write the word as they think it is spelled. Then the student asks the teacher or another student if it is spelled correctly. If it is incorrect, the student will tell the other student which letters are in the correct place, and the student will try again. After the third try, the teacher can either tell the students how to spell the word and add this to the list of words the student has to learn, or work on the necessary spelling strategy.

Skill 8.9   Applies knowledge of the benefits of technology for teaching writing (e.g., word processing, desktop publishing software)

Technological advances have greatly increased teachers' ability to work with individual students. Software such as desktop publishing and word processing has proven to be of tremendous value in teaching students how to correct the spelling and grammar in their writing. It has also helped students who are not so adept at handwriting produce legible papers and receive higher grades. When students type their first draft of a piece of writing, they can save it and return to it to make corrections on the same page without having to rewrite the piece over and over with each round of editing and revision. Students with difficulties in writing can benefit from speech-to-print software that writes the words a student speaks into a microphone or headset.

However, these technologies cannot do everything, and in no way should they be expected to replace teachers in the classroom. They can only help with correcting spelling and grammar and do not provide instruction as to how to proceed through the stages of the writing process. Students still need instruction on how to organize their ideas, how to construct paragraphs, and how to elaborate on the ideas they want to present.

Skill 8.10 **Knows how to formally and informally monitor and assess students' writing development, including their use of writing conventions, and how to use assessment results to develop focused instruction that is responsive to students' strengths, needs, and interests to reinforce students' writing skills**

By assessing students' writing, teachers are able to monitor the progress and growth they make in writing over a period of time. Assessing also helps the teachers identify areas where the students need more help in developing as writers. Teachers should keep a comprehensive record of student writing progress to build an effective writing program and provide instruction according to student needs.

As a preliminary assessment, teachers may ask students to provide a writing sample on a topic of their own choosing or teacher provided. This sample will then be assessed to see how well the students can communicate in writing, to identify strengths and weaknesses, and to identify areas where instruction is needed. This initial assessment provides a wealth of information to tteachers about where they need to start with writing instruction for the whole class and small groups. Some of the things teachers can look for in this writing sample include:

- Students' scope of vocabulary
- Spelling strengths and needs
- Use of conventional grammar
- Absence or presence of details and descriptions
- The length of the piece and the time used to complete it

Teachers should respond to each piece of writing, telling the student what it reveals. The emphasis should not be on giving a grade to each piece of writing, but rather on giving the students information about how to improve as writers. Teachers should help the students set goals for their writing. Both teachers and students should record the goals and use them as the focal points for assessment. By looking at student goals, teachers can assess how well the students are progressing in this area.

Some of the methods teachers can use to observe and assess student progress in writing include:

- Writing conference
- Writing folder
- Writing portfolio and student reflections on the work in the portfolio

Students should also know the criteria teachers are using in assessing the writing. When students have this before they start writing, they know what standards they have to meet.

Skill 8.11   Demonstrates knowledge of delays or differences in students' writing and spelling development and when such delays/differences warrant further assessment and additional intervention

As with reading, there will be students experiencing delays and difficulties with writing. These students need models of what good writing looks like, and they need extra time to complete the writing. Some students are exceptionally slow when they have to write by hand, and allowing them to use a word processor for their writing will not only speed up the process, but will help to improve their self-confidence as writers.

Some students may need extra intervention in terms of building background knowledge to enable them to formulate ideas for writing. They may be lacking the essential strategies of organizing their thoughts into sentences and paragraphs and may need one-on-one help with these aspects of the writing process.

When working with students who have difficulties or delays, teachers need to work on one strategy at a time and practice this strategy until the students internalize it. When conferencing about student writing, teachers can focus on only one aspect, such as capitalization, and have students find all the mistakes. Another conference could focus on spelling mistakes.

Software designed for writing is also helpful for use with these students, such as programs that write what students say. There are also prompting programs and programs that provide maps and webs to use in prewriting.

DOMAIN II.	INSTRUCTION AND ASSESSMENT: RESOURCES AND PROCEDURES

COMPETENCY 9.0 ASSESSMENT

Skill 9.1   Demonstrates knowledge of the reciprocal nature of assessment and instruction and uses multiple and varied reading assessments before, during, and after instruction to monitor progress and design and modify instruction

Assessment is the practice of collecting information about children's progress, and evaluation is the process of judging the children's responses to determine how well they are achieving particular goals or demonstrating reading skills.

Assessment and evaluation are intricately connected in the literacy classroom. Assessment is necessary because teachers need ways to determine what students are learning and how they are progressing. In addition, assessment can be a tool which can also help students take ownership of their own learning and become partners in their ongoing development as readers and writers. In this day of public accountability, clear, definite and reliable assessment creates confidence in public education.

There are two broad categories of assessment. Informal assessment utilizes observations and other non-standardized procedures to compile anecdotal and observation data/evidence of children's progress. It includes but is not limited to checklists, observations, and performance tasks. Formal assessment is composed of standardized tests and procedures carried out under circumscribed conditions. Formal Assessments include: state tests, standardized achievement tests, NAEP tests, and the like.

To be effective, assessment should have the following characteristics:

l. It should be an ongoing process with the teacher making informal or formal assessments on an ongoing basis. The assessment should be a natural part of the instruction and not intrusive.

2. The most effective assessment is integrated into ongoing instruction. Throughout the teaching and learning day, the child's written, spoken and reading contributions to the class or lack thereof, need to and can be continually noted.

3. Assessment should reflect the child's actual reading and writing experiences. The child should be able to show that he or she can read and explain or react to a similar literary or expository work.

4. Assessment needs to be a collaborative and reflective process. Teachers can learn from what the children reveal about their own individual assessments. Children, even as early as grade two, should be supported by their teacher to continually and routinely ask themselves questions assessing their reading. They might ask: "Am I understanding what the author wanted to say?," " What can I do to improve my reading?" and "How can I use what I have read to learn more about this topic?"

Teachers need to be informed by their own professional observation AND by children's comments as they assess and customize instruction for children.

5. Quality assessment is multidimensional and may include but not be limited to samples of writings, student retellings, running records, anecdotal teacher observations, self-evaluations, and records of independent reading. From this multidimensional data, the teacher can derive a consistent level of performance and design additional instruction that will enhance the child's reading performance.

6. Assessment must take into account children's age and ethnic/cultural patterns of learning.

7. Assess to teach children from their strengths, not their weaknesses. Find out what reading behaviors children demonstrate well and then design instruction to support those behaviors.

8. Assessment should be part of children's learning process and not done TO them, but rather done WITH them.

Skill 9.2   Applies knowledge of the characteristics, advantages, and limitations of types of reading assessment (e.g., norm referenced, criterion referenced, formal and informal inventories, constructed response, portfolios, running records, miscue analyses, observations, anecdotal records, journals, technology-based assessments) and their uses in monitoring and evaluating student progress in the components of reading (e.g., oral language, phonological and phonemic awareness, concepts of print, alphabetic principle, word identification, fluency, comprehension, vocabulary development, and written language)

Characteristics and Uses of Criterion-referenced and Norm-referenced Tests to Assess Reading Development and Identify Reading Difficulties

Criterion-referenced – tests where the children are measured against criteria or guidelines which are uniform for all the test takers. Therefore by definition, no special questions, formats or considerations are made for the test taker who is either from a different linguistic/cultural background or is already identified as a struggling reader/writer. On a criterion-referenced test, it is possible that a child test taker can score 100% because the child may have actually been exposed to all of the concepts taught and mastered them. A child's score on such a test would indicate which of the concepts have already been taught and what he or she needs additional review or support to master.

Two criterion-referenced tests that are commonly used to assess children's reading achievement are the Diagnostic Indicators of Basic Early Literacy Skills (DIBELS) and the Stanford Achievement Test. DIBELS measures progress in literacy from kindergarten to grade three. It can be downloaded from the Internet free at dibels.uoregon.edu. The Stanford is designed to measure individual children's achievement in key school subjects. Subtests covering various reading skills are part of this test. Both DIBELS and the Stanford Achievement Test are group-administered.

DEGREES OF READING POWER (DRP) –This test is targeted to assess how well children understand the meaning of written text in real life situations. This test is supposed to measure the process of children's reading, not the products of reading such as identifying the main idea and author's purpose.

CTPIII- This is a criterion-referenced test which measures verbal and quantitative ability in grades 3-12. It is targeted to help differentiate among the most capable students, i.e., those who rank above the 80th percentile on other standardized tests. This is a test that emphasizes higher order thinking skills and process-related reading comprehension questions.

Norm-referenced –test in which the children are measured against one another. Scores on this test are reported in percentiles. Each percentile indicates the percent of the testing population whose scores were lower than or the same as a particular child's score. Percentile is defined as a score on a scale of 100 showing the percentage of a distribution that is equal to it or below it. This type of state standardized norm-referenced test is being used in most districts today in response to the No Child Left Behind Act. While this type of test does not help tract the individual reader's progress in his/her ongoing reading development, it does permit comparisons across groups.

There are many more standardized norm-referenced tests to assess children's reading than there are criterion-referenced. In these tests, scores are based on how well a child does compared to others, usually on the local, state and national level. IF the norming groups on the tests are reflective of the children being tested (e.g. same spread of minority, low income, gifted students), the results are more trustworthy.

One of the best known norm-referenced test is the Iowa Test of Basic Skills. It assesses student achievement in various school subjects and has several subtests in reading. Other examples of norm-referenced tests used around the country are the Metropolitan Achievement Tests, the Terra Nova-2, and the Stanford Diagnostic Reading Test-4. These are all group tests. An individual test that reading specialists use with students is the Woodcock Reading Mastery Test.

Concepts of Validity, Reliability, and Bias in Testing

Validity is how well a test measures what it is supposed to measure. Teacher made tests are therefore not generally extremely valid, although they may be an appropriate measure for the validity of the concept the teacher wants to assess for his/her own children's achievement.

Reliability is the consistency of the test. This is measured by whether the test will indicate the same score for the child who takes it more than once.

Bias in testing occurs when the information within the test or the information required to respond to a multiple choice question or constructed response (essay question on the test) is information that is not available to some test takers who come from a different cultural, ethnic, linguistic or socio-economic background than do the majority of the test takers. Since they have not had the same prior linguistic, social or cultural experiences that the majority of test takers have had, these test takers are at a disadvantage in taking the test and no matter what their actual mastery of the material taught by the teacher, can not address the "biased" questions. Generally other "non-biased" questions are given to them and eventually the biased questions are removed from the examination.

To solidify what might be abstract to the reader, on a recent reading test in my school system, the grade four reading comprehension multiple choice had some questions about the well known fairy tale of the gingerbread boy. These questions were simple and accessible for most of the children in the class. But two children who were recent new arrivals from the Dominican Republic had learned English there. They were reading on grade four level, but in their Dominican grade school, the story of the Gingerbread Boy was not a major one. Therefore a question about this story on the standardized reading test did demonstrate examiner bias and was not fair to these test takers.

The Characteristics and Uses of Formal and Informal Assessments

Informal Assessments

A running record of children's oral reading progress in the early grades K-3 is a pivotal informal assessment. It supports the teacher in deciding whether a book a child is reading is matched to his/her stage of reading development. In addition this assessment allows the teacher to analyze a child's miscues to see which cueing systems and strategies the child uses and to determine which other systems the child might use more effectively. Finally the running record offers a graphic account of a child's oral reading.

Generally, a teacher should maintain an annotated class notebook with pages set aside for all the children or individual notebooks for each child. One of the benefits of using running records as an informal assessment is that they can be used with any text and can serve as a tool for teaching, rather than an instrument to report on children's status in class.

Another good point about using running records is that they can be taken repeatedly and frequently by the teacher, so that the educator can truly observe a pattern of errors. This in turn provides the educator with sufficient information to analyze the child's reading over time. As any mathematician or scientist knows, the more samples of a process you gather over time, the more likely the teacher is to get an accurate picture of the child's reading needs.

Using the notations which Marie Clay developed and shared in her *An Observation Study of Early Literacy Achievement*, Sharon Taberski offers in her book, *On Solid Ground*, a lengthy walk through keeping a running record of children's reading. She writes in the child's miscue on the top line of her running record above the text word. Indeed she records all of the child's miscue attempts on the line above the text word. Sharon advises the teacher to make all the miscue notations as the child reads, since this allows the teacher to get additional information about how and why the child makes miscue choices. Additionally, the teacher should note, self corrections (coded SC) when the child is monitoring his/her own reading, crosschecks information, and uses additional information.

As part of the informal assessment of primary grade reading, it is important to record the child's word insertions, omissions, requests for help, and attempts to get the word. In informal assessment the rate of accuracy can be estimated by dividing the child's errors by the total words read.

Results of a running record assessment can be used to select the best setting for the child's reading. If a child reads from 95%-100% correct, the child is ready for independent reading. If the child reads from 92% to 97% right, the child is ready for guided reading. Below 92% the child needs a read-aloud or shared reading activity. Note that these percentages are slightly different from those one would use to match books to readers.

One of the increasingly popular and meaningful forms of informal assessment is the compilation of the literacy portfolio. What is particularly compelling about this type of informal portfolio is that artists, television directors, authors, architects and photographers use portfolios in their careers and jobs. This is a most authentic format for documenting children's literacy growth over time. The portfolio is not only a significant professional informal assessment tool for the teacher, but a vehicle and format for the child reader to take ownership of his or her progress over time. It models a way of compiling one's reading and writing products as a lifelong learner, which is the ultimate goal of reading instruction.

Portfolios can include the following six categories of materials:

Work samples: These can include children's story maps, webs, K-W-L charts, pictures, illustrations, storyboards, and writings about the stories which they have read.

Records of independent Reading and Writing: These can include the children's journals, notebooks or logs of books read with the names of the authors, titles of the books, date completed, and pieces related to books completed or in progress.

Checklists and Surveys: These include checklists designed by the teacher for reading development, writing development, ownership checklists, and general interest surveys.

Self Evaluation Forms: These are the children's own evaluations of their reading and writing process framed in their own words. They can be simple templates with starting sentences such as: "I am really proud of the way I ...

I feel one of my strengths as a reader is _____

To improve the way I read aloud I need to _____

To improve my reading I should _____

Generally at the beginning of a child's portfolio in grade 3 or above there is a letter to the reader explaining the work that will be found in the portfolio and from fourth grade level up, children write a brief reflection detailing their feelings and judgments about their growth as readers and writers.

When teachers are maintaining the portfolios for mandated school administrative review, district review, or even for their own research, they often prepare portfolio summary sheets. These provide identifying data on the children and then a timeline of their review of the portfolio contents plus professional comments on the extent to which the portfolio documents satisfactory and ongoing growth in reading.

Portfolios can be used beneficially for child-teacher and of course, parent/teacher conversations to review the child's progress, discuss areas of strength, set future goals, make plans for future learning activities and evaluate what should remain in the portfolio and what needs to be cleared out for new materials.

Rubrics

Holistic scoring involves assessing a child's ability to construct meaning through writing. It uses a scale called a RUBRIC which can range from 0 to 4.

O- This indicates the piece can not be scored. It does not respond to the topic or is illegible.

1- The writing does respond to the topic, but does not cover it accurately.

2- This piece of writing does respond to the topic but lacks sufficient details or elaboration.

3- This piece fulfills the purpose of the writing assignment and has sufficient development (which refers to details, examples, and elaboration of ideas).

4- This response has the most details, best organization, and presents a well expressed reaction to the original writer's piece.

MISCUE ANALYSIS

This is a procedure that allows the teacher a look at the reading process. By definition, the miscue is an oral response different from the text being read. Sometimes miscues are also called unexpected responses or errors. By studying a student's miscues from an oral reading sample, the teacher can determine which cues and strategies the student is correctly using or not using in constructing meaning. Of course, the teacher can customize instruction to meet the needs of this particular student.

INFORMAL READING INVENTORIES (IRI)

These are a series of samples of texts prearranged in stages of increasing difficulty. Listening to children read through these inventories, the teacher can pinpoint their skill level and the additional concepts they need to work on.

Characteristics and uses of Group versus Individual Reading Assessments

In assessment, tests are used for different purposes. They have different dimensions or characteristics whether they are given individually or in a group and whether they are standardized or teacher-made. The chart below shows the relationships of these elements.

	Standardized	**Teacher-made**
Individual	*Characteristics* • is uniformly administered *Uses* • is best for younger children • helps with placement for special services	*Characteristics* • has more flexibility *Uses* • assists teaching decisions • used for diagnostic purposes
Group	*Characteristics* • is uniformly administered • is time efficient *Uses* • permits comparisons across groups • used for policy decisions by administrators	*Characteristics* • has high face validity • is time efficient *Uses* • informs teach-reteach & enrichment decisions • documents students' learning

Techniques for Assessing Particular Reading Skills

Sharon Taberski recommends that the teacher build in one-on-one time for supporting individual children as needed in considering what makes sense, sounds right and matches the letters.

She has noted that emergent and early readers tend to focus on meaning without adequate attention to graphophonic cues. She suggests using the following prompts for children who are having problems with graphophonic cues:

Does what you said match the letters?

If the word were what you said ___, what would it have to start with?
Look carefully at the first letters... then look at the middle letters. . then look at the last letters. What could it be?

If it were _____, what would it end with?

Oral retellings can be used to test children's comprehension.

Children who are retelling a story to be tested for comprehension should be told that that is the purpose when they sit down with the teacher.
It is a good idea to let the child start the retelling on his or her own, because then the teacher can see whether he or she needs prompts to retell the story. Many times more experienced readers summarize what they have read. This summary usually flows out along with the characters, the problem of the story and other details.
Other signs that children understand what they are reading when they give an oral retelling include their use of illustrations to support the retelling, references to the exact text in the retelling, emotional reaction to the text, making connections between the text and other stories or experiences they the readers have had, and giving information about the text without the teacher's asking for it.

Awareness of Text Leveling

The classroom library in the context of the balanced literacy approach to reading instruction is focused on leveled books. These are books which have been leveled with the support of Fountas and Pinnell's Guided Reading: *Good First Teaching for All Children* and *Matching Books to Readers: Using Leveled Reading in Guided Reading*, K-3.

The books which are leveled according to the designations in these reference books need to be stored in bins or crates with front covers facing out. This makes them much easier for the children to identify. In that way the children can go through the appropriate levels and find those books that they are particularly interested in which are also at the right level for them to read. These are those books which the children can read with the right degree of reading accuracy. When young children can see the cover of a book, they are more likely to flip through the book until they can independently identify an appealing book. Then they will read a little bit of the book to see if it's "just right."
"Just right" leveled books, that children can read on their own, need to be available for them to read during independent reading. The goal is for the more fluent readers to select books on their own. Ultimately the use of leveled books helps the children, in addition to the teacher, decide which books are "good" or "just right" for them.

Levels are indicated by means of blue, yellow, red, and green dot stickers at their right upper corners which parallel emergent, early, transitional, and fluent reading stages. They are then kept in containers with other "blue," "yellow," "red," and "green" books.

Other lists and resources other than Fountas and Pinnell which can be used to match children with "just right" books include the Reading Recovery level list. Ultimately, the teacher has to individualize whatever leveling is used in the library to address the individual child learners' needs.

Awareness of the Challenges and Supports in a Text

Illustrations can be key supports for emergent and early readers. Teachers should not only use wordless stories (books which tell their narratives through pictures alone), but can also make targeted use of Big Books for read-alouds, so that young children become habituated to the use of illustrations as an important component for constructing meaning. The teacher should model for the child how to reference an illustration for help in identifying a word in the text the child does not recognize. Of course, children can also go on a picture walk with the teacher as part of a mini-lesson or guided reading and anticipate the story (narrative) using the pictures alone to construct meaning.

Decodability: Use literature which contains examples of letter sound correspondences you wish to teach. First, read the literature with the children or read it aloud to them. Then take a specific example from the text and have the children reread it as the teacher points out the letter-sound correspondence to the children. Then ask the children to go through the now familiar literature to find other letter-sound correspondences. Once the children have correctly made the letter-sound correspondences, have them share similar correspondences they find in other works of literature.

Cooper (2004) suggests that children can become word detectives so that they can independently and fluently decode on their own. The child should learn the following word detective routines so that he or she can function as an independent fluent reader who can decode words on his/her own. First the child should read to the end of a sentence. Then the child should search for word parts which he or she knows. The child should also try to decode the word from the letter sounds. As a last resort, the child should ask someone for help or look up the word in the dictionary.

Techniques for Determining Students' Independent, Instructional and Frustration Reading Levels

Instructional reading is generally judged to be at the 95 percent accuracy level, although, Taberski places it at between 92 and 97 percent. Taberski tries to enhance the independent reading levels by making sure that readers on the instructional reading levels read a variety of genres, and have a range of available and interesting books within a particular genre to read.

Taberski's availability for reading conferences helps her to both assess first hand her children's frustration levels and to model ongoing teacher/reader book conversations by scheduling child-initiated reading conferences when she personally replenishes their book bags.

In order to allay children's frustration levels in their reading and to foster their independent reading, it is important to some children that the teacher personally take time out to hear them read aloud and to check for fluency and expression. Children's frustration level can be immeasurably lessened if they are explicitly told by the teacher after they have read aloud that they need to read without pointing and that they should try chunking words into phrases which mimic their natural speech.

Assessment of the Reading Development of Individual Students

For young readers who are from ELL backgrounds, even if they have been born in the United States, the use of pictures validates their story authoring and story telling skills and provides them with access and equity to the literary discussion and book talk of their native English speaking peers. These children can also demonstrate their storytelling abilities by drawing sequels or prequels to the story detailed in the illustrations alone. They might even be given the opportunity to share the story aloud in their native language or to comment on the illustrations in their native language.

Since many stories today are recorded in two or even three languages at once, discussing story events or analyzing pictures in a different native language is a beneficial practice which can be accomplished in the 21st century marketplace.

Use of pictures and illustrations can also help the K-3 educator assess the capabilities of children who are struggling readers if the children's learning strength is spatial. Through targeted questions about how the pictures would change if different plot twists occurred or how the child might transform the story through changing the illustrations, the teacher can begin to assess struggling reader's deficits and strengths.

Children from ELL backgrounds can benefit from listening to a recorded version of a particular story which they can read along with the tape. This gives them another opportunity to "hear" the story correctly pronounced and presented and to begin to internalize its language structures. In the absence of taped versions of some key stories or texts, the teacher may want to make sound recordings her or himself.

Highly proficient readers can also be involved in creating these literature recordings for use with ELL peers or younger peers. This of course develops oral language proficiency and also introduces these skilled readers into the intricacies of supporting ELL reading instruction. When they actually see their tapes being used by children, they will be tremendously gratified.

Skills to Evaluate:

- Ability to use syntactic cues when encountering an unknown word. Good readers will expect the word to fit the syntax they are familiar with. Poor readers may substitute a word that does not fit the syntax and will not correct themselves.

- Ability to use semantic cues to determine the meaning of an unknown word. Good readers will consider the meanings of all the known words in the sentence. Poor readers may read one word at a time with no regard for the other words.

- Ability to use schematic cues to connect words read with prior knowledge. Good readers will incorporate what they know with what the text says or implies. Poor readers may think only of the word they are reading without associating it with prior knowledge.

- Ability to use phonics cues to improve ease and efficiency in reading. Good readers will apply letter and sound associations almost subconsciously. Poor readers may have one of two kinds of problems. They may have underdeveloped phonics skills and use only an initial clue without analyzing vowel patterns before quickly guessing the word. Or they may use phonics skills in isolation, becoming so absorbed in the word "noises" that they ignore or forget the message of the text.

- Ability to process information from text. Students should be able to get information from the text and store, retrieve, and integrate it for later use.

- Ability to use interpretive thinking to make logical predictions and inferences.

- Ability to use critical thinking to make decisions and develop insights about the text.

- Ability to use appreciative thinking to respond to the text, whether emotionally, mentally, ideologically, or etc.

Methods of Evaluation:

- Assess students at the beginning of each year to determine grouping for instruction.
- Judge whether students recognize when a word does not make sense.
- Monitor whether students correct themselves and if they know when to ignore and read on or when to reread a sentence.
- Looks for skill such as recognizing cause and effect, finding main ideas, and using comparison and contrast techniques.
- Use oral reading to assess reading skills. Pay attention to word recognition skills rather than readers' ability to communicate the author's message. Strong oral reading sounds like natural speech, utilizes phrasing and a pace that match the meaning of the text, and uses pitch and tone to interpret the text.
- Keep dated records to follow individual progress. Focus on a few students each day. Grade them on a scale of 1-5 according to how well they perform certain reading tasks (e.g. Logically predict coming events). Also include informal observations, such as "Ed was able to determine the meaning of the word 'immigrant' by examining the other words in the sentence."

Remember that evaluation is important, but enjoyment of reading is the most important thing to emphasize. Keep reading as a pressure-free, fun activity so students do not become intimidated by reading. Even if students are not meeting excellent standards, if they continue wanting to read each day, that by itself is a success!

Skill 9.3 Uses information from reading assessments for various purposes (e.g., screening, in-depth assessment, continuous progress monitoring, formative an summative evaluation)

Assessment can be done at various times during instruction. A comprehensive assessment consists of formative and summative assessment. Formative assessment takes place during a unit or theme so that teachers can provide immediate feedback to help students improve and achieve the outcomes. It does not involve giving grades, but rather it is intended to drive the instruction. Through formative assessment, teachers can find out what the students' needs are and make changes to the instruction in order to meet those needs.

Summative assessment is done at the end of a unit or theme and is used to find out how much students have learned through the instruction. Through summative assessment, teachers can determine whether or not students have achieved the objectives of the lesson or unit. This assessment will show how much the students have progressed since the first assessment. It will also show teachers whether or not their instructional changes have been effective to help the students demonstrate learning over time.

Skill 9.4   Knows how to identify students' independent, instructional, and frustrational reading levels and listening comprehension and to adjust instruction to accelerate student learning

When considering both formal and informal assessment data gathered on students, it is important to quantify the information into terms easily recognized by other teachers, administrators, and parents. In reading, general practice is to categorize the information into levels of reading. These levels go across both kinds of assessments. They are compromised of a combination of a word-accuracy percentage and a comprehension percentage.

Independent. This level is the level at which children can read text totally on their own. When reading books at the independent level, students will be able to decode between 95 and 100% of the words and comprehend the text with 90% accuracy or better. Many bodies of research indicate that about 98% accuracy makes for a good independent reader; however, there is other research that goes as low as 95% accuracy.

Instructional. This is the level at which students should be taught because it provides enough difficulty to increase their reading skills without providing so much that it becomes too cumbersome to finish the selection. Typically, the acceptable range for accuracy is between 85-94% with 75% or greater comprehension. Some standards rely on the number of errors made instead of the accuracy percentage, with no more than one error out of twenty words read being the acceptable standard.

Frustration. Books at students' frustration level are too difficult for them and should not be used. The frustration level is any text with less than 85% word accuracy and/or less than 75% comprehension. The use of independent, instructional and frustration levels allow educators to provide children with texts of different ranges depending on the skills necessary to be completed. Typically, standardized or formal assessments test to the instructional level. Therefore, if reading a standardized assessment such as an Iowa Test of Basic Skills, the reported reading level would be the instructional level for that student.

Additionally, some formal and informal test results use alternate methods of reporting information. Some use the grade level and month equivalent, where a 3.2 reading level would indicate that children are reading at the third grade level second month or, typically, October. Still others use their own leveling system. The Developing Readers Assessment (DRA) has its own unique method of coding book levels based on the work of Fountas and Pinnell. Regardless of the levels listed, the work can easily be translated into independent, instructional and frustration levels by examining the comprehension and the word reading accuracy portions of the assessment.

The classroom library in the context of the balanced-literacy approach to reading instruction is focused on leveled book pots. These are books which have been leveled with the support of Fountas and Pinnell's Guided Reading: *Good First Teaching for All Children* and *Matching Books to Readers: Using Leveled Reading in Guided Reading,* K-3.

The books are leveled according to the designations in these reference books and need to be stored in pots with their front covers facing out. This makes them much easier for the children to find. In this way, the children can go through the appropriate levels and find those books that they are particularly interested in at the right level for them to read. These are books which the children can read with the right degree of reading accuracy. When young children can see the cover of a book, they are more likely to flip through the book until they can independently identify an appealing book. Then they will read a little bit of the book to see if it's "just right."

"Just right" leveled books that children can read on their own need to be available for them to read during independent reading. The goal is for the more fluent readers to select books on their own. Ultimately the use of leveled books helps the children, in addition to teachers, decide which books are "good" or "just right" for them.

Leveled books are leveled by means of blue, yellow, red, and green dot stickers at their right upper corners which parallel emergent, early, transitional, and fluent reading stages. They are then kept in book pots with other "blue," "red," "yellow," and "green" books. Another list which can be used to match children with "just right" books is the Reading Recovery level list. Ultimately, the teacher has to incorporate whatever leveling is used in the library to address individual needs.

Adjustment of Reading Instruction Based on Ongoing Assessment

The running records taken of children help the teacher learn about the cueing systems that children use. It is important for the teacher to adjust reading instruction based on the pattern of miscues gathered from several successive reading records. When the teacher carefully reviews a given student's substitutions and self corrections, certain patterns begin to surface. A child may use visual cues as he or she reads and adds meaning to self correct. To the alert teacher, the reliance on visual miscues indicates that the reader doesn't make sense of what she is reading. This means that the teacher needs to check to see what cueing system the child uses when he or she is reading "just right" books. Children, who use meaning and structure but not visual/graphophonic cues, need to be reminded and facilitated to understand the importance of getting and reconstructing the author's message. They have to be able to share the author's story, not their own.

Not only can and should the teacher use the material in the children's ongoing assessment notebook to adjust the child's current instruction but the material also serves to document for the child his/her growth as a successful reader over time. In addition, if the same concerns surface over the use of a particular cueing system or high frequency word, the teacher can adjust the class wall chart and even devote a whole class lesson to the particular element.

Strategies for Selecting and Using Meaningful Reading Materials at Appropriate Levels of Difficulty

Matching young children with "just right" books fosters their reading independently, no matter how young they are. The teacher needs to have an extensive classroom library of books. Books that emergent readers and early readers can be matched with should have fairly large print, appropriate spacing, so that the reader can easily see where word begins and ends, and few words on each page so that the young reader can focus on all important concerns of top-to bottom, left-to-right, directionality, and the one-to-one match of word to print.

Illustrations for young children should support the meaning of the text and language patterns and predictable text structures should make these texts appealing to young readers. Most important of all the content of the story should relate to the children's interests and experiences as the teacher knows them.

Only after all these considerations have been addressed, can the teacher select "just right" books from an already leveled bin or list. In a similar fashion, when the teacher is selecting books for transitional and fluent readers, the following ideas need to be taken into account:

The book should take at least two sittings to read, so children can get used to reading longer books. The fluent and transitional reader needs to deal with more complex characters and more intricate plotting. Look for books that set the stage for plot development with a compelling beginning. Age appropriateness of the concepts, plot and themes is important so that the child will sustain interest in the book. Look for book features such as a list of chapters to help children navigate through the book.

Series books are wonderful to introduce at this point in the children's development

Skill 9.5 **Applies knowledge of a variety of methods for assessing students' reading, study, and inquiry skills across content areas**

See Skill 4.3

Skill 9.6 **Demonstrates knowledge of instructional strategies that promote students' use of self-assessment to enhance literacy development**

As proficient readers, students must master strategies to monitor their own comprehension. Teaching these to students is a critical task that requires explicit modeling in order for students to make the transition to independent use within their own reading.

Self-Questioning. In this technique, the students will ask themselves a series of questions about the text to ensure that they are understanding the progression of events. These questions generally revolve around the major story elements: characters, plot, setting, events, climax, and resolution. Teachers model for students how to develop questions.

Think Alouds. As previously discussing, thinking aloud is one of the most effective strategies for both teaching comprehension and for working through complex concepts presented in some texts. When using the think-aloud approach, teachers are simply speaking out loud every thought that would normally be going on silently in their head. They demonstrate the connections they make while reading and show the students how they arrived at these connections. Integrating new information with the old information is a valuable skill for students to attain.

Visualization. Visualization is the process of putting a picture to the words on the page. Generally, good readers have a mental image of what they are reading. The phrasing and author's voice provide clear details that allow multiple readers to have the same basic vision. When working with visualization, it can sometimes be helpful for students to take the additional step of drawing out the picture as they see it in their mind. If key concepts are missing, working with teachers can help the students to better make comprehension steps forward.

Graphic Organizers. Providing students with a visual means of organizing and tracking all of the information contained in a text is very helpful. The next level of appropriate use involves teaching the students how to develop their own method of organizing the events and information contained in a text. By becoming less reliant on teacher-prepared organizers, the students will have tools that can be used when teachers do not provide organizers or when the students are reading on their own.

Reading Strategies. It is imperative that students understand and are able to utilize the many different types of reading strategies before they can monitor them on their own. Taking the time to teach the skills can provide the foundation to allow students the ability to begin monitoring their own comprehension. These skills include inferring, questioning, drawing conclusions, making connections, weeding out useless information, and, finally, synthesizing information.

Skill 9.7   Analyzes factors that may impact student performance on various types of assessment (e.g., text characteristics, testing environment, and student characteristics, such as language, culture, prior knowledge, disabilities)

There are many factors that can affect how well students perform on various types of assessments. When there are other factors coming into play, it is possible that teachers will not get a valid assessment of what students can actually do.

<u>Text Characteristics</u>
As children progress to the older grades (3-6), it is important for teachers to model for them that in research on a social studies or science exploration, it may not be necessary to read every single word of a given expository text. For instance, if children are trying to find out about hieroglyphics, they might only read through those sections of a book on Egyptian or Sumerian civilization which dealt with picture writing. Teachers should model how to go through the table of contents and the index of the book to identify only those pages which deal with picture writing. In addition, children should come to the front of the room or to the center of the area where the reading group is meeting. They should then, with the support of the teacher, skim through the book for illustrations or diagrams of picture writing, the focus of their need.

Children can practice the skills of skimming texts and scanning for particular topics that connect with their grade's social studies, science and mathematics content-area interests.

Certainly, children need to understand and to be comfortable with the fact that not every single expository text is meant to be read thoroughly and completely. Traditionally, the aspects of expository-text reading comprehension have been taught in a dry format using reference books from the school or public library, particularly the atlas; the almanac; dusty, large geography volumes; etc. to teach these necessary and meaningful skills.

Although these worthy library and, perhaps, classroom library books can still be used, it is much easier to take a simple newspaper to introduce and provide children with daily, ongoing, authentic experiences in learning these necessary skills as they also keep up with real world events that positively and negatively affect their daily lives.

They can go on a chronological hunt through the daily newspaper and discover the many formats of schedules contained therein. For instance, some newspapers include a calendar of the week; with literary, sports, social, movie, and other public events. Children can also go on scavenger hunts through various sections of the newspaper and, on certain days, find full-blown timelines detailing famous individuals' careers, business histories, milestones in the political history of a nation, or even key movies made by a famous movie director up for an Oscar.

The nature of the newspaper reportage and the public's need to know the why and wherefore behind the story of natural disasters, company takeovers, political downfalls and uprisings lead newspapers to represent events graphically and to use cause /effect diagramming and comparison/contrast wording. If teachers specifically want to make certain that the students come away with this material, they can pre-clip "teaching" stories from the news for the children and post the stories in a special NEWS center.

After children have been walked through these comparison/contrast news writings and cause/effect diagramming as it has appeared in the newspaper, they can be challenged to find additional examples of these text structures in the news or challenged to reframe or rewrite familiar stories using these text structures. They can even use desktop publishing to re-author the stories using the same text structures.

If a class participates in a local Newspapers-in-Education program, where the children receive a newspaper for free two to three times a week within the classroom, the teacher can teach index skills using the index of the newspaper and having children race to find various features.

Map and chart skills take on much more relevance and excitement when the children work on these skills using sport charts detailing the batting averages and pass completion percentages of their favorite players or perhaps the box scores of their older siblings' football and baseball games. Maps dealing with holiday weather become meaningful to children as they anticipate a holiday vacation. If students are not familiar with the different text characteristics that they may encounter on a test, they may not score as highly as they should in reading.

Testing Environment

The testing environment certainly plays a part in how well students do on any test. Whether the room is too warm or cold, whether the lighting is adequate, or whether the seats are comfortable all have an impact on how the students feel at the time of the test. Teachers also have to consider how the students feels emotionally and socially when the test is taking place. Testers who walk around and stand behind students may make them feel uncomfortable as if the students are under scrutiny. Many people do not like to have someone stand over them as they do a test. The number of people in the room can also impact the result of the test. If students are being tested individually, they may not feel comfortable with a tester whom they do not trust. At the same time, students may not feel comfortable in a room with a large number of people.

Student Characteristics

There are certain characteristics of the students that can impact the results of tests as well. Students whose first language is not English may have difficulty understanding the context of certain words and therefore not answer the questions correctly. Students' prior knowledge also comes into play if they do not have the background knowledge required to answer the questions on the test. Disabilities play a large part in the results when students are not able to read the test or are unable to understand the directions. Students with reading disabilities may need a reader or a scribe, but in some reading tests it is impossible to provide a reader and still obtain valid results.

Skill 9.8   Applies knowledge of assessment-related concepts and issues (e.g., reliability, validity, utility, bias, confidentiality) and common standardized testing terminology (e.g., raw score, scaled score, percentile, grade equivalency, stanine, normal curve equivalency {NCE} growth scale)in selecting and using assessments and interpreting results

Validity is how well a test measures what it is supposed to measure. Teacher-made tests are therefore not generally extremely valid, although they may be an appropriate measure for the validity of the concept teachers want to assess for their own students' achievement.

Reliability is the consistency of the test. This is measured by whether the test will indicate the same score for children who take it twice.

Bias in testing occurs when the information within the test or the information required to respond to a multiple-choice question or constructed response (an essay question on the test) is information that is not available to some test takers who come from a different cultural, ethnic, linguistic, or socio-economic background than do the majority of the test takers. Since they have not had the same prior linguistic, social, or cultural experiences that the majority of test takers have had, these test takers are at a disadvantage in taking the test, and (no matter what their actual mastery of the material taught) can not address the "biased" questions. Generally, other "non-biased" questions are given to them, and eventually the biased questions are removed from the examination.

The results of formal testing are also confidential. Teachers have to relay the results to the students and parents/guardians. In order to release the testing results to any other persons, whether they are professionals in the field of education or in the medical field, teachers must first get the parents/guardians to sign a release paper explaining how the test results will be used and agree to let others see the results..

All tests must have a purpose. The utility of the test will give teachers an idea of where the students are in regard to understanding the concepts associated with language arts – reading, writing, listening, speaking, viewing, and representing.

Terminology for standardized testing

Achievement Test – a standardized test designed to find out how much learning has occurred as a result of classroom instruction

Alternative Assessment – assessment that differs from the traditional, standardized, norm-referenced or criterion-referenced test that utilizes open-ended questions, working out problems, performing a task, or producing work that is different from pencil and paper tests.

Benchmark – an established standard of student performance on a scale

Cut Score – score used to determine the minimum level of performance needed to pass a test

Grade Equivalent – a score that determines the approximate grade level of a student based on an average score. For example, a student with a grade equivalent of 5.5 is said to be able to function at the midpoint of Grade 5.

Item Analysis – analyzing the answers students give to questions on a test to determine the proportion of students giving the same answer

Mean – one of the ways of representing a group with a single score. The scores of all the students in a class are added up and divided by the number of students in the class to find the class average. However, this can be distorted by extremely high and low scores.

Median – the point on a scale that divides a group into sub-groups.

Norm- a distribution of scores obtained from a norm group. The norm is the midpoint of the scores of the number of students in that group.

Norm group – a random group of students selected by a tester to complete a test to establish the percentiles of performance to be used in establishing standards

Normal Curve Equivalent – a score that ranges from 1 – 99 used by testers to compare different tests for the same group of students and between different groups of students taking the same test. An NCE is a normalized test score of 50 with a standard deviation of 21.06. For comparative purposes, an NCE should be used instead of percentiles.

Percentile – a ranking score from 1 – 99 with a median score of 50. A percentile rank indicates the percentage of a reference or norm group obtaining scores equal to or less than the test-taker's score. A percentile score does not refer to the percentage of questions that the student answered correctly. It refers to the student's standing relative to the standard of the norm group.

Profile – how well an individual does on a group of assessments compiled on a graph

Quartile – the breakdown of an aggregate of percentile rankings broken down into four categories (0.25, 25-5-0, 50-75, 75-100)

Quintile – the breakdown of an aggregate of percentile rankings broken down into five categories (1-20, 20-40, 40-60, 60-80. 80-100)

Raw Score- the original result a student obtains on a test, such as the number of questions answered correctly.

Scaled Score – the mean score for each grade and content area

Stanine – a method of scaling test scores on a nine point standard with a mean of 5 and a standard deviation of 2.

Skill 9.9   Knows state and federal requirements related to reading assessment and diagnosis

Visit http://www.tsbvi.edu/Education/ for more information.

Skill 9.10   Applies skills for communicating to various stakeholders the results and instructional applications of formal and informal assessments

Effective teachers use advanced communication skills such as clarification, reflection, perception, and summarization to facilitate communication. Teachers who are effective communicators are also good listeners. Teachers who make eye contact, focus on student body language, clarify students' statements, and use "I" messages are effective listeners. The ability to communicate with students, listen effectively, identify relevant and non-relevant information, and summarize students' messages facilitates establishing and maintaining an optimum classroom learning environment.

Any assessment done on students must be documented and samples kept so that the parents and other teachers can understand their import. Communicating the findings of assessment is not something that has to wait for parent-teacher interviews or the report card. It is something that teachers should report to parents on a regular basis, such as in monthly notes or telephone calls, arranged meetings, or even simple chats.

Guidance and speech counselors should communicate the results of assessments to teachers and parents as soon as possible after testing is complete. In many districts, this is called a debriefing and takes the form of an arranged meeting. In this meeting, counselors discuss the findings and make suggestions about how to best meet the needs of the child.

Skill 9.11   Knows grade-level expectation for literacy and when delays or differences in language and literacy development warrant referral for additional evaluation or intervention

The grade level expectations for literacy are published online at http://www.k12.wa.us/curriculuminstruct/reading/pubdocs/ReadingEALR-GLE.pdf. It is the duty of all teachers to know the grade-level expectations for their individual grade levels and, if possible, for the grades above and below that level. Reading specialists need to be familiar with the grade-level expectations for all grades because they will be dealing with students from all grades ranging from early entry through Grade 12.

When teachers are aware of what students are expected to do at each grade level, they can better assess where the students are on that continuum. It is normal to have students operating on a range of three different grade levels within one classroom, which means teachers need to differentiate instruction so that all students are operating at their own level. When students are more than two grade levels behind or ahead, then it is time to look at other methods of intervention rather than simply individualizing instruction. Students who are progressing at a faster rate than their peers need just as much individualization and help in being challenged as students who are below grade level. Reading specialists have to be able to provide instruction suited to gifted students in the classroom as well as to those with delays.

For information on how to refer students to other specialists, see Skill 6.11

COMPETENCY 10.0 INSTRUCTIONAL METHODS AND RESOURCES

Skill 10.1   Knows about state and national standards and requirements that relate to reading and writing curriculum and instruction

Visit **http://www.tea.state.tx.us/rules/tac/ch110_128a.html** for more information.

Skill 10.2   Knows how to develop systematic, sequential age-appropriate literacy instruction that reflects content and performance standards, components of a comprehensive literacy program, students' strengths and needs, and a convergence of research evidence

Decoding

In the late l960's and the l970's, many reading specialists, most prominently Fries (l962), believed that successful decoding resulted in reading comprehension. This meant that if children could sound out the words, they would then automatically be able to comprehend the words. Many teachers of reading and many reading texts still subscribe to this theory.

Asking questions

Another theory or approach to the teaching of reading that gained currency in the late sixties and the early seventies was the importance of asking inferential and critical thinking questions of the reader which would challenge and engage the children in the text. This approach to reading went beyond the literal level of what was stated in the text to an inferential level of using text clues to make predictions and to a critical level of involving the child in evaluating the text. While asking engaging and thought-provoking questions is still viewed as part of the teaching of reading, it is only viewed currently as a component of the teaching of reading.

Comprehension "Skills"

As various reading theories, practices, and approaches percolated during the l970's and l980's, many educators and researchers in the field came to believe that the teacher of reading had to teach a set of discrete "Comprehension Skills" (Otto et al, l977). Therefore the reading teacher became the teacher of each individual comprehension skill. Children in such classrooms came away with: main idea, sequence, cause and effect, and other concepts that were supposed to make them better comprehenders. However, did it make them lifelong readers?

Transactional Approach

During the late I970's and early I980's, researchers in the field of education, psychology and linguistics, began to examine how the reader comprehends. Among them was Louise Rosenblatt who posited that reading is a transaction between the reader and the text. It is Rosenblatt (I978) who explained successful reading as the reader constructing a meaning from the text that reflected both the reader and the text. She described two general purposes for reading: *efferent* and *aesthetic*. Efferent reading is looking for and remembering information to use functionally. Examples would be filling out a job application, reading a story in preparation for a test, or reading a newspaper article to find out who won the state basketball championship. Aesthetic reading is done to connect one's own life to the text, to be swept away by the beauty of a poem, or to respond emotionally to a book such as *Bridge to Terabithia*.

These differing purposes call for somewhat different reading strategies: one might skim the newspaper article for basketball information but read a poem closely ten times and create mental images of different passages. Lastly, when children are asked to read all fiction differently (What's the setting? What's the main conflict in the plot? There will be a test on this on Thursday!), it can thwart a child's joy in the written word and work against the student's desire to be a lifelong reader.

Bottom-up, Top-down, Interactional Theories of Reading

Bottom-up theories of reading assume that children learn from part-to-whole starting with the smallest segments possible. Instruction begins with a strong phonics approach, learning letter-sound relationships and often using basal readers or *decodable books*. Decodable books are vocabulary-controlled using language from word families with high predictability. Thus we get sentences like "Nan has a tan fan." Reading is seen as skills-based, and the skills are taught one at a time.

Top-down theories of reading suggest that reading begins with the reader's knowledge, not the print. Children are seen as having a drive to construct meaning. This stance views reading as moving from the whole to the parts. An early top-down theory was the *whole word* approach. Children memorized high-frequency words to assist them in reading the Dick and Jane books of the 30s. Then teachers helped children discover letter-sound correpondences in what they read. A more recent top-down theory is the *whole language* approach. This approach was influenced by research on how young children learned language. It was thought that children could learn to read as naturally as they learned to talk. Children were surrounded by print in their classrooms, using quality literature often printed in Big Books and were viewed as writers from the start. Hence journals kept by kindergarten children. Advocates of whole language viewed the "skill'em-drill'em-and kill'em" approach based on bottom-up theories as a deadly dull introduction to the world of reading.

Interactive theories of reading combine the strengths of both bottom-up and top-down approaches. Teachers need to be able to teach decoding, vocabulary, and comprehension skills to support children's drive for meaning and desire for a stimulating exchange with high-quality literary texts from their earliest days in school. Strategies include shared, guided, and independent reading, Big Books, reading and writing workshops, and the like. Today this approach is called the *balanced literacy approach.* It is considered to be a synthesis of the best from bottom-up and top-down methods.

Literacy and Literacy Learning

To be literate in the 21st century world means more than being able to read and write. To live well and happily in today's society an individual has to be able to read, not only newspapers and books, but emails, blogs, directions for how to use one's cell phone, and the like. There has evolved a "disconnect" between the isolated reading comprehension skills the schools were teaching and the literacy skills including listening and speaking that are crucial for employment and personal and academic success. Thornburg (1992, 2003) has also noted that technology capacities and the ability to communicate online are now integral parts of our sense of literacy.

Cooper (2004) views literacy as reading, writing, thinking, listening, viewing, and discussing. These are not viewed as separate activities or components of instruction, but rather as developing and being nurtured simultaneously and interactively. Children learn these abilities by engaging in authentic explorations, readings, projects and experiences.

Just as in learning how to ride a bike, the learner goes through various approximations before learning how to actually ride the bike, so too does the reader with the scaffold (support) of the teacher go through various approximations before developing his/her own independent literacy skills and capacities.

Emergent Literacy: the concept that young children are emerging into reading and writing with no real beginning or ending point. Children are introduced into the word of print as soon as their parents read board books to them at the age of one or two. When children scribble write or use invented spelling during the preschool years, they reveal themselves as detectives of the written word, having watched parents and teachers make lists, write thank-you notes, or leave messages. This view of the reader assumes that all children have a drive to make meaning in print and will begin doing it almost on their own if surrounded by a print-rich environment.

Reading Readiness: an approach which is antithetical to emergent literacy in that it assumes that all children must have mastered a sequence of reading skills before they can begin to read. This approach stands in contrast to emergent literacy.

Language Acquisition: continuous and never-ending. From the perspective of this theory and research, all children come to school with a language base which the school must build on. As a consequence of the connection between oral language and reading, it is important that schools build literacy experiences around the language the child brings to the school.

Prior Knowledge, Schemata, Background, and Comprehension

Schemata are structures which represent generic concepts stored in our memory (Rumelhart, 1980). Young children develop their schemata through experiences. Prior knowledge and the lack of experiences in some cases influence comprehension. The more closely the reader's experiences and schemata approximate those of the writer, the more likely the reader is to comprehend the text. It is obvious that for many children from non-native English language speaking backgrounds and perhaps for those from struggling socio-economic family structures schemata deficits indicate the need for intense teacher support as these children become emergent and early readers.

Often the teacher will have to model and scaffold for the child the steps to form a schemata from the information provided in a text.

Comprehension

Cooper defines comprehension as: "a strategic process by which readers construct or assign meaning to a text by using the clues in the text and their own prior knowledge. " We view comprehension as a process where the reader transacts with the text to construct or assign meaning. Reading and writing are both interconnected and mutually supportive. Comprehension is a strategic process in which readers adjust their reading to suit their reading purpose and the type or genre of text they are reading. Narrative and expository texts require different reading approaches because of their different text structures.

Strategic readers also call into play their metacognitive capacities as they analyze texts so that they are self aware of the skills needed to construct meaning from the text structure.

The Role of Literature in Developing Literacy

The balanced literacy approach advocates the use of "real literature"—recognized works of the best of children's fiction and non-fiction trade books and winners of such awards as the Newberry and Caldecott medals for helping children develop literacy.

Balanced literacy advocates argue that:

- Real literature engages young readers and assures that they will become lifelong readers.

- Real literature also offers readers a language base that can help them expand their expressiveness as readers and as writers.

- Real literature is easier to read and understand than grade-leveled texts

There are districts in the United States where the phonics-only approach is heavily embedded. However, the majority of school districts would describe their approach to reading as the balanced literacy approach which includes phonics work as well as the use of real literature texts. To contrast the phonics and balanced literacy approaches as opposite is inaccurate, since a balanced approach includes both.

It is important to go online and to visit the key resources of the NCTE, National Council of Teachers of English, and the IRA, International Reading Association, to keep abreast of the latest research in the field.

Skill 10.3   Applies knowledge of educational theories that underlie instructional practices and components of effective instructional design

Over the years, theories regarding language development have been very vocal and have clashed on many levels. The major disagreement can be tracked back to the 1950's, where two predominant theories emerged.

Behaviorism developed and asserted that language was the direct result of the situations surrounding the child. Behaviorists believed that the environment controlled all language and that these outside forces alone influenced its development.

On the other hand, nativism theorists believed that all language was determined by factors similar to genetic traits. They believed that language was determined before birth and developed in a similar manner to other innate characteristics. They ruled out that any outside factors could influence the development process.

Currently, these two opposing viewpoints have been combined to form the interactionist theories. This term indicates that children's language skills are a direct result of inherent, predetermined skills and the surrounding environment. It is this combination approach that is most accepted in today's society. In relation to reading, it is important to understand the fact that reading is language based. Children who struggle in language developmental will almost certainly have difficulty obtaining a solid foundation in reading skills.

As language develops, students begin to understand how sounds blend together to form words, how words go together to form sentences, and how sentences go together to form stories. It is through these stories and sentences that meaning is conveyed from one party to another.

If students are unable to convey that meaning or draw conclusions from the message that someone else is sending, they miss a key component of language development. With this skill missing, the natural progression that text conveys meaning is also missed. Since the ultimate goal of reading is comprehension, one can see the significant deficit these children experience.
Speech pathologists, who specialize in language development, can therefore be essential components in preventing (and helping children with) language disorders. In this way, these trained specialists can also help in preventing and remediating language issues, which will help reading skills.

In summary, language development is crucial to the progress students will experience in reading. Language and reading go hand in hand, and this fact should be remembered when bringing in professionals with expertise to help work with children who are struggling.

Various subject areas have added to philosophical debates regarding teaching. For example, reading teachers have long debated whether phonics or whole language was more appropriate as an instructional methodology. Language arts teachers have debated the importance of the canon (famous works of literature); some teachers feel that the canon is irrelevant and that the only reason to teach literature is to teach thinking skills and an appreciation of good literature. Math teachers have debated the extent to which application is necessary in math instruction; some feel that it is more important to teach structure and process, while others feel it is only important to teach math skills in context.

In reading, there has been no greater debate than the approach to teaching reading. Educators speak of the great pendulum in reading instruction swinging between three major philosophies: literature-based, phonics, and whole language.

Literature-Based- In this method, teachers incorporate all reading instruction through true literature pieces. Using trade books, poetry, or other forms of literature, the students are exposed and taught all of the necessary skills to be successful readers.

Phonics- Phonics instructional approach involves teaching very explicitly and sequentially the phonics skills children need to be readers. In this way, the children read controlled texts, which revolve around the current phonics skill being introduced and practiced. These controlled texts provide numerous repetitions of the skills.

Whole Language- Whole language instruction revolves around a readers' workshop approach. In this manner, the students have assigned tasks to complete that take them through reading skills. The teacher works with the children to guide them through the necessary tasks, but does not explicitly teach skills. It is though through the process of reading many different texts that students will learn the necessary skills to become readers.

There is not one approach that is right or wrong; all of these methods have great value and should not be discounted. It is important to understand clearly the different philosophies involved in reading to be able to work with many different teachers. Understanding the approaches helps reading specialists to be able to provide curricular suggestions to help students make the necessary progress. The balanced reading approach is taking on new meaning after the now well-known report from the National Reading Panel. A comprehensive and well-balanced reading program is becoming more and more complex and difficult to define.

In general, it should include instruction in phonemic awareness, phonics, fluency, comprehension, and vocabulary. There also needs to be times when teachers read to the children, when they read with the children, and when the children read for themselves. The catch phrase 'To, With and By' has often been used to remind teachers of the types of reading that must occur within the classroom.

In reading <u>to</u> students, generally teachers use a read-aloud approach. The read aloud helps build vocabulary and listening comprehension. It allows modeling of fluent reading and builds a love of reading.

When reading <u>with</u> students, teachers use two different approaches: shared reading and guided reading. Shared reading allows teachers to share more difficult texts with the students than they might be able to read on their own. Teachers generally focus on comprehension skills and will often complete think alouds or use other comprehension strategies to increase the development of these skills. Vocabulary development and modeling appropriate fluency are also key factors in shared reading. In guided reading, the students are reading texts on their instructional levels. In these small groups, skill development occurs regularly. This is when the phonics skills and phonemic awareness skills can be focused on specifically for a small group of students.

Finally, independent reading, or the '<u>by</u> students,' provides each child the opportunity to practice all of the parts of reading. They are able to get multiple repetitions of the same skills taught elsewhere to build automaticity.

No one part of the reading program as described above would be sufficient to help the students develop and become proficient readers. It is the inter-relationship of them all that makes it work. It is the combination and reliance on each other which makes for success. If one part is removed, not only are skills missed, but also the practice opportunities and modeling opportunities are lost. While all of the components of good reading instruction can be taught or practiced in each section individually, it is when they are combined that the most economical use of the time occurs.

Skill 10.4   Applies knowledge of instructional methods and resources to provide effective literacy instruction that addresses various student dialects, learning preferences and modalities

Reading, writing, listening, and speaking are the four main components of language arts at any grade level. They are interrelated, and they complement each other. By ensuring that all four of these strands are woven into language arts classes, teachers can ensure that they provide a balance of experiences to give students the instruction and support that they need. With such a balance, the students are able to integrate all of the English language processes and build on their prior knowledge and experiences.

Speaking and listening may be viewed as separate from reading and writing, but all four form the main communication system of the English language. They are interdependent, and all other forms of communication depend on the ability to speak and listen. They are also the foundation for many other language skills, which is why teachers should provide ample opportunities for students to speak and listen in class as part of the daily routine. Classrooms are places where talk flows freely; and, by taking advantage of this talk to find out where students are in their thinking about topics, themes, and responses to literature, teachers can easily assess this component of language arts. When students can express ideas in their own words, it helps them to make meaning of their experiences with reading.

Although students don't have a lot of problems with speaking in class, listening is something that has to be nurtured and taught. Good listeners will respond emotionally, imaginatively, and intellectually to what they hear. Students need to be taught how to respond to presentations by their classmates in ways that are not harmful or derogatory in any way. There are also different types of listening that the teacher can develop in the students:

- Appreciative listening to enjoy an experience
- Attentive listening to gain knowledge
- Critical listening to evaluate arguments and ideas

Within the classroom setting, many opportunities will present themselves for students to speak and listen for various purposes; and, often, these may be spontaneous. Activities for speaking and listening should be integrated throughout the language arts program, but there should also be times when speaking and listening are the focus of the instruction. By incorporating speaking and listening into the language arts program, students will begin to see the connection between the two and, therefore, be able to improve their reading skills with more efficiency.

Some of the ways that speaking and listening can be integrated include:

- Conversations
- Small group discussions
- Brainstorming
- Interviewing
- Oral reading
- Readers' Theatre
- Choral speaking
- Storytelling
- Role playing
- Booktalks
- Oral reports
- Class debates
- Listening to guest speakers

Reading and writing are two interrelated aspects of language development. Students will read print and then realize that they can convey similar messages by using written language. The connections to the generally more formal language in reading and the same type of language the students will be asked to produce in writing are plentiful. Students can begin to draw phrases from text and the conventions of written language from reading before they are able to apply those same strategies in writing. By combing the two and explicitly showing students these connections, teachers can develop both skills in a more rapid manner.

Skill 10.5   Knows how to select materials and provide instruction that promotes respect for cultural and linguistic diversity and fosters all students' literacy development

See Skills 6.4 and 8.1

Skill 10.6 **Knows how to implement effective instructional strategies that focus on specific literacy components (e.g., oral language, phonological and phonemic awareness, concepts of print, alphabetic principle, word identification, fluency, comprehension, vocabulary development, written language) and identifies specific short-term and long-term interventions to address student needs in each component**

In 2000, the National Reading Panel released its now well-known report on teaching children to read. In a way, this report slightly put to rest the debate between phonics and whole-language. It argued, essentially, that word-letter recognition was important, as was understanding what the text means. The report's "big 5" critical areas of reading instruction are as follows:

- Phonemic Awareness: The acknowledgement of sounds and words. For example, a child's realization that some words rhyme. Onset and rhyme, for example, are skills that might help students learn that the sound of the first letter "b" in the word "bad" can be changed with the sound "d" to make it "dad." The key in phonemic awareness is that when you teach it to children, it can be taught with the students' eyes closed. In other words, it's all about sounds, not about ascribing written letters to sounds.
- Phonics: As opposed to phonemic awareness, the study of phonics must be done with the eyes open. It's the connection between the sounds and letters on a page. In other words, students learning phonics might see the word "bad" and sound each letter out slowly until they recognize that they just said the word.
- Fluency: When students practice fluency, they practice reading connected pieces of text. In other words, instead of looking at a word as just a word, they might read a sentence straight through. The point of this is that in order for students to comprehend what they are reading, they would need to be able to "fluently" piece words in a sentence together quickly. If students are NOT fluent in reading, they would sound each letter or word out slowly and pay more attention to the phonics of each word. Fluent readers, on the other hand, might read a sentence out loud using appropriate intonations. The best way to test for fluency, in fact, is to have students read something out loud, preferably a few sentences or more in a row. Sure, most students just learning to read will probably not be very fluent right away; but with practice, they will increase their fluency. Even though fluency is not the same as comprehension, it is said that fluency is a good predictor of comprehension. Think about it: If you're focusing too much on sounding out each word, you're not going to be paying attention to the meaning.

- Comprehension: Comprehension simply means that readers can ascribe meaning to text. Even though students may be good with phonics and even know what many words on a page mean, some of them are not good with comprehension because they do not know the strategies that would help them to comprehend. For example, students should know that stories often have structures (beginning, middle, and end).
  They should also know that when they are reading something and it does not make sense, they will need to employ "fix-up" strategies involving going back into the text they just read and looking for clues. Teachers can use many strategies to teach comprehension, including questioning, asking students to paraphrase or summarize, utilizing graphic organizers, and focusing on mental images.
- Vocabulary: Students will be better at comprehension if they have a strong working vocabulary. Research has shown that students learn more vocabulary when it is presented in context rather than in vocabulary lists. Furthermore, the more that students get to use particular words in context, the more they will (a) remember each word, and (b) utilize it in the comprehension of sentences that contain the word.

Methods used to teach these skills are often featured in a "balanced literacy" curriculum that focuses on the use of skills in various instructional contexts. For example, with independent reading, students independently choose books that are at their reading levels; with guided reading, teachers work with small groups of students to help them with their particular reading problems; with whole group reading, the entire class will read the same text, and the teacher will incorporate activities to help students learn phonics, comprehension, fluency, and vocabulary. In addition to these components of balanced literacy, teachers incorporate writing so that students can learn the structures of communicating through text.

Skill 10.7 Identifies appropriate strategies for addressing the literacy needs and accelerating the achievement of students who are reading below grade level

If we have learned anything in education over the last few decades, it is that students do not all learn in the same way. Furthermore, we have learned that a steady diet of lecture and textbook reading is an extremely ineffective method of instruction. While students definitely should be exposed to lecture and textbooks, they will greatly benefit with the creativity and ingenuity of teachers who find outside resources to assist in the presentation of new knowledge.

Let's first discuss some possibilities: textual and media references, hands-on materials, and technology. Lately, some people have referred to the concept of "multiple texts" as a method of bringing into the classroom multiple types of texts. For example, a social studies teacher might ask students to read an historical novel to complement a unit of study.

In addition to texts, appropriately-selected video or audio recordings may be useful. For example, a science teacher may wish to show a short clip of a video that demonstrates how to conduct a particular experiment before students do it on their own. Or, a language arts teacher may bring in an audio recording of a book to present a uniquely dramatized reading of the book.

Hands-on materials are very important to student learning. For example, math teachers may introduce geometric principles with quilt blocks. The very idea of a science experiment is that hands-on materials and activities more quickly convey scientific ideas to students than do lectures and textbooks.

Finally, technologies, such as personal computers are very important for student learning. First, it is extremely important that students learn new technologies so that they can easily adapt to the myriad of uses found in business and industry. Second, technology can provide knowledge resources that go beyond what a school library, for example, may be able to offer. Students will need increasingly to learn how to search for, evaluate, and utilize appropriate information in the Internet.

Choosing an appropriate reference, text, material, or technology depends on many factors. First, realize that whatever is brought into the class should be done so based on the knowledge that the item will assist students in learning academic standards. There is no reason for teachers, for example, to show a movie to their students that is not for the explicit purpose of helping students reach specific academic objectives tied to the curriculum. Second, consider the developmental level of the students you are working with. You would not want to introduce complex experiments to second graders; likewise, you would not want to assume that twelfth graders have no knowledge of the Internet.

Skill 10.8 **Recognizes the value of using flexible grouping to promote literacy growth for all students and knows how to assist other educators in implementing flexible grouping**

Teachers need to look at flexible grouping within the classroom setting. Although students may be grouped for ability at different times, this should not be the standard. Some of the various instructional grouping strategies that teachers can use in the classroom are:

- Whole Class Instruction – used to introduce new materials and strategies to the whole class
- Small group Instruction – used for small groups of students who need more instruction on an objective
- Students working alone in teacher-directed activities – this enables the teacher to give one-on-one instruction or to assess how students are progressing
- Collaborative groups – students working together on a project
- Circle sharing – student discussion, such as author's chair
- Partner groups – paired reading, think par share, etc.

There are many different practices which can be utilized to deliver reading instruction. Each practice is in itself a valid method for helping students become more successful readers. There is never a one-fit approach that will work with all students, instead it is a combination approach which allows the teacher to better meet the needs of all students in their classroom.

The reading specialist is responsible for not only being able to implement various techniques to deliver reading instruction, but also for being able to instruct other teachers in delivering the same methods. In this way, the reading specialist must have an in-depth understanding of them.

Modeling- Modeling involves teachers demonstrating a strategy for the students. This may involve thinking aloud, or orally taking the students step-by-step through the teacher's thinking process. It may also involve demonstrating how to attack an unknown word with a variety of reading techniques including phonics, context cues, reading ahead, skipping unknown words, and developing meaning other ways such as looking for little-known words found in bigger unknown words.

Direct Instruction- This approach uses a formal, scripted dialogue between the teacher and student. The scripts allow the students to have highly-explicit, specific, and continuant instruction in all areas of reading. The students are able to take this very structured approach and make generalizations to other, less-formalized reading. Many teachers find the scripted language a nuisance and stilted. The purpose of this type of program is to provide teachers with a complete understanding of the types of activities, number of repetitions, and appropriate vocabulary to be used with students to improve their skills. While not for everyone, the approach has a significant research base that demonstrates its value.

Independent Practice-This is the time provided for students to rehearse and tone the skills they have learned through the modeling and direct-instructional processes. Such practice should only be provided when the students will be more than ninety-five percent successful. If they are less successful, the students may begin to practice skills incorrectly. This is important to avoid. It generally takes ten to twenty repetitions for new learning to be considered mastered. When a student practices something wrongly, after twenty times of doing it that way, it becomes the mastered way. It then takes somewhere close to three hundred repetitions to undo the incorrect learning. In this respect, it is important for children to not practice incorrect methods of reading.

USES OF LARGE GROUP, SMALL GROUP and INDIVIDUALIZED READING INSTRUCTION

The framework for organizing the balanced-literacy classroom is referred to as the one-book-whole class, flexible-groups' mode. What this means is that everyone in the class has experiences with the same book. Everyone in the class will discuss the literature. Each child will have a copy of the text being read. The teacher will start by activating prior knowledge and developing the context or background for the piece of literature. Some of the children within the class may have no prior knowledge or context with which to frame the book. The teacher will need to provide a preview of the book or develop key concepts to provide a stronger base for what the class will read together.

Some children will have to work with a paraprofessional or with a reading tutor before the class studies the book. Different modes of reading are accommodated within the class by the books being read as a read-aloud, as part of shared reading, or as guided reading. Student-reader choices can also include cooperative reading (reading with a partner), partners, or independent reading.

Following the reading, the children have to make a response to the reading, which can be done through a literature circle, the whole class, or in writing. In kindergarten, discussion groups are short, but in other grades, 1-6, they last from 5 to10 minutes.

In order to create personalized learning communities, educators must use information from the school experience to create relationships that create bridges of collaboration between school and community resources. The interaction chart of personalized learning shows the research of Clarke and Frazer (2003) in evaluating the developmental needs for students in school communities:

Interactions in Personalized Learning

Personal Needs	Relationships	School Practices
Self- Expression	Recognition from school	Provides equity
Creating self-identity	Acceptance-feeling of belonging	Shared community
Choosing one's own path	Creating trust	Range of options for student development
Freedom to take risks	Respect from community	Taking responsibility
Using one's imagination to view self projections	Fulfilling one's purpose in life	Creating greater challenges
Successful mastery	Confirm one's progress and goals	Having clear expectations for performance

(as adapted from Clarke and Frazer, 2003)

In a personalized learning community, students must feel a sense of connection to teachers and staff. Teachers know students by name and individual expression. Greeting students in the morning with names and a special recognition such as, "Jamie, thanks for participating the school's recycling program," or "Great job, David, in that last quarter touchdown at last Friday's football game," will go a long way in creating an affirming and connected school environment.

Skill 10.9   Knows how to evaluate, select, and incorporate various types of reading materials, including children's and young adult literature, expository texts, and other instructional materials for a range of reading levels, purposes, and interests

See Skill 10.5

Skill 10.10 Knows how to support students' learning in all content areas by teaching them to apply various strategies for comprehending expository and narrative texts and by promoting their acquisition and use of study and inquiry skills (e.g., note taking, outlining, skimming and scanning, using graphic organizers, setting purposes for reading, self-assessing, locating and evaluating multiple sources of information)

Reading does not end when one leaves the reading classroom; it, in fact, is an inherent component of every subject area taught in schools today. Content-area reading (science, social studies, math, etc.) can sometimes be much more difficult for students. Typically, the information is nonfiction, and there is a great deal of knowledge contained in a small amount of text. Deciphering content-area reading requires a unique set of strategies in order to best acquire the necessary information.

Text Format. Teaching children that nonfiction texts are laid out significantly differently than fictional texts is an important goal. Oftentimes, the format of the text helps provide an automatic organizational tool to help chunk information. Key words or section headings can help provide students with catch phrases with which they can remember the information. They can also help students to scan a large amount of information to find the precise information that they require to answer comprehension questions. Indexes and table of content skills can provide additional support with this.

Summarizing. As stated before, content subjects generally attempt to convey a great deal of information in a small amount of text. This is where the idea of summarizing can be so valuable and productive. Teaching the students to be able to take larger amounts of information and break it down into four or five sentences allows them to manage more details and learning. It also helps them to make connections and compartmentalize the information.

Graphic Organizers. There a numerous different forms of graphic organizers. They can be defined as a pictorial method of organizing information to help the student remember it more efficiently. Graphic organizers can be complex or simple, provided to the student or drawn from memory. The key is that the method or organizing tool used will help the students classify the information to be learned into smaller pieces with common characteristics. They also help the students to begin to see relationships between the concepts. Graphic organizers work well as study aids to help students acquire more information. Some graphic organizers can use pictures or other visual cues to help the students remember the items to be learned.

Semantic Mapping. In this strategy of organizing information, the students will use a visual representation to show how words or concepts are interrelated. This is a form of graphic organizer. In semantic mapping, the new knowledge is directly linked to the prior information. Sometimes called concept mapping, semantic maps allow the learner to see relationships between words or concepts and tie them to their own background knowledge in a meaningful manner.

Graphic Aids - It is important to teach students how to interpret the graphic aids typically included in content area texts. This may involve teaching some other subject area skills (e.g. reading a graph or chart), but it is necessary for students to understand these additions to the text. Graphic aids often help to clarify the text and provide another format to help with accurate interpretation.

With the advent of the Internet, research and study skills in texts are becoming lost. They are, however, skills that need to be emphasized and explained to students. Understanding reference materials will provide the students with the necessary foundational skills to better prepare them for future learning. Students need to be able to locate the information that they need for projects or to further their learning. In order to be able to find the information they need, students will need knowledge of using indexes, table of contents, and other time-saving helpers.

Furthermore, students need to be taught how to read and interpret graphs, charts, and maps that will be found within reference materials and content-specific materials. Being able to correctly interpret these types of information will better allow the students to draw the appropriate conclusions. It will enhance the knowledge the students gain from reading and provide further clarification.

Once the children understand how to access and interpret the information contained in content-specific materials or reference materials, they can begin to analyze it to clarify their thinking process and make the connections to their own life or information from other texts. Sometimes, the students will find conflicting pieces of information that they will be able to look at more in depth. Processing information in this way takes the level of reading to an even higher, more involved level. It also requires students to find their own method for integrating it into their personal schema for later recall.

Teaching students specific study skills like note taking, summarizing, using graphic organizers, semantic mapping, and time management will allow for effective use of the reference materials available to them.
Reading expository, nonfiction texts requires a significant set of different skills than other types of reading. Though there may be subplots or other story lines included, fiction reading generally has one main plot ,. The entire story in fiction reading is interrelated. However, expository text is written with the purpose of conveying information about a topic.

Generally, there is so much known information about topics that authors employ special organizational tactics to try to share all of that information with the reader. Since there is a large amount of information to be conveyed, authors use specific organizational information within the text to break it into smaller more manageable chunks. These different structures require the reader to make adjustments to their own personal reading style in order to successfully manage the intake of the new learning.

Note Taking- Learning how to take notes when reading is a tough skill to master and teach. It requires readers to understand the main ideas in a passage and be immediately able to summarize those ideas into something meaningful to themselves. This process requires a great deal of higher-order thinking and may need to be scaffolded for younger students. A method of providing support is to provide a rough outline with some information missing and that the students can find when they are reading.

Mapping- Mapping is a strategy that can be used to reach all learning styles and, therefore, is an important one to teach. It is exactly what its name implies, a map of the reading. A road map helps the driver get from point A to point B, and it is the same for a reading map. It helps readers maneuver through the information in a meaningful manner. Maps can use words with key ideas connected to smaller chunks of information. They can also use pictures instead of words to help the more visual learners. Adding color to a map can help certain ideas stand out more. This can be particularly helpful for students to begin to understand the process of prioritization in skills. Combining words and pictures is probably the most commonly used type of map. Lines are drawn between connecting concepts to show relationships, and, because readers are creating it themselves, it is meaningful to them alone. Maps are individual creations and revolve around readers' learning and prior knowledge.

Text Structure- Readers need to understand that nonfiction work often provides its own outline system in the way the text itself is organized. Most nonfiction text has headings and sub-headings that are bold. Students who use these as the main points can than fill in additional learning by reading the information below that heading. Also, if looking for a specific piece of information, students can utilize tables of contents and indexes, generally included in expository texts.

Skill 10.11   Knows how to promote students' comprehension, literary response and analysis using various genres

Development of Literary Response Skills

Literary response skills are dependent on prior knowledge, schemata, and background. Schemata (the plural of schema) are those structures which represent generic concepts stored in our memory.

Without schemata and experiences to call upon as they read, children have little ability to comprehend. Of course, the reader's schemata and prior knowledge have more influence on the comprehension of plot or character information that is not directly stated, than on plot or character information which is directly stated. Effective comprehenders of text, whether they are adults or children, use both their schemata and prior knowledge PLUS the ideas from the printed text for reading comprehension.

There are numerous strategies for developing and assessing students' responses to various types of literature.

Guided Reading. As a technique to provide small group instruction to students on their reading levels, Fountas and Pinnell introduced guided reading. It involves forming groups based on reading ability. During these groups, teachers choose specific texts and take the students through a process to build their reading skills. Running records are taken on a regular basis and used as the major assessment method.

Reading Logs. Reading logs can be used to encourage students to complete reading outside of the classroom setting and can take many different forms. A simple log of amount of time spent reading is on the basic end of the spectrum. On the other end might be reader-response logs, where the child is asked to respond specifically to something in the text they read. While these both seem like extremes, both strategies encourage students to develop their reading skills and responses to literature.

Literature Discussion. Literature discussion groups, sometimes known as literature circles, provide the students the opportunity to not only reflect on the reading, but also to drive the discussion. In this strategy, teachers are ancillary members of the discussion. The content and its depth and breadth come directly from the participation of the students and their views on the items in the reading.

Making Reading Connections. As with all learning, it is important for good readers to connect the item being read to other events. Guiding students to make these connections is the role of the teacher. It is important that first, students draw from their background knowledge to better understand the vocabulary and content of the story. Sharing information across students can be helpful to those who may be lacking in certain background information. Connections also need to be made across texts. This can be done by comparing and contrasting more than one story. Sometimes it is helpful to look at the use of language by a specific author. In this case, it would be beneficial to draw these comparisons across to books written by the same author. The most memorable connections are those that children make between the text and their own lives. It is when they can relate to something on a personal level that the students can then truly understand the situations and ideas presented.

Points to consider in analyzing story elements:
- Setting – Where does the story take place? Does it change throughout the story? What effect does the setting have on the story?
- Plot – What happens in the beginning, middle and the end of the story?
- Characters – Who are the people in the story? Who are the main characters? How does what they say and do reveal about them?
- Theme – What is the message of the story?
- Conflict – What is the problem in the story?
- Solution – How is the problem resolved?
- Mood – How does the author make you feel as you read the story – happy sad, angry, etc.?

Figurative language

Personification – giving human characteristics to inanimate objects
Similie – comparison using like or as
Metaphor – comparison by saying that something is another
Hyperbole – exaggeration

Students can also consider whether or not the story is indicative of a particular culture or time period. Teachers need to help the students find clue words in the story to help them make this analysis.

Development of Literary Response Skills

Literary response skills are dependent on prior knowledge, schemata and background. Schemata (the plural of schema) are those structures which represent concepts stored in our memory.

Without schemata and experiences to call upon as they read, children have little ability to comprehend. Of course, the reader's schemata and prior knowledge have more influence on the comprehension of plot or character information that is implied rather than directly stated.

Prior Knowledge

Prior knowledge can be defined as all of an individual's prior experiences, learning, and development which precede his/her entering a specific learning situation or attempting to comprehend a specific text. Sometimes prior knowledge can be erroneous or incomplete. Obviously, if there are misconceptions in a child's prior knowledge, these must be corrected so that the child's overall comprehension skills can continue to progress. Prior knowledge of children includes their accumulated positive and negative experiences both in and out of school.

These might come from wonderful family travels, watching television, visiting museums and libraries, to visiting hospitals, prisons and surviving poverty. Whatever the prior knowledge that the child brings to the school setting, the independent reading and writing the child does in school immeasurably expands his/her prior knowledge and hence broadens his/her reading comprehension capabilities.

The teacher must consider as he/she prepares to begin any imaginative/literary text the following about the students' level of prior knowledge:

1. What prior knowledge needs to be activated for the text, theme or for the writing to be done successfully?
2. How independent are the children in using strategies to activate their prior knowledge?

Holes and Roser (1987) have suggested five techniques for activating prior knowledge before starting an imaginative/literary text:
Free Recall: Tell us what you know about...

Unstructured Discussion: Let's talk about...

Structured Question: Who exactly was Jane Aviles in the life of the hero of the story?

Word Association: When you hear these words--hatch, elephant, who, think-- What author do you think of?

Recognition: Mulberry Street...What author comes to mind?

Previewing and predicting and story mapping are also excellent strategies for activating prior knowledge.

Development of Literary Analysis Skills

There are many exciting ways to sensitize and to teach children about the features and formats of different literary genres.

Strategy One: Genre Switch-Reader and Writer Transformation

This strategy should be introduced as a read aloud with young children or with children who are struggling readers. In a similar fashion, it would be introduced as a read-aloud for ELL learners. Older children in grades 3-6 might just be "started off" by a teacher prompt and do the required reading on their own.

To begin, the teacher selects a particular genre book. If it is close to Halloween, a goblin or suspense story will do well. The teacher begins to read the story with the open invitation to the students to determine as the story is being read, what type of story it is and what makes it that type of story.

Older children take notes in their reading journals, while younger children and those more in need of explicit teacher support contribute their ideas and responses as part of the discussion in class. Their responses are recorded on a chart.

As the reading continues, the story type components are listed on the chart (most of the responses are those which have been elicited from the children).

At some point in what is either an oral read aloud, guided reading or independent reading, the teacher directs the children's attention to the components which have emerged on the chart. They then use these components which are generally components of character - setting, plot, style, conflict, language – to identify the story genre.

The teacher provides the children with an opportunity to expound at length on why this story is an example of the genre which they have identified.
Once they have done so, the teacher challenges them to consider how this story with its set of given characters, plot, and setting would be changed if the genre were different. The teacher can challenge the class as a whole with the idea of changing the story to a radically different genre—i.e. from suspense to a fairy tale or a comedy or allow the children to come up another genre.

Then depending on the children's developed writing abilities, they might be given time to rewrite the story on their own or re-tell it in class prior to writing and illustrating it.

In the balanced literacy approach, this transformation of the story into another genre is done as part of the Writing Workshop component which uses the same reading material as the source for writing. The strategy results in the children having had the experience of an in-depth analysis of a particular genre as well as hands-on writing (or telling, if they can not yet write or can not yet write in English) experience of restyling that basic plot and characters into another genre. This authenticates the children's participation as readers and writers.

Strategy Two: Analyzing Story Elements

Story elements include plot (including conflict and resolution, setting (including time and place), characters (flat and round/static and dynamic), and theme (the main idea of the story). Students can use graphic organizers such as story maps, compare/contrast displays, and sequence boxes to display their understanding of these critical features of fiction.

Strategy Three: Analyzing Character Development

Characters in children's literature may be flat or round. A flat character is one-dimensional and is often defined by one characteristic. Rosie in *Rosie's Walk* is an example. A round character seems like someone you know, such as Jess in *Bridge to Terabithia*. Static characters do not change from the beginning to the end of the story, while dynamic ones do. Characters reveal themselves through their actions, their interactions, and through what they say.

Strategy Four: Interpreting Figurative Language
Similes are direct comparisons between two things using "like" or "as." "Her eyes were like stars" is a simile. Metaphors are indirect comparisons, such as "The earth is a big blue marble." Personification is giving human characteristics to non-animal beings. Frances, Shrek, or the animals in *Mr. Gumpy's Outing* are all examples of personification.

Strategy Five: Identifying Literary Allusions

Children can understand allusions best when they read a lot. A literary allusion when it appears in a story is also called *intertextuality.* That is when a reference, character, or symbol from one story appears or is alluded to in another. Recently, many popular children's books use literary allusions, from the Ahlbergs' *Each Peach Pear Plum* to Jon Scieszka's *The True Story of the Three Little Pigs.* Note that any character or plot element can become allusions, not just references from fairy tales.

Strategy Six: Analyzing the Author's Point of View

In fiction, point of view is the vantage point from which the narrator tells the story. We determine point of view by asking, where is the narrator standing in relation to the characters? Is the narrator inside or outside of the story? If inside, is the narrator one of the characters? This is *first person point of view.* If outside, can the narrator "see" into anyone else's mind besides his/her own? If the narrator cannot see into the mind and heart of other characters, then the point of view is *third person limited.* Narrators who can see what other characters are thinking and feeling are using *third person omniscient point of view.*

Use of Comprehension Strategies Before, During, and After Reading

Cooper (2004), Taberski (2000), Cox (2005) and other researchers recommend a broad array of comprehension strategies before, during, and after reading.

Cooper (2004) suggests a broad range of classroom posters on the walls plus explicit instruction to give children prompts to monitor their own reading. An example follows: My Strategic Reading Guide

I. Do I infer/predict important information, use what I know, think about what may happen or what I want to learn?
2. Can I identify important information about the story elements?
3. Do I generate questions and search for the answers?
4. Does this make sense to me? Does this help me meet my purpose in reading?
5. If lost, do I remember fix-ups?
   Re-read, read further ahead, look at the illustrations, ask for help, and think about the words, and evaluate what I have read.
6. Do I remember to think about how the parts of the stories that I was rereading came together?

Storyboard panels, which are used by comic strip artists and by those artists who do advertising campaigns as well as television and film directors, are perfect for engaging children K-6 in a variety of comprehension strategies before, during, and after reading. They can storyboard the beginning of a story, read aloud, and then storyboard its predicted middle or end. Of course, after they experience or read the actual middle or ending of the story, they can compare and contrast what they produced with its actual structure. They can play familiar literature identification games with a buddy or as part of a center by storyboarding one key scene or characters from a book and challenging a partner or peer to identify the book and characters correctly.

Use of Oral Language Activities to Promote Comprehension

Retelling

Retelling needs to be very clearly defined so that the child reader does not think that the teacher wants him or her to spill the WHOLE story back in the retelling. A child should be able to talk comfortably and fluently about the story he or she has just read. He or she should be able to tell the main things that have happened in the story.

When a child retells a story to a teacher, the teacher needs ways to help him or her assess the child's understanding. Ironically, the teacher can use some of the same strategies he or she suggests to the child to assess the child's understanding of a book which is not familiar to the teacher. These strategies include: back cover reading, scanning the table of contents, looking at the pictures, and reading the book jacket.

If the child can explain how the story turned out and provide examples to support these explanations, try not to interrupt him or her with too many questions. Children can use the text of the book to reinforce what they are saying and they can even read from it if they wish. It is also important to note that some children need to re-read the text twice and their re-reading of it is out of enjoyment.

When the teacher plans to use the retelling as a way of assessing the child, then the following ground rules have to be set and made clear to the child. The teacher explains the purpose of the retelling to determine how well the child is reading at the outset of the conference.

The teacher maintains in the child's assessment notebook or in his/her assessment record what the child is saying in phrases, not sentences. Just enough is recorded to indicate whether the child actually understood the story. The teacher also tries to analyze from the retelling why the child can not comprehend a given text. If the child's accuracy rate with the text is below 95 per cent, then the problem is at the word level, but if the accuracy rate for the text is above 95 per cent, the difficulty lies at the text level.

Development of the Reading Comprehension Skills and Strategies of Individual Students

ELL Learners bring to their classrooms different prior knowledge concerns than do their native English language speaking peers. Some of the ELL students have extensive prior knowledge in their native language and can read well on or above their chronological age level in their native language. Other ELL learners come to the United States from cultures where reading was not emphasized or circumstances did not give families native language literacy opportunities.

Rigg and Allen (1999) offer the following four principles regarding the literacy development and prior knowledge of ELL-second language learners:

1. In learning a language you learn to do the things you want to do with people who are speaking that language.
2. A second language, like the first, does not develop linearly, but rather globally.
3. Language can develop in rich context.
4. Literacy develops parallel to language, so as speaking and listening for the second language develop, so do writing and reading.

As far as retelling, it needs to be noted that English language learners have the problem of not bringing rich oral English vocabulary to the stories they are decoding. Therefore, often they "sound the stories out" well, but can not explain what they are about, because they do not know what the words mean.

Use of Oral Reading Fluency in Facilitating Comprehension

At some point it is crucial that just as the nervous, novice bike rider finally relaxes and speeds happily off, so too must the early reader integrate graphophonic cues with semantic and structural ones. Before this is done, the oral quality of early reader's has a stilted beat to it, which of course does not promote reading engagement and enjoyment.

The teacher needs to be at his/her most dramatic to model for children the beauties of voice and nuance that are contained in the texts whose print they are tracking so anxiously. Children love nothing more than to mimic their teacher and can do so legitimately and without hesitation, if the teacher takes time each day to recite a poem with them. The poem might be posted on chart paper and be up on the wall for a week.

First the teacher can model the fluent and expressive reading of this poem. Then with a pointer, the class can recite it with the teacher. As the week progresses, the class can recite it on their own.

Use of Writing Activities to Promote Literary Response and Analysis

In addition to the activities already mentioned, the activities below will promote literary response and analysis:

  *   Have children take a particular passage from a story and retell it from another character's perspective.

- Challenge children to suggest a sequel or a prequel to any given story they have read.

- Ask the children to recast a story in which the key characters are male into one where the key characters are female (or vice versa). Have them explain how these changes alter the narrative, plot, or outcome.

- Encourage the children to transform a story or book into a Reader's Theater format and record it complete with sound effects for the audio-cassette center of the classroom.

- Have the children produce a newspaper as the characters of a given story would have reported the news in their community.

- Transform the story into a ballad poem or a picture book version for younger peers.

- Give ELL children an opportunity to translate stories into their native language or to author in English with a buddy a favorite story that was originally published in their native language.

Skill 10.12   Knows how to design and implement instruction in interpreting, analyzing, and evaluating information (e.g., maps, charts, graphics, video segments, technology presentations) and how to use media to produce visual images, messages, and meanings

Preview-Review. Background knowledge is essential when reading for adequate comprehension to occur. Before reading a text, it can be helpful to preview vocabulary, phonics concepts, or other language-arts elements with the students. This preview provides them a heads-up, so to speak, and the ability to have some minor background knowledge. After reading the selection, it is just as important to go back and review the information to ensure understanding.

Visual Aids, Charts, and Real Objects. For all students, but particularly those learning English as a second language, whenever it is possible to provide a nonverbal, visual representation, it will enhance the instruction. Oftentimes, the students have a framework of understanding about certain topics, but do not have the language skills or vocabulary to define that concept. With pictorial representations, the language component is eliminated, and, therefore, the students can draw more conclusions and better understand the concepts. The visual may be a picture, a chart, or (if reasonable) the real object.

Word Organizers. Semantic mapping can help to provide students with a deeper understanding of the interrelationship between words and concepts. Seeing these relationships on paper can help the students make additional generalizations and draw conclusions.

Graphic Organizers. The flexibility of graphic organizers to span multiple subjects makes them an invaluable tool to students and teachers. The fact that a graphic organizer puts a visual representation to a concept or arranges multiple concepts in a more manageable manner provides the student learning English with the opportunity to connect new learning with old learning or to connect English with their native language.

Outlining. Outlining is an organizational tool that is very sequential and concrete. The use of this tool with students for whom English is a second langue provides a clear path for them to follow. Whether it be a prepared outline showing the concepts to be covered and with room for the students to take notes, or their own prepared outline for an upcoming writing assignment, students will find the sequential nature of the outline to leave little room for misinterpretation.

DOMAIN III.   **MEETING THE NEEDS OF INDIVIDUAL STUDENTS**

COMPETENCY 11.0 INSTRUCTION FOR ENGLISH LANGUAGE LEARNERS

Skill 11.1   **Demonstrates knowledge of expected stages and patterns of first- and second-language learning and issues and concepts related to the transfer of literacy competency from one language to another**

The strategies necessary to develop vocabulary in students for whom English is not the primary language mirror the strategies that work for other students. There is no one set of approaches that works best for second language students; it is only through a combination of strategies and approaches that students' success can be assured.

Keep in mind, as previously discussed, that students who are learning English as a second language require some additional time in order to make the transition. For those students who have received education in their primary language, the time is shortened, typically five years. Students who have received no formal instruction in their primary language may take as long as seven years.

Vocabulary development, in any case, needs to be meaning-based instruction. With or without schooling in their primary language, these students do have a mental framework of what words mean and of concepts. It is tying the new information to these existing structures that allows the students to progress and gain more skills in English.

This transfer between languages is not an easy process and requires time and both meaning-based and explicit teaching strategies. The general list of vocabulary words to memorize along with their meanings will not be a useful strategy for these students. A more significant approach is to tie the vocabulary into the context of the reading or situation. It is through contextual situations that students will better be able to progress.

Since the English language has many roots derived from the Latin and Greek languages, these parallels can be explicitly shown to students. Through this, they will be able to find the necessary hooks in their own language with which to connect the English variation. Students whose primary language also has many Latin and Greek derivatives will make the transition to English easier than those whose primary language is not from these roots.

As in any group of students, diversity is going to be present and a key factor in the educational process. Using teaching methodologies of a variant nature will be the most successful approach to helping second-language students become fluent in English. Vocabulary instruction needs to be flexible: sometimes explicit, and other times based in context.

Skill 11.2   Applies knowledge of issues and procedures in assessing English language Learners' reading strengths and needs, and when to collaborate with other specialists to aid in assessment

Children who come from family backgrounds where English is not spoken lack a solid understanding of its syntactic and visual structure. Therefore, as they are being recorded for progress using the oral running record, they may need additional support from their teachers and from ESL teachers in examining the structure and meaning of English. Children from a non-native-English-language-speaking background may often pronounce words that make no sense to themselves and just go on reading. They have to learn to stop to construct meaning. They may have to be prompted to self-correct.

Children from non-native-English-language-speaking backgrounds can benefit from independent reading opportunities to listen to a familiar story on tape and read along. This also gives them practice in listening to standard-English oral reading. Often these children can begin to internalize the language structures by listening to the book on tape several times.

Highly proficient readers can sometimes support early readers through a partner relationship. Some children, particularly the emergent and beginning early readers, benefit from reading books with partners. The partners sit side-by-side and each one takes a turn reading the entire text.

Use of talking books and author web resources provides special needs learners having visual or auditory handicapping conditions immediate contact with authors and with direct sharing in the joy of story telling. In addition to the accessibility of the keyboard, their responses to literature can be shared with a broad network of other readers, including close and distant peers. Technology literally enfranchises special needs learners into the circle of connected readers and writers.

In the classroom, there are numerous ways to determine which students are in need of additional assistance. The most effective methods are to examine the classroom performance, to review the available assessment data, and to work individually with the student.

Regular classroom teachers often have numerous concerns about the students they are working with in the classroom. They will seek help from reading specialists for additional strategies and support to help increase the reading skills. It is important that the specialists be able to determine what difficulties require additional assistance and in which specific areas of reading to provide that assistance.

As previously discussed, running records are of tremendous value in helping in this area because they provide a fast and efficient way to examine the errors the students are making and the number of errors they are making. Also, the levels at which the students are able to read can be a warning flag. If a student is struggling with material several grade levels below their current grade, it is important to determine the cause.

Once a general warning flag appears, it may be necessary for specialists to look in depth and administer additional skill-specific assessments or to examine the data present more in depth. In general, it's good to keep in mind the five larger areas of reading as a method of narrowing down the problem. These include phonemic awareness, phonics, fluency, comprehension, and vocabulary.

Identifying which of these areas is causing the problems helps teachers and specialists to determine an appropriate plan of action to address the skill deficits. Many children will demonstrate deficits in more than one area, so it is critical to follow the appropriate skill sequence to move the students forward in the most efficient manner possible.

Even knowing the broad area of difficulty may not be enough in itself. Sometimes very skill-specific assessment or identification will need to occur before the instruction can begin. Other times, a more global approach would be prudent. An example of a time when a global approach might be more beneficial when a student has all of the phonics skills in isolation, but has difficulty applying them in text. In this case, spending more time teaching the phonics skills will not benefit the child, but rather spending the time helping the child to use other cueing systems beyond phonics and in a broader sense through many passages and texts would be a more suitable use of time.

One of the first things that teachers learn is how to obtain resources and help for their students. All schools have guidelines for receiving this assistance, especially since the implementation of the Americans with Disabilities Act. The first step in securing help is for teachers to approach the school's administration or exceptional education department for direction in attaining special services or resources for qualifying students. Many schools have a committee designated for addressing these needs, such as a Child Study Team or Core Team. These teams are made up of both regular and exceptional education teachers, school psychologists, guidance counselors, and administrators. The particular student's classroom teachers usually have to complete some initial paper work and will need to do some behavioral observations.

Teachers will take this information to the appropriate committee for discussion and consideration. The committee will recommend the next step to be taken. Often, subsequent steps include a complete psychological evaluation along with certain physical examinations such as vision and hearing screening and a complete medical examination by a doctor.

The referral of students for this process is usually relatively simple for classroom teachers and requires little more than some initial paper work and discussion. The services and resources the students receive as a result of the process typically prove to be invaluable to those with behavioral disorders. Collaborative teams play a crucial role in meeting the needs of all students, and they are an important step to identifying students with special needs. Under the Individuals with Disabilities Act (IDEA), which federally mandates special education services in every state, it is the responsibility of public schools to ensure consultative, evaluative, and (if necessary) prescriptive services to children with special needs. In most school districts, a collaborative group called the Child Study Team (CST) handles this responsibility. If teachers or parents suspect children to have academic, social or emotional problems, the children are referred to the CST where a team consisting of educational professionals (including teachers, specialists, the school psychologist, guidance, and other support staff) review the case and situation through meetings with teachers and/or parents/guardians. The CST will determine what evaluations or tests are necessary, if any, and will also assess the results. Based on these results, the CST will suggest a plan of action.

One plan of action is an Academic Intervention Plan (AIP). An AIP consists of additional instructional services that are provided to students who have met certain criteria (such as scoring below the state reference point on standardized tests or performing more than two levels below grade-level) in order to help them better achieve academically.

Another plan of action is a 504 plan. A 504 plan is a legal document based on the provisions of the Rehabilitation Act of 1973 (which preceded IDEA). A 504 plan is a plan for instructional services to assist students with special needs in a regular education classroom setting.

Students with physical, emotional, or other impairments (such as Attention Deficit Disorder) impacting their ability to learn in a regular education classroom setting can be referred for a 504 meeting. Typically, the CST (and perhaps even the student's physician or therapist) will participate in the 504 meeting and review to determine if a 504 plan will be written.

Finally, children referred to CST may qualify for an Individualized Education Plan (IEP). An IEP is a legal document which delineates the specific, adapted services students with disabilities will receive. An IEP differs from a 504 plan in that children must be identified for special education services to qualify for an IEP, and ALL students who receive special education services must have an IEP. Each IEP must contain statements pertaining to the their present performance level, annual goals, related services and supplementary aids, testing modifications, a projected date of services, and assessment methods for monitoring progress. Each year, the CST and guardians must meet to review and update the IEP.

At times, teachers must go beyond the school system to meet the needs of some students. An awareness of special services and resources and how to obtain them is essential to all teachers and their students. When the school system is unable to address the needs of students, teachers often must take the initiative and contact agencies within the community. Frequently there is no special policy for finding resources.

It is simply up to individual teachers to be creative and resourceful in finding whatever helps students. Meeting the needs of all students is certainly a team effort that is most often spearheaded by classroom teachers.

When considering students for whom English is not the primary language, it is critical to understand the natural development of second language acquisition before applying the general knowledge of reading assessments to this subgroup of students.

In general, second-language students can take up to seven years to become proficient in the second language. This factors in the acculturation process of speaking, listening, reading and writing. Students who are fluent and able to read in their primary language before starting the second language are more likely to become fluent in the second language than those who are not fluent in the primary language.

Students attempting to learn in a second language generally tend to lag behind in vocabulary particularly. The connection between words and their meanings is essential to understand what is being read. Students who can make the transition easily between the two languages have the advantage of seeing or hearing a word, translating it in their mind to the same or a similar word in their native language, then making the connection and being able to access that information to help them understand the text. Though this is a slow and labor-intensive process, in the end the students are able to understand.

However, students who are unable to complete these numerous steps will require additional support, particularly in vocabulary development. Helping to build background knowledge is critical when introducing texts to these students, using as concrete a process as is possible. The more concrete examples teachers can provide, the better for the students.

In looking at the other areas of reading, phonics and phonemic awareness skills can also pose problems. Students will sometimes substitute the sounds from their native language in the middle of the process or at other times. Additionally, they may have no connection within their native language because there may be no letters/combinations that make those sounds.

In the end, good reading assessment and instruction is essential when working with students acquiring a second language. However, it must be married well with the body of research into how one learns a second language. Remembering that oral language will develop first (receptive before expressive) and after oral language reaches a conversational level, one can begin the reading instruction. One of the most important things to know about the differences between L1 (first language) and L2 (second language) acquisition is that people usually will master L1, but they will almost never be fully proficient in L2. However, if children can be trained in L2 before about the age of seven, their chances at full mastery will be much higher. Children learn language with so little effort, which is why they can be babbling one year and speaking with complete, complex ideas just a few years later. It is important to know that language is innate, meaning that our brains are ready to learn a language from birth. Yet a lot of language learning is behavioral, meaning that children imitate adult.

L2 acquisition is much harder for adults. Multiple theories of L2 acquisition have come about. Some of the more notable ones come from Jim Cummins. Cummins argues that there are two types of language that usually need to be acquired by students learning English as a second language: Basic Interpersonal Communication Skills (BICS) and Cognitive Academic Language Proficiency (CALP). BICS is general, everyday language used to communicate simple thoughts, whereas CALP is the more complex, academic language used in schools. It is harder for students to acquire CALP, and many teachers mistakenly assume that students can learn complex academic concepts in English if they have already mastered BICS. The truth is that CALP takes much longer to master, and in some cases, particularly with little exposure in certain subjects, it may never be mastered.

Another set of theories is based on Stephen Krashen's research in L2 acquisition. Most people understand his theories based on five principles:

1. The acquisition-learning hypothesis: This states that there is a difference between learning a language and acquiring it. Children "acquire" a first language easily—it's natural. But adults often have to "learn" a language through coursework, studying, and memorizing. One can acquire a second language, but often it requires more deliberate and natural interaction within that language.
2. The monitor hypothesis: This is when the learned language "monitors" the acquired language. In other words, this is when a person's "grammar check" kicks in and keeps awkward, incorrect language out of a person's L2 communication.
3. The natural order hypothesis: This suggests that the learning of grammatical structures is predictable and follows a "natural order."
4. The input hypothesis: Some people call this "comprehensible input." This means that a language learner will learn best when the instruction or conversation is just above the learner's ability. That way, the learner has the foundation to understand most of the language, but still will have to figure out, often in context, what that extra, more difficult, element means.
5. The affective-filter hypothesis: This suggests that people will learn a second language when they are relaxed, have high levels of motivation, and have a decent level of self-confidence.

Skill 11.3   Applies knowledge of how to develop systematic, sequential age-appropriate reading instruction that is based on a convergence of research evidence and that is responsive to individual students' strengths, needs, and interests

Teaching students who are learning English as a second language poses some unique challenges, particularly in a standards-based environment. The key is realizing that no matter how little English a student knows, the teacher should teach with students' developmental level in mind. This means that instruction should not be "dumbed-down" for ESOL students. Different approaches should be used, however, to ensure that these students (a) get multiple opportunities to learn and practice English and (b) still learn content.

Many ESOL approaches are based on social learning methods. By being placed in mixed-level groups or by being paired with a student of another ability level, students will get a chance to practice English in a natural, non-threatening environment. Students should not be pushed in these groups to use complex language or to experiment with words that are too difficult. They should simply get a chance to practice with simple words and phrases.

In teacher-directed instructional situations, visual aids (such as pictures, objects, and video) are particularly effective at helping students make connections between words and items they are already familiar with.

ESOL students may need additional accommodations with assessments, assignments, and projects. For example, teachers may find that written tests provide little to no information about a student understanding of the content. Therefore, an oral test may be better suited for ESOL students. When students are somewhat comfortable and capable with written tests, a shortened test may actually be preferable; take note that they will need extra time to translate.

From high school and college experiences, most of us think that learning a language strictly involves drills, memorization, and tests. While this is a common method used (some people call it a structural, grammatical, or linguistic approach). While this works for some students, it certainly does not work for all.

Although there are dozens of methods that have been developed to help people learn additional languages, we will focus on some of the more common approaches used in today's K-12 classrooms. Cognitive approaches to language learning focus on concepts. While words and grammar are important, when teachers use the cognitive approach, they focus on using language for conceptual purpose rather than learning words and grammar for the sake of simply learning new words and grammatical structures. This approach focuses heavily on students' learning styles, and it cannot necessarily be pinned down as having specific techniques. Rather, it is more of a philosophy of instruction.

There are many approaches that are noted for their motivational purposes. In a general sense, when teachers work to motivate students to learn a language, they do things to help reduce fear and to assist students in identifying with native speakers of the target language. A very common method is often called the functional approach. In this approach, the teacher focuses on communicative elements. For example, a first grade ESOL teacher might help students learn phrases that will assist them in finding a restroom or asking for help on the playground. Many functionally-based adult ESOL programs help learners with travel-related phrases and words.

Another very common motivational approach is Total Physical Response. This is a kinesthetic approach that combines language learning and physical movement. In essence, students learn new vocabulary and grammar by responding with physical motion to verbal commands. Some people say it is particularly effective because the physical actions create good brain connections with the words.

In general, the best methods do not treat students as if they have a language deficit. Rather, the best methods build upon what students already know, and they help to instill the target language as a communicative process rather than a list of vocabulary words that have to be memorized.

Skill 11.4 Knows how to work with other professionals in selecting and using appropriate formal and informal assessments of English Language Learners and in planning effective literacy instruction, including selecting instructional materials and strategies that reflect cultural diversity

As a teacher you will experience many forms of evaluations. Through student teaching to formal evaluations completed by supervisors, ongoing critical looks at your performance will be a part of the regular process. One area that is often under-utilized but is, perhaps, more valuable than outside evaluations is the self-assessment.

Examining with a critical eye one's own performance is the highest level of reflection. There are several forms that self-assessments can undertake. One format is to videotape yourself completing a lesson with the students. Then replaying the tape for yourself at a later time. Before watching the tape, you should have specific questions or areas in mind. Simply watching the tape itself is much less valuable than when you watch it with a purpose. The questions might include things like: "Did I keep the students engaged throughout the lesson?" "Was I clear in explaining the content I wanted them to understand?" "What could I do to improve the understanding of this concept for the students?"

Another method of self-assessment might include providing your students with surveys to complete. When compiling the data from the questions, you will have a better understanding of how you are perceived by your students and what skills you can work on to improve the weak areas. Carefully written questions focused on the items you are interested in learning about are necessary.

Sometimes a self-assessment could be as simple as keeping a reflection journal. With this strategy, teachers simply keep a regular notebook and after each day or week (or even lesson) takes a few minutes to write down their thoughts and feelings. Writing down what went well, what did not go well, what could have been done differently, or what was a surprise can provide valuable insight into teaching style and improvement. The drawback to this strategy is finding the time to use this it. Self reflection has been found to provide the most immediate and effective changes to instructional practice. If used authentically and kept confidential, it can be one of the best tools for improvement available to an educator.

Regular use of self-evaluation tools allows teachers to understand what goals and objectives to include in the personal improvement plan. These ideas then become a part of the professional development plan. Remembering to review the state standards and using them as a guide for the self-evaluation will provide further guidance and a place to start for the development of such plans.

Skill 11.5 **Knows how to work with other professionals to plan, implement, and monitor instruction that reflects an awareness of appropriate instructional progressions and that facilitates students' transfer of oral language skills and literacy from their primary language to English while maintaining literacy in their primary language**

As a specialist of any kind within a school building, it is imperative that collaboration among all staff be of top priority. It is not enough to simply service the students who are assigned through whatever means the district or building uses. Current educational trends have collaboration of the utmost priority. In some cases, reading specialists are becoming literacy coaches and responsible for working closely with regular educators to increase the reading skills of the students across the building. This collaborative model has reading specialists working in the classroom beside the teacher in a team-teaching model. At times, lessons may be modeled to demonstrate new or innovative ideas or different ways to structure lessons. Still other times, the two professionals would work together to provide instruction to groups of students.

This coaching model also provides out-of-the-classroom time where professional development activities may occur. These may take the form of study groups, individual discussion sessions, or workshop offerings for different strategies. For this to be a successful implementation, it is important for all parties to realize that this is a learning session for everyone and that one party is not evaluating another.

Another less formal collaboration model simply involves regular meetings where children and their needs are discussed. These meetings may be formal or informal. Usually they revolve around the assessment data gathered on the students, but may not. As the data and needs of the students are reviewed, the teachers present will discuss items indicating various needs. This allows for the most appropriate professional development to occur.

As they are directly related to an immediate need for teachers with their current students, the skills learned are more likely to be implemented. In an informal setting, anyone with knowledge can share his or her ideas, suggestions, strategies or skills. It is in this format that all parties feel less threatened and more comfortable sharing.

As reading specialists, it is vital to collaborate with other reading specialists as much as possible. Today's use of technology and the availability of email can make this a much less cumbersome task. Collaboration is a vital part of growth for all teachers and should not be seen as a negative. It should instead be viewed as opportunity to be part of a team of professionals working together to ensure that all students receive the most appropriate educational experience possible.

Skill 11.6   **Applies strategies for collaborating with teachers, specialists, parents/guardians, students, and administrators to promote and maintain English language Learners literacy in English and their primary language**

See Skills 11.4 and 11.5

Skill 11.7 Recognizes the importance of distinguishing between language differences and reading disabilities and knows when additional assessment or intervention is needed

Students whose first language is not English have more difficulty than usual trying to succeed in the schools of the United States. Teachers need to learn to recognize when the difficulty stems from a difference in the language and when it is an actual reading disability. Some students may not have adequate access to effective English-as-a-second-language resources outside of the school and rely on the school to provide them with the English instruction that they need. If students are from a low socio-economic background, they may not be able to function well in a school that assumes that all children come from middle-class backgrounds. Therefore the instruction the students receive needs to be modified to meet their specific needs.

Still other students do have a reading disability that severely impairs their ability to succeed in school no matter what the language of instruction may be. Quite often teachers do not have the proper assessment tools for students who are learning English and may have to refer them to more specialized experts for help in getting a valid assessment. Reading specialists in the school should have access to all sorts of assessment tools that will help diagnose whether these students need help with learning the language or need intervention with reading difficulties.

It is important to establish a school environment that focuses on the success of students learning English. This means the school should have strong administrative leadership, high expectations for all students, ongoing and systematic assessment of students, and shared decision-making opportunities for ESL teachers. All teachers should have a knowledge base about working with these students, recognition of the importance of preserving the students' first language, programs rich in opportunities for the students, and effective instruction.

Recognition of the students' native language is paramount in the instruction. By availing of translators, teachers can translate the material into the students' language to assess student knowledge. Teachers need to integrate approaches that draw on the students' prior knowledge to help them make connections between English and the mother tongue. Direct instruction is important when dealing with ESL students as teachers teach the skills and concepts and reinforce them on a daily basis. Teams of teachers with ESL students in their classrooms should have the opportunity to meet on a regular basis to discuss problems they are experiencing and developing solutions to the problems to the advantage of the students.

COMPETENCY 12.0 INSTRUCTION FOR STUDENTS WITH READING DIFFICULTIES, DYSLEXIA, AND READING DISABILITIES

Skill 12.1 **Applies knowledge of the characteristics and instructional implications of reading difficulties, dyslexia, and reading disabilities in relation to the development of reading experience**

There are various reasons why children experience reading difficulties in the school system. Some may have medical difficulties, challenges in the home environment, dyslexia, or attention-deficit difficulties that will impede their language learning. While most children progress at a normal rate, there are those who learn at a slower rate than their peers, and even those progressing normally may experience a block in the learning from time to time.

The difficulties children have with reading may be identified as soon as they enter kindergarten, while for others it may take longer. However, research shows that children who experience reading difficulties beyond third grade have a difficult time catching up in the later grades. For some children, it may be a problem with fluency or word recognition. Teachers often have to go back to the basics and reteach skills that the students didn't quite grasp in earlier grades.

Students may come to your classroom having been diagnosed with dyslexia. Dyslexia is a learning disability that causes difficulties for students in the areas of reading and writing. The underlying cause is believed to be brain based and is identified in students who fail to read despite all types of reading and writing instruction and interventions and in the absence of any medical condition. These students appear to be bright, intelligent, and articulate, but are unable to read. Their intelligence is average, and they may show exceptional talents in other areas, such as art or music.

Extensive educational tutoring in the area of phonemic awareness is the usual route with teaching dyslexic students. The earlier this intervention takes place, the better for the students. There are also other methods, such as the Davis Dyslexia Correction, which uses modeling clay to teach students the letters of the alphabet and Fast ForWord, a software program to help children learn the sounds of language. Vision therapy has also been used in the form of colored lenses.

Skill 12.2 **Knows about state and federal laws, regulations, guidelines, and procedures regarding assessment and provision of services for students with reading difficulties, dyslexia, and reading disabilities**

Visit http://www.tsbvi.edu/Education/ for more information.

Skill 12.3 **Knows how to work with other professionals to select and administer appropriate informal and formal assessments of students with reading difficulties, dyslexia, and reading disabilities and analyze results to plan effective literacy instruction that is responsive to individual students' strengths, needs, and interests**

See Skill 11.5

Skill 12.4 **Uses results from formal and informal assessments to determine when in-depth evaluation and additional intervention are warranted**

See Skill 2.5

Skill 12.5 **Applies knowledge of convergent research about practices for providing effective literacy instruction to students with reading difficulties, dyslexia, and reading disabilities, including both prevention and intervention strategies**

There are several educational learning theories that can be applied to classroom practices. One classic learning theory is Piaget's stages of development, which consists of four learning stages: sensory motor stage (from birth to age 2); pre-operation stages (ages 2 to 7 or early elementary); concrete operational (ages 7 to 11 or upper elementary); and formal operational (ages 7-15 or late elementary/high school). Piaget believed children passed through this series of stages to develop from the most basic forms of concrete thinking to sophisticated levels of abstract thinking.

Some of the most prominent learning theories in education today include brain-based learning and the Multiple Intelligence Theory. Supported by recent brain research, brain-based learning suggests that knowledge about the way the brain retains information enables educators to design the most effective learning environments. As a result, researchers have developed twelve principles that relate knowledge about the brain to teaching practices. These twelve principles are:

- The brain is a complex adaptive system
- The search for meaning is innate
- We use patterns to learn more effectively
- Emotions are crucial to developing patterns
- Each brain perceives and creates parts and whole simultaneously
- Learning involves focused and peripheral attention
- Learning involves conscious and unconscious processes
- We have at least two ways of organizing memory
- Learning is developmental
- Complex learning is enhanced by challenged (and inhibited by threat)

Educators can use these principles to help design methods and environments in their classrooms to maximize student learning in the area of reading.

The Multiple Intelligence Theory, developed by Howard Gardner, suggests that students learn in (at least) seven different ways. These include visually/spatially, musically, verbally, logically/mathematically, interpersonally, intrapersonally, and bodily/kinesthetically.

The most current learning theory of constructivist learning allows students to construct learning opportunities. For constructivist teachers, the belief is that students create their own reality of knowledge and how to process and observe the world around them. Students are constantly constructing new ideas, which serve as frameworks for learning and teaching. Researchers have shown that the constructivist model is comprised of the four components:

1. Learner creates knowledge
2. Learner constructs and makes meaningful new knowledge to existing knowledge
3. Learner shapes and constructs knowledge by life experiences and social interactions
4. In constructivist learning communities, the student, teacher and classmates establish knowledge cooperatively on a daily basis.

Kelly (1969) states, "Human beings construct knowledge systems based on their observations parallels Piaget's theory that individuals construct knowledge systems as they work with others who share a common background of thought and processes." Constructivist learning for students is dynamic and ongoing. For constructivist teachers, the classroom becomes a place where students are encouraged to interact with the instructional process by asking questions and posing new ideas to old theories. The use of cooperative learning that encourages students to work in supportive learning environments using their own ideas to stimulate questions and propose outcomes is a major aspect of a constructivist classroom.

The metacognition learning theory deals with "the study of how to help the learner gain understanding about how knowledge is constructed and about the conscious tools for constructing that knowledge" (Joyce and Weil 1996). The cognitive approach to learning involves teachers understanding that teaching the student to process their own learning and mastery of skills provides the greatest learning and retention opportunities in the classroom. Students are taught to develop concepts and teach themselves skills in problem-solving and critical thinking. The student becomes an active participant in the learning process, and the teacher facilitates that conceptual and cognitive learning process.

Social and behavioral theories look at the social interactions of students in the classroom that instruct or impact learning opportunities in the classroom. The psychological approaches behind both theories are subject to individual variables that are learned and applied either proactively or negatively in the classroom. The stimulus of the classroom can promote conducive learning or evoke behavior that is counterproductive for both students and teachers. Students are social beings that normally gravitate to action in the classroom, so teachers must be cognizant in planning classroom environments that provide both focus and engagement in maximizing learning opportunities.

Designing classrooms that provide optimal academic and behavioral support for a diversity of students can be daunting for teachers. The ultimate goal for both students and teachers is creating a safe learning environment where students can construct knowledge in an engaging and positive classroom climate of learning.

No one of these theories will work for every classroom, and a good approach is to incorporate a range of learning styles in a classroom. Still, under the guidance of any theory, good educators will differentiate their instructional practices to meet the needs of their students' abilities and interests in reading using various instructional practices.

Teachers and reading specialists need to know how to diagnose children with dyslexia as early as possible so that those children can get the help they need at an early age. Since this condition does not come to light until children come to school, it is the teacher that refers them to other professionals. Based on research on dyslexia, teachers now know that children with the following characteristics need to be assessed to determine whether or not they have this learning disability:

- There is a noticeable difference between the child's intelligence and ability to read and write
- There is a family history of learning disabilities
- The child has difficulty learning to spell
- There is confusion between left and right
- The child writes numbers and/or letters backwards

- The child has difficulty following directions with 2 or 3 steps

For children experiencing difficulties in reading, it is important for teachers to accentuate the positive and praise even the smallest advances. Because these children learn differently, they may not complete assignments exactly according to the instructions. Teachers should select the aspects that are correct and really stress these while explaining where other problems lie. These students need longer than others to complete the work. By looking at the work on regular intervals and guiding the students as to where they should go next, teachers can help influence the students' sense of self-esteem and experiences with success.

Teachers need to be exceptionally understanding. Patience is the key when dealing with these students because they often appear to be slow and unmotivated when it is the disability that is at fault. Holding frequent meetings with the students, discussing areas of improvement, and establishing goals keeps the students focused and on track.

Skill 12.6   Uses assessment results to design age-appropriate instruction that promotes reading skills and strategies by building on strengths and addressing needs of students with reading difficulties, dyslexia, and reading disabilities

The information contained within student records, teacher observations, and diagnostic tests are only as valuable as teachers' ability to understand it. Although the students' cumulative records will contain this information, it is the responsibility of teachers to read and interpret the information. Diagnostic test results are somewhat uniform and easy to interpret. They usually include a scoring guide that tells teachers what the numbers actually mean. Teachers also need to realize that these number scores leave room for uncontrollable factors and are not the ultimate indicator of children's ability or learning needs. Many factors influence these scores, including the rapport the children had with testers, how they were feeling when the test was administered, and how they regarded the value or importance of the test. Therefore, teachers should regard these scores as "ball park" figures.

When teachers read other teachers' observations, it is important to keep in mind that people bring to an observation certain biases. Readers may also influence the information contained within an observation with their own interpretations. When using teacher observations as a basis for designing learning programs, it is necessary to be aware of these shortcomings.

Student records may provide the most assistance in guiding instruction. These records contain information that was gathered over a period of time and may show student growth and progress. They also contain information provided by several people including teachers, parents, and other educational professionals. By reading this compilation of information, teachers may get a more accurate impression of a student needs. All of this information is only a stepping-stone in determining how children learn, what they know, and what they need to know to further their education.

There are many ways to evaluate children's knowledge and assess their learning needs. In recent years, the emphasis has shifted from mastery testing of isolated skills to authentic assessments of what children know. Authentic assessments allow teachers to know more precisely what each individual student knows, can do, and needs to do. Authentic assessments can work for both students and teachers in becoming more responsible for learning.

One of the simplest, most efficient ways for teachers to get to know their students is to conduct an entry survey. This is a record that provides useful background information about the students as they enter a class or school. Collecting information through an entry survey will give valuable insights into student background knowledge and experience. Teachers can customize entry surveys according to the type of information considered valuable. Some of the information that may be incorporated include student's name and age, family members, health factors, special interests, strengths, needs, fears, parent expectations, languages spoken in the home, what the child likes about school, and etc.

At the beginning of each school term, teachers will likely feel compelled to conduct some informal evaluations in order to obtain a general awareness of their students. These informal evaluations should be the result of a learning activity rather than a test and may include classroom observations, collections of reading and writing samples, and notations about the students' cognitive abilities as demonstrated by classroom discussions and participation including the students' command of language. The value of these informal evaluations cannot be underestimated. These evaluations, if utilized effectively, will drive instruction and facilitate learning.

After initial informal evaluations have been conducted and appropriate instruction follows, teachers will need to fine tune individual evaluations in order to provide optimum learning experiences. Some of the same types of evaluations can be used on an ongoing basis to determine individual learning needs as were used to determine initial general learning needs. It is somewhat more difficult to choose an appropriate evaluation instrument for elementary-aged students than for older students. Therefore, teachers must be mindful of developmentally-appropriate instruments. At the same time, teachers must be cognizant of the information that they wish to attain from a specific evaluation instrument. Ultimately, these two factors—students' developmental stage and the information to be derived—will determine which type of evaluation will be most appropriate and valuable. There are few commercially designed assessment tools that will prove to be as effective as the tool that is constructed by the teacher.

Students need to be surrounded by good literature appropriate to the various reading levels of the students. Students who are fluent readers will need more challenging reading materials, and students who have not yet mastered the decoding skills will need easier reading materials. It is important that all students are reading at a level where they can experience success and expand their reading knowledge at the same time.

In order for reading instruction to be effective, students must be monitored with frequent evaluation. A good rule of thumb to remember is that if students cannot automatically recognize 95% of the words in a text, then it is too hard for them. Frequent conferencing and listening to the students read are important techniques for teachers to employ.

When working with small groups, students should be allowed to progress at their own rate. Too often teachers are too concerned with making sure they cover the curriculum to slow down and wait for students. As a result, students get lost in the shuffle. Groups should change as students progress so that they can also see improvement in their reading.

While students should be allowed to choose their own books, they could be reading significantly above or below their reading level. It does take considerable effort on the part of teachers to keep the students in the right range of books. If students are continually reading easy books, they do not get the exposure they need to challenging vocabulary. Teachers should use a uniform standard for determining the reading level of books, such as that proposed by Fountas and Pinnell. By using running records on a regular basis, teachers can determine when students can move on to the next level.

Skill 12.7   Applies strategies for collaborating with teachers, specialists, parents/guardians, students, and administrators to promote literacy for individual students with reading difficulties, dyslexia, and reading disabilities

A positive self-concept for children is a very important element in terms of students' ability to learn and to be integral members of society. If students think poorly of themselves or have sustained feelings of inferiority, they probably will not be able to optimize their potentials for learning. It is, therefore, part of teaching to ensure that students develop a positive self-concept.

A positive self-concept does not imply feelings of superiority, perfection, or unjustified competence/efficacy. Instead, a positive self-concept involves self-acceptance as a person, self-appreciation, and self-respect. Teachers who encourage these factors have contributed to the development of a positive self-concept in students.

Teachers may take a number of approaches to enhancement of self-concept among students. One such scheme is the process approach, which proposes a three-phase model for teaching. This model includes a sensing function, a transforming function, and an acting function. These three factors can be simplified into the words by which the model is usually given: reach, touch, and teach. The sensing, or perceptual, function incorporates information or stimuli in an intuitive manner. The transforming function conceptualizes, abstracts, evaluates, and provides meaning and value to perceived information. The acting function chooses actions from several different alternatives to be set forth overtly. The process model may be applied to almost any curricular field.

An approach that aims directly at the enhancement of self concept is designated Invitational Education. According to this approach, teachers and their behaviors may be inviting or disinviting. Inviting behaviors enhance self-concept among students, while disinviting behaviors diminish self-concept.
Disinviting behaviors include those that demean students and those that may be chauvinistic, sexist, condescending, thoughtless, or insensitive. Inviting behaviors are the opposite of these and characterize teachers who act with consistency and sensitivity. Inviting teacher behaviors reflect an attitude of "doing with" rather than "doing to." Students are "invited" or "disinvited" depending on these teacher behaviors.

Invitational teachers exhibit the following skills (Biehler and Snowman, 394):

   a. reaching each student (e.g., learning names, having one-to-one contact)
   b. listening with care (e.g., picking up subtle cues)
   c. being real with students (e.g., providing only realistic praise, "coming on straight")
   d. being real with oneself (e.g., honestly appraising your own feelings and disappointments)
   e. inviting good discipline (e.g., showing students you have respect in personal ways)
   f. handling rejection (e.g., not taking lack of student response in personal ways)
   g. inviting oneself (e.g., thinking positively about oneself)

Cooperative learning situations, as practiced in today's classrooms, grew out of searches conducted by several groups in the early 1970's. Cooperative learning situations can range from very formal applications such as STAD (Student Teams-Achievement Divisions) and CIRC (Cooperative Integrated Reading and Composition) to less formal groupings known variously as "group investigation," "learning together," "discovery groups." Cooperative learning as a general term is now firmly recognized and established as a teaching and learning technique in American schools.

Since cooperative learning techniques are so widely diffused in the schools, it is necessary to orient students in the skills by which cooperative learning groups can operate smoothly, and thereby enhance learning. Students who cannot interact constructively with other students will not be able to take advantage of the learning opportunities provided by the cooperative learning situations and will furthermore deprive their fellow students of the opportunity for cooperative learning.

These skills form the hierarchy of cooperation in which students first learn to work together as a group so that they may then proceed to levels at which they may engage in simulated-conflict situations. This cooperative setting allows different points of view to be constructively entertained.

Effective teaching and learning for students begins with teachers who can demonstrate sensitivity for diversity in teaching and relationships within school communities. Student portfolios include work that has a multicultural perspective and inclusion where students share cultural and ethnic life experiences in their learning. Teachers are responsive to including cultural and diverse resources in their curriculum and instructional practices.

Exposing students to culturally-sensitive room decorations and posters that show positive and inclusive messages is one way to demonstrate inclusion of multiple cultures. Teachers should also continuously make cultural connections that are relevant and empowering for all students and communicate academic and behavioral expectations. Cultural sensitivity is communicated beyond the classroom with parents and community members to establish and maintain relationships.

Diversity can be further defined as the following:

- Differences among learners, classroom settings and academic outcomes
- Biological, sociological, ethnicity, socioeconomic status psychological needs, learning modalities and styles among learners
- Differences in classroom settings that promote learning opportunities such as collaborative, participatory, and individualized learning groupings
- Expected learning outcomes that are theoretical, affective, and cognitive for students

Teachers establish a classroom climate that is culturally respectful and engaging for students. In a culturally sensitive classroom, teachers maintain equity and fairness in student interactions and curriculum implementation. Assessments include cultural responses and perspectives that become further learning opportunities for students. The Florida Teacher Standard Code 6A-5.065 shown below further exemplifies the importance of diversity in the classroom.

The effective teacher is cognizant of students' individual learning styles and human growth and development theory and applies these principles in the selection and implementation of appropriate instructional activities. In regards to the identification and implementation of appropriate learning activities, effective teachers select and implement instructional activities consistent with principles of human growth and development theory.

Learning activities selected for younger students (below age eight) should focus on short time frames in highly simplified form. The nature of the activity and the content in which the activity is presented affects the approach that the students will take in processing the information. Younger children tend to process information at a slower rate than older children (age eight and older).

On the other hand, when selecting and implementing learning activities for older children, teachers should focus on more complex ideas as older students are capable of understanding more complex instructional activities. Moreover, effective teachers maintain a clear understanding of the developmental appropriateness of activities selected for providing educational instructions to students and select and present these activities in a manner consistent with the level of readiness of their students.

Effective teachers take care as to select appropriate activities and classroom situations in which learning is optimized. Classroom teachers should manipulate instructional activities and classroom conditions in a manner that enhances group and individual learning opportunities. For example, classroom teachers can organize group learning activities in which students are placed in a situation in which cooperation, sharing ideas, and discussion occurs. Cooperative learning activities can assist students in learning to collaborate and share personal and cultural ideas and values in a classroom learning environment.

Effective teachers select learning activities based on specific learning objectives. Ideally, teachers should not plan activities that fail to augment the specific objectives of the lesson. Learning activities should be planned with a learning objective in mind. Objective-driven learning activities tend to serve as a tool to reinforce teachers' lesson presentation. Additionally, selected learning objectives should be consistent with state and district educational goals that focus on National educational goals (Goals 2000) and the specific strengths and weaknesses of individual students assigned to the class.

Effective teachers plan their learning activities so as to introduce them in a meaningful instructional sequence. Teachers should combine instructional activities so as to reinforce information by providing students with relevant learning experiences through instructional activities.

The major questions for parents in understanding student performance, criterion-referenced data assessment are, "Are students learning?" and "How well are students learning?" Providing parents with a collection of student learning assessment data related to student achievement and performance is a quantifiable response to the questions. The National Study of School Evaluation (NSSE) 1997 research on School Improvement: Focusing on Student performance adds the following additional questions for parent focus on student learning outcomes:

- What are the types of assessments of student learning that are used in the school?
- What do the results of the data assessments indicate about the current levels of student learning performance? About future predictions? What were the learning objectives and goals?
- What are the strengths and limitations in student learning and achievement?
- How prepared are students for further education or promotion to the next level of education?
- What are the trends seen in student learning in various subject areas or overall academic learning?

At each grade level, the same testing format and scoring is used for subject areas tested in Reading, Mathematics, Science and Writing. The scale scores range from 100-500 points.

Developmental scores noting the annual progress of students are also given with the actual student scores on each section of the testing process. The developmental scores are given from grade to grade level and range from 86 to 3008, so a student taking the test as a 10th grader in 2006 would have a developmental score of 2006. The range of testing scores includes the following:

- High range: 400-500
- Middle range: 325-399
- Low range: 130-324

Students who received scores in the high range in each testing subject area can receive Certificates of Achievement that demonstrate outstanding or notable performances on the Florida Sunshine State Standards. At each grade level of the FCAT, the topic areas are the same, so for example in Science, the tested areas would be:

- Physical and Chemical Science
- Earth and Space Sciences
- Life and Environmental Sciences
- Scientific Thinking

Providing parents with opportunities to attend in-service workshops on data discussions with teachers and administrators creates additional opportunity for parents to ask questions and become actively involved in monitoring their students' educational progress. With state assessments, parents should look for the words "passed" or "met/exceeded standards" in interpreting the numerical that data on student reports. Parents who maintain an active involvement in their students' education will attend school opportunities to promote their understanding of academic and educational achievement for students.

Other artifacts that could reflect teacher/student sensitivity to diversity might consist of the following:

- Student portfolios reflecting multicultural/multi-ethnic perspectives
- Journals and reflections from field trips/ guest speakers from diverse cultural backgrounds
- Printed materials and wall displays from multicultural perspectives
- Parent/guardian letters in a variety of languages reflecting cultural diversity
- Projects that include cultural history and diverse inclusions
- Disaggregated student data reflecting cultural groups
- Classroom climate of professionalism fosters diversity and cultural inclusion

The target of diversity allows teachers a variety of opportunities to expand their experiences with students, staff, community members, and parents from culturally-diverse backgrounds, so that their experiences can be proactively applied in promoting cultural diversity inclusion in the classroom. Teachers are able to engage and challenge students to develop and incorporate their own diversity skills in building character and relationships with cultures beyond their own. In changing the thinking patterns of students to become more cultural-inclusive in the 21st century, teachers are addressing the globalization of our world.

The home and community play an important part in the reading development of children. "It takes a village to raise a child" is an old adage that has great ramifications for a successful school. At the beginning of the year, teachers should hold an information session for parents explaining how they can help their children at home. Some of the suggestions teachers can use include:

- Having children write out the grocery list
- Writing "Thank You" cards or letters for gifts
- Writing notes to the child
- Reading to children at home
- Listening to children reading
- Discussing what they learned at school
- Reading the newspaper

People from the community can become active volunteers in school working with small groups of children – reading to them and listening to them read. They can also help the children in the writing groups by working with them when they are publishing their stories or teaching them to do crafts.

Quite often, the only communication between the school and parents takes the form of end of term reports and parent-teacher interviews. Parents are often reluctant to come to the school because they feel that the teachers are more knowledgeable than they are. In order to have good literacy communication between the school and parents, teachers and reading specialists can employ different techniques. These include:

- Holding a curriculum night during the first two weeks of school. At this time, teachers can explain how the children will be taught and the textbooks and materials that will be used.
- Having an open door policy where parents can feel free to come into the classroom and observe what is happening.
- Telephoning or emailing the parents on a regular basis. Parents dread getting a call from teachers because it usually means that their children have been in trouble or are experiencing problems in school. When you make these phone calls to report progress, parents become allies in helping their children at home.
- Notes to parents in the child's agenda are also helpful in keeping parents informed about how to help at home and about how well their children are doing.
- Inviting parents or members of the community into the classroom to help with literacy centers gives those outside the school a chance to experience what is happening in the classroom. This could be listening to children read, helping them revise and edit writing or even helping them choose books to take home.

Skill 12.8   Knows how to monitor and evaluate the effectiveness of an intervention and how to determine when additional or alternative interventions are appropriate

See Skill 12.6

DOMAIN IV.   PROFESSIONAL KNOWLEDGE AND LEADERSHIP

COMPETENCY 13.0 THEORETICAL FOUNDATIONS AND RESEARCH-BASED CURRICULUM

Skill 13.1   Demonstrates knowledge of major theories of language acquisition, reading, cognition, and learning (e.g., behaviorism, cognitive theory, constructivism, transactional theory) and how they relate to approaches and practices in literacy instruction

See Skill 6.1

Skill 13.2   Analyzes the impact of physical, perceptual, emotional, social, cultural, linguistic, environmental, and intellectual factors on learning, language development, and reading competence

See Skill 12.7

Skill 13.3   Demonstrates knowledge of the significance of the interactions among the reader, the text, and the content of the reading situation

See Skill 10.11

Skill 13.4   Knows the role of societal trends and technological innovations in shaping literacy needs (e.g., Internet, reading electronic texts)

With a surplus of educational software on the market, it is important for educators to be able to evaluate programs before purchasing them. Software can vary greatly in content, presentation, skill level, and objectives; and it is not always possible to believe everything that is advertised on the package. If teachers are in the position of having to purchase a computer program for use in the classroom without any prior knowledge of the program itself, it is useful to have some guidelines to follow.   Once a program has been purchased and the shrink-wrap has been removed, many vendors are reluctant to allow its return because of a possible violation of copyright laws or damage to the software medium. For this reason, it is important to preview the software personally before buying it. If a vendor is reluctant to allow teachers to preview a program prior to its purchase, it is sometimes possible to get a preview copy from the publisher.

Many school districts have addressed this problem by publishing a list of approved software titles for each grade level in much the same way that they publish lists of approved text books and other classroom materials. In addition, most districts have developed a software evaluation form to be used by any instructors involved in the purchase of software that is not already on the "approved" list. Use of a software evaluation form can eliminate a lot of the risk involved when shopping for appropriate titles for the classroom. In many districts, all software is evaluated by the actual instructors who will use the software, and the completed evaluation forms are made available for the perusal of other prospective buyers.

The first thing that must be considered before purchasing software is its compatibility with the computer on which it is to be used. If the program will not run efficiently on the computer in the classroom because of hardware limitations, there is no need to continue the evaluation process. Some of the restrictions to consider are the operating system (MS-DOS, Windows, or MacIntosh) for which the particular software package was developed, the recommended memory size, the required hard drive space, the medium type (floppy disk or CD-ROM), the type of monitor, and the need for any special input devices such as a mouse, joystick, or speech card. If a network is used in the classroom or school for which the program is to be purchased, it is also important to know if the program is networkable. Often, programs with a lot of graphics encounter difficulties when accessed from a network.

There are three general steps to follow when evaluating a software program. First, one must read the instructions thoroughly to familiarize oneself with the program, its hardware requirements, and its installation.

Once the program is installed and ready to run, the evaluator should first run the program as it would be run by successful students--without deliberate errors, but making use of all the possibilities available to the student. Thirdly, the program should be run making deliberate mistakes to test the handling of errors. One should try to make as many different kinds of mistakes as possible, including those for incorrect keyboard usage and testing the validity of user directions.

Most software evaluation forms include the same types of information. There is usually a section for a general description of the program, consisting of the intended grade level, additional support materials available, the type of program (game, simulation, drill, etc), stated goals and objectives, and the clarity of instructions. Other sections will provide checklists for educational content, presentation, and type and quality of user interaction with the program. Once a software package has been thoroughly tested, teachers will be able to make intelligent decisions regarding purchase.

When dealing with large class sizes and at the same time trying to offer opportunities for students to use computers, it is often necessary to use a lot of ingenuity. If the number of computers available for student use is limited, the teacher must take a tip from elementary school teachers who are skilled at managing centers. Students can be rotated singly or in small groups to the computer centers as long as they are well oriented in advance to the task to be accomplished and with the rules to be observed. Rules for using the computer should be emphasized with the whole class prior to individual computer usage in advance and then prominently posted.

If a computer lab is available for use by the curriculum teacher, the problem of how to give each student the opportunity to use the computer as an educational tool might be alleviated, but a whole new set of problems must be dealt with. Again the rules to be observed in the computer lab should be discussed before the class ever enters the lab, and students should have a thorough understanding of the assignment. When a large group of students is visiting a computer lab, it is very easy for the expensive hardware to suffer from accidental or deliberate harm if the teacher is not aware of what is going on at all times. Students need to be aware of the consequences for not following the rules because it is so tempting to experiment and show off to their peers.

Unfortunately, students who have access to computers outside of school often feel like they know everything already and are reluctant to listen to instruction on lab etiquette or program usage. The teacher must be constantly on guard to prevent physical damage to the machines from foreign objects finding their way into disk drives, key caps from disappearing from keyboards (or being rearranged), or stray pencil or pen marks from appearing on computer systems. Experienced students also get a lot of enjoyment from saving games on hard drives, moving files into new directories or eliminating them altogether, creating passwords to prevent others from using machines, etc.

At the same time, the other students need a lot of assistance to prevent accidents caused by their inexperience. It is possible to pair inexperienced students with more capable ones to alleviate some of the problem. Teachers must constantly rotate around the room, and students must be prepared before their arrival in the lab so that they know exactly what to do when they get there to prevent them from exercising their creativity.

Literacy practices have expanded in an attempt to respond to the technological advances in society. As a result of these advances, there are different sorts of literacy practices to use than existed two decades ago. Word processing, web searches, scanning documents, and even cutting and pasting relevant information are all skills that today's students need to learn.

Teachers should incorporate technology into their literacy instruction. Some of the ways they can do this include:

- Use the Internet for online learning and as a source for instruction
- Teach students how to navigate the web
- Encourage students to use the Internet as a way of supporting their research and writing
- Teach students how to make use of all the features of word processing when they are writing
- Showing students how to share pieces of writing with students from other schools in the local region and from other parts of the country
- Encourage the use of email for students to communicate with students from all over the world
- Use CD-Roms, videos and films in literacy so that students can access different types of information
- Use books on tape

Skill 13.5 Applies knowledge of convergent research on reading and literacy instruction for all students, and identifies sources for locating information about convergent research on reading and literacy instruction

Educational journals are full of literacy research. These are often available at the school if the district has a subscription. As the reading specialist you should have a subscription to these, which include:
- The Reading Teacher
- Educational Leadership
- Adolescent Learning

In addition, experts are writing about the findings of research into literacy and there are many published books on the subject. Consider the writings of:
- Marie Clay
- Donald Graves
- Regi Routman
- Susan Taberski

Participating in professional organizations that promote literacy will put teachers in touch with experts in the field and give them resources that they can draw upon to help them in their classrooms. Such participation offers teachers the opportunities to work with these professionals and to hear speakers on all aspects of literacy. They can gain valuable information and tips for dealing with the various issues that arise in their classrooms and provide them with a sounding board for ideas they would like to try out.

Many of the methods teachers try in the classroom turn out to be exceptional ways of promoting literacy. By writing about them, they can get a chance to give advice to other teachers and often they are invited to speak at conventions about their findings.

It is imperative one keeps up on the current research validated methods for working in the field of reading. This can be best done through membership to professional organizations such as International Reading Association (IRA) or the National Reading Conference (NRC). Joining these or other similar organizations will help the professional stay current with methodologies and provide appropriate literature and other publications for review.

Technology and the availability of the Internet also provide staff with materials and strategies to help keep abreast of the issues and current literature in the field of reading. Online journals, search engines, study groups, and chat groups can be integral to ongoing professional development. Coursework at the graduate level will also help educators continue to build their understandings, as does mentoring and collaborative teaching. In fact, finding an experienced mentor in the same field can provide more information as to roles, issues and current topics in the field of reading than a variety of other sources.

Other specific skills in reading, such as Reading Recovery©, require additional training specifically in their program. These types of programs usually have a rigorous, ongoing professional development plan that require numerous hours over years.

It is important to seek out conferences and workshops specifically designed for reading specialists because districts typically provide inservices to the majority of their populations, which would be regular education teachers, often overlooking the lower-incidence employees. Sometimes, therefore, the standard professional development of the district will not pertain to this area of expertise. Other times, reading specialists may be asked to provide inservices to groups of teachers.

Having a professional development plan can be an integral component of staying current. In this plan, reading teachers look ahead down the road at what skills they would like to attain and then develop a plan over the years to help achieve these goals. Looking into the future as an educator and having a set plan for what goals and objectives to achieve helps tremendously in implementing the current research.

As with any educational profession, thinking of yourself as an appropriate role model for your students is paramount. Appropriate ethics and demonstration regularly of those ethics are key components of professionalism.

Today, teachers are immediately faced with the challenge of deciding whether they believe that the classroom should be run as teacher-centered or student-centered. While the most probable answer is that an appropriate combination of both is preferred, most teachers must negotiate which areas of their instruction should be teacher-centered and which areas should be student-centered. Teacher-centered classrooms generally focus on the concept that knowledge is objective and that students must learn new information through the transmission of that knowledge from the teacher. Student-centered classrooms are considered to be "constructivist," in that students are given opportunities to construct their own meanings to new pieces of knowledge. Doing so may require that students are more actively involved in the learning process. Indeed, constructivism is a strong force in teaching today, but it does get misinterpreted a lot. Good constructivist teachers do NOT just let their students explore anything they want in any way they choose; rather they give students opportunities to learn things in more natural ways, such as experiments, hands-on projects, discussion, etc.

For quite some time, a movement called "multiple intelligences" was popular in many classrooms. This theory suggested that there are at least seven different types of intelligence, and that verbal and quantitative intelligences, the two types that are most often associated with intellect, should be re-considered as less important as they once were. Other intelligences included kinesthetic, inter-personal, musical, intra-personal, and spatial. This theory helped teachers understand that while some students may not be expert in one style of learning, it is entirely possible that they are incredibly gifted in another.

Various subject areas have added to philosophical debates of teaching. For example, reading teachers have long debated whether phonics or whole language was more appropriate as an instructional methodology. Language arts teachers have debated the importance of the canon (famous works of literature); some teachers feel that the canon is irrelevant and that the only reason to teach literature is to teach thinking skills and an appreciation of good literature. Math teachers have debated the extent to which application is necessary in math instruction; some feel that it is more important to teach structure and process, while others feel it is only important to teach math skills in context.

Skill 13.6 Applies knowledge of the foundations of basic research design, methodology, and application to critically review research on reading and to select research findings for the purpose of improving reading instruction

See Skill 10.3

Skill 13.7   Knows how to prepare written documentation of literacy assessment data, analysis of instructional needs, and accommodations for instruction

A written documentation of literary assessment data for each student is called an Individual Educational Plan. Teachers take a look at all the literacy assessment the students have had over the years and writes them from the earliest to the most recent. Then teachers list the strengths in literacy and the areas of weakness. Teachers work with the students and the parents to set at least three goals for the school year. These goals must be specific in that they are measurable so that everyone involved will know when or if they have been achieved. The goals must be ones that the students can achieve in small steps. The plan must also detail how the instruction will be delivered- whether it will be in the classroom with generalist teachers, with the aid of assistants, or in a one-to-one setting with reading specialists.

Once the plan is written, teachers and reading specialists schedule a meeting with all the stakeholders to review the plan and sign it. The parents attend these meetings along with the children and, in the case of older students, the students also sign the plan.

COMPETENCY 14.0 COLLABORATION, COMMUNICATION, AND PROFESSIONAL DEVELOPMENT

Skill 14.1   Demonstrates knowledge of how to use leadership, communication, and facilitation skills and strategies to effect positive changes in the school reading program and literacy instruction

Reading specialists, administrators and teachers should take a critical look at the policies in place within the school for meeting the reading needs of all students. Part of this should include a school-wide reading initiative such as 15 minutes of silent reading in every classroom every day. During this time, teachers can be reading as a model for the students or can be conferencing with individual students about what they are reading. This can take the form of listening to students read or asking them questions to ensure they comprehend what they are reading.

Guided Reading materials should be in place in every classroom with books at the students' reading levels. Teachers or reading specialists can work with small groups of students on a particular reading strategy and provide them with the opportunity to practice the strategy.

Students from grades 1 to 6 can also participate in a weekly rotation where they work with students of the same reading ability. Within this group, students can work on projects related to the reading material, engage in writing activities, or craft products demonstrating comprehension.

Literacy centers in the classroom allow students to work on different projects, as does a Reading/Writing workshop. Conferencing with students on a regular basis helps to ensure that students are understanding what they are reading as well as employing various strategies to help them become fluent readers

The standards mandated by the state should be the beginning point for any instructional design. These are what the students need to know in order to progress to the next level or grade. The curriculum guide is the Bible of teaching – not the textbook or reading program. The standards should be communicated to students in words they understand so that they know exactly what they have to learn. By employing "assessment for learning," teachers can assess the students before instruction to find out exactly where their deficiencies lie and gear the instruction toward them.

When planning for instruction, teachers should begin with the end in mind. This may mean deconstructing the outcomes to make them more manageable. Assessment should also be in the forefront – for example, ask yourself what students will have to do to demonstrate they have achieved the objective of the lesson. Once you know what you want students to do, then you can plan accordingly

Skill 14.2   Demonstrates knowledge of principles, guidelines, and professional ethical standards related to collegial and professional collaborations, and applies skills and procedures for facilitating effective interactions among groups and individuals to improve literacy instruction for all students

Whenever teachers are dealing with colleagues, parents, or other professionals, the main goal is to improve the literacy instruction for the students. They should approach all communication with a sense of professionalism and employ the following:
- Patience
- Respect for the views of others
- A sense of openness to new ideas
- Confidentiality in not revealing any information that is to be kept private

Skill 14.3   Knows how to communicate research findings and make recommendations based on a convergence of research evidence to colleagues and the wider community

See Skill 9.10

Skill 14.4   Knows how to communicate local data and information related to literacy issues and, when appropriate, make recommendations to district staff and community stakeholders

Any assessment done on students must be documented and samples kept so that the parents and other teachers can understand what you mean. Communicating the findings of assessment is not something that has to wait for parent-teacher interviews or the report card. It is something that teachers should report to parents on a regular basis, such as in monthly notes or telephone calls, arranged meetings, or even simple chats.

Guidance and speech counselors should communicate the results of assessments to teachers and parents as soon as possible after the testing is completed. In many districts, this is called a debriefing and takes the form of an arranged meeting. In this meeting, counselors discuss the findings and make suggestions as to how best meet the needs of children.

Skill 14.5   Applies strategies for working with other educators to involve parents/guardians in cooperative efforts to support students' reading and writing development

Although working with parents/guardians may be challenging in some situations, they do need to be included in literacy initiatives. Once parents know the ideas teachers have for helping the children, they will be more than happy to become involved. Parents are the child's first teachers and often need to be instructed in how to help the child at home with reading. Some parents are not aware of the importance of reading to children from an early age, so schools should take the initiative in encouraging and broadening parents' experience with reading to their children.

Parents need to know how children learn language instead of just taking it for granted or leaving it to the school to take over the instruction. Teachers need to constantly keep in touch with parents through interviews, conversations, reports, and cooperative projects. They also need to inform the parents about the strategies they use in the classroom so that when parents see their children reading silently or aloud or editing and revising their writing, they have some idea of how to help them at home.

Encourage parents to read with or to their children on a daily basis. Bringing parents into the school as volunteers, especially in the library, helps them know the types of books appropriate for different age groups. Parents can also assist in the classroom helping children with reading difficulties, and they can help in writing questionnaires and analyzing the results of the testing teachers do with their children.

Skill 14.6   Knows how to use local data to identify and prioritize professional development needs and provide sound professional development experiences that address the needs of participants, are sensitive to school constraints (e.g., class size, limited resources), and use multiple indicators to monitor and evaluate the effectiveness

Literacy programs are most effective in schools where the whole teaching staff shares the same philosophy of literacy learning. In order to create a culture of change, there must be a community of teachers committed to literacy improvement. This involves making changes in classroom routines, scheduling, and roles and responsibilities.

There are a number of ways to initiate a whole-school approach to literacy:

- Review all literacy programs in the school to make sure that all the teachers have the same approach to planning, assessment and professional development
- Teachers should be encouraged and given time to reflect upon their instruction and the ways they monitor, track, and report student improvements
- Preparation time must be sufficient for teachers to be able to get together to plan for instruction
- There should be the same amount of time devoted to literacy in all classes
- Literacy classroom should include time for reading aloud, silent reading, reading conferences, book talks, guided and independent writing, and mini-lessons on skills and concepts
- Assistance for at-risk students should be provided wherever it is needed
- Classrooms should be organized for flexible groupings

Skill 14.7   Demonstrates knowledge of strategies for facilitating positive change in instructional practices through professional development and for working with other educators to initiate, implement, and evaluate professional development and its impact on instructional practice

Professional development does not mean teachers attending meetings where they hear speakers talking about various aspects of literacy development and improvement. Collaborative networks of teachers across grade levels or content areas help teachers from different schools get together to draw on one another experiences and to plan for improvement. These could involve weekly meetings with a lead teacher where the group shares ideas and asks for specific kinds of help.

Resource teachers are a great source of information for professional development as they have the expertise needed to help teachers in the classroom. These experts can provide the reading material teachers need or can even come into the classroom to help out.

District consultants are specialists in specific areas of the curriculum. They are also a wealth of information and can provide inservices on a school- or district-wide basis. There are also many private consultants who have a high level of expertise because they deal with different schools and even different school districts. Many of these people work for educational publishers and have access to new materials. They can organize many different professional development events for teachers.

Skill 14.8   **Applies knowledge of procedures for effectively mentoring and coaching educators to promote the successful implementation and sustained application of instructional practices addressed in professional development**

See Skill 14.6.

Skill 14.9   **Knows how to expand knowledge of literacy through a variety of professional activities (e.g., reading professional publications, participating in conferences) and recognizes the value of participating in local, state, national, and international professional organizations whose mission is the improvement of literacy**

See Skill 14.5

GLOSSARY

These definitions are critical for success on all multiple choice questions on the examinations. Proper use of these terms, is crucial for success in tackling a constructed response involving balanced literacy.

ABILITY GROUPING- grouping of children with similar needs for instructional purposes. Ability groups do not remain constant throughout the year, but change as the children's needs within them change.

ALLITERATION- occurs when words begin with the same consonant sound, as in *Peter Piper picked a pair of pickled peppers.*

ALPHABETIC PRINCIPLE- the idea that written spellings represent spoken words.

ANCHOR BOOK- a balanced literacy term for a book that is purposely read repeatedly and used as part of both the reading and writing workshop.

It is a good idea to use certain books that become the children's familiar and cherished favorites for both reading and then to inspire children's writing.

ASSONANCE- Occurs when words begin with the same vowel sound.

AUTHENTIC ASSESSMENT- assessment activities which reflect the actual workplace, family community and school curriculum.

BALANCED LITERACY LESSON FORMAT- The Balanced Literacy Approach has its own specific format for the delivery of the literacy lesson, whether it is a reading or writing workshop lesson. The format begins with a 10-15 minute mini-lesson which the teacher delivers to the whole class. This mini-lesson is then followed by a thirty-minute small group (when the children break into small groups to work) lesson. It concludes with a 10-minute share during which the whole class reconvenes to share what they have done in the small groups.

One can refer to this format as the whole-small-whole group approach.

BENCHMARKS- school state, or nationally mandated statements of the expectations for student learning and achievement in various content areas.

BICS-BASIC INTERPERSONAL COMMUNICATION SKILLS (ELL term-Bilingual Education)- learning second language skills and becoming proficient in a second language through face to face interaction-translation through speaking, listening, and viewing.

BLENDING- the process of hearing separate phonemes and being able to merge them together to read the word.

BOOK FEATURES- children need to be familiar with the following book features: front and back cover, title and half- title page, dedication page, table of contents, prologue and epilogue, and foreword and after notes. For factual books, children need to be familiar with: labels, captions, glossary, index, headings and subheadings of chapters, charts and diagrams, and sidebars.

CHECKLIST- an assessment form which lists targeted learning and social behaviors as indicators of achievement, knowledge or skill. They can be professionally- or teacher-prepared.

CINQUAIN- a five line poem that can be read and then used as a model for writing. Generally line 1 of this format is a single word, line 2 has 2 words, which describe the title of line 1, line 3 is comprised of 3 words which are movement words, line 4 has 4 words which express feeling and line 5 has a single word which is a synonym for line 1's single word.

COMPREHENSION- this occurs when the reader correctly interprets the print on the page and constructs meaning from it. Comprehension depends on activating prior knowledge, cultural and social background of the reader, and the reader's ability to use comprehension monitoring strategies.

CONCEPTS ABOUT PRINT- include: how to handle a books, how to look at print, directionality, sequencing, locating skills, punctuation, and concepts of letters and words.

CONSONANT DIAGRAPHS- two consecutive consonants that represent one new speech sound. In the word "digraph" the *ph* which sounds like /f/ is a digraph.

CONTEXTS- sentences deliberately prepared by the teacher which include sufficient contextual clues for the children to decipher meaning.

CONTEXTUAL REDEFINITION- using context to determine word meaning.

COOPERATIVE READING- Children read with a partner or buddy. It can be silent or oral reading.

CRISSCROSSERS- an ELL term for second language learners who have a positive attitude toward both first language and second language learning. These second language learners, children from ELL backgrounds, are comfortable navigating back and forth between the two languages as they learn.

CUES- as they self monitor their reading comprehensions, readers have to integrate various sources of information or cues to help them construct meaning from text and graphic illustrations.

DECODING-"sounding out" a printed sequence of letters based on knowledge of letter sound correspondences.

DIPHTHONGS- two vowels in one syllable where the two sounds are heard. For instance in the word *house* both the "o" and the "u" are heard.

DIRECTIONALITY-children use their fingers to indicate left to right direction and return sweep to the next line.

DIFFERENTIATED INSTRUCTION- The need for the teacher, based on observation of individual student's work, progress, test results, fluency, and other reading/literacy behaviors, to provide modified instruction and alternative strategies or activities. These activities are specifically developed by the teacher to address the individual student's different needs.

EARLY READERS- recognize most high frequency words and many simple words. They use pictures to confirm meaning. Using meaning, syntax, and phonics, they can figure out most simple words. They use spelling patterns to figure out new words. They are gaining control of reading strategies. They use their own experiences and background knowledge to predict meanings. They occasionally use story language in their writing. This stage follows emergent reading.

EMERGENT READERS- the stage of reading in which the reader understands that print contains a consistent message. The reader can recognize some high frequency words, names, and simple words in context. Pictures can be used to predict meaning. The emergent reader begins to attend to left to right directionality and features of print and may identify some initial sounds and ending sounds in words.

ENCODE- to change a message into symbols. For example, readers encode oral language into writing.

ENGLISH as a SECOND LANGUAGE- a way of teaching English to speakers of other languages using English as the language of instruction.

EXPOSITORY TEXT-. is non-fiction that provides information and facts. This text type is what newspapers, science, mathematics and history texts use. Currently there is much focus, even in elementary schools, on teaching children how to comprehend and author expository texts. They must produce brochures, guides, recipes, and procedural accounts on most elementary grade levels. The teaching of reading of expository texts requires working with a particular vocabulary and concept structure that is very different from that of the narrative text. Therefore time must be taken to teach the reading of expository texts and contrast it with the reading of narrative texts.

FIRST LANGUAGE- an ELL term for the language any child acquires in the first few years of life. It is through this acquired language that the child acquires phonological and phonemic awareness.

FLUENT READERS- identify most words automatically. They can read chapter books with good comprehension. They consistently monitor, cross-check, and self-correct reading. They can offer their own interpretations of text based on personal experiences and prior reading experiences. Fluent readers are capable of reading a variety of genres independently. Furthermore, they can respond to texts or stories by sharing pertinent examples from their lives. They can also readily make connections to other books which they have read. Finally, they are capable of beginning to create spoken and written writings which are in the style of a particular author.

FORMAL ASSESSMENT- a test or an observation of a performance task which is done under controlled and regulated conditions.

FUNCTIONAL READING- the reading of instructions, recipes, coupons, classified ads, notices, signs, and other documents which we have to read and correctly interpret in school and in society.

GRADE EQUIVALENT/GRADE SCORE- a score transformed from a raw score on a standardized test into the equivalent score earned by an average student in the norming group.

GRAPHIC ORGANIZERS- graphic organizers express relationships among various ideas in visual form including: sequence, timelines, character traits, fact and opinion, main idea and details, differences and likenesses. Graphic organizers are particularly helpful for visual learners.

GUIDED READING- one of the key modes of instruction in the balanced literacy theory approach. During guided reading, the teacher "guides" the child through silent reading of a text by giving them prompts, target questions, and even helping the child start an answer to a specific prompt or question. At the end of each guided reading section or excerpt of the text, the child stops to talk with the teacher about the text. By definition, guided reading is an interactive discussion between the child and the teacher. This mode of reading instruction is generally used when children need extra support in constructing meaning because the text is complex or because their current independent reading capacities are still limited.

HIGH FREQUENCY- frequently used words. These words appear many more times than do other words in ordinary reading material. Examples of such words include: *as, in, of,* and *the.* These words are also sometimes called service words. These words are also part of sight vocabulary words. A classic best-known high frequency word list was generated by Dolch (1936).

INDEPENDENT READING- a set period of time within the daily literacy block when children read books with 95%-100% accuracy on their own. This reading of books by themselves which they can understand without teacher support promotes lifelong literacy and love of learning, which enhances reading mileage, builds fluency, and helps children orchestrate integrated cue strategies.

INFORMAL ASSESSMENT- observations of children made under informal conditions; these can include kid watching, checklists, and individual child/teacher conversations.

INFORMAL READING INVENTORY (IRI) - a series of reading excerpts that can be used to determine a child's reading strengths and needs in comprehension and decoding. Many published reading series have an IRI to go with their series.

JUSTIFIED PRINT- the positioning of print on the page so that each line ends either a sentence or a phrase.

KID WATCHING- term used within the balanced literacy approach for the teacher's deliberate, detailed, and recorded observations of individual student and class literacy behaviors., often done during small group work. The teacher then reconfigures lessons on experiences to meet the students' individual and group needs.

KINESTHETIC- learning is tactile; as contrasted with an activity where the learner sits still or attempts to sit still in one place. Cutting and moving syllable or word strips or using sandpaper letters are kinesthetic activities.

LANGUAGE EXPERIENCE- Children giving dictation to the teacher who writes their words on a chart or their drawings. This shows children that words can be written down.

LEARNING LOGS- daily records of what students have learned.

LISTENING POST- sets of headphones attached to a single tape player. Children can go to centers where they listen to audiotapes of books while reading the print book. These posts are in many libraries as well.

LITERATURE CIRCLES- a group discussion involving four to six children who have read the same work of literature (narrative or expository text). They talk about key parts of the work, relate it to their own experience, listen to the responses of others, and discuss how parts of the text relate to the whole.

MANIPULATION- moving around or switching sounds within a word or words within a phrase or sentence.

MEANING VOCABULARY- words whose meanings children understand and can use.

MISCUE- an oral reading error made by a child which differs from the actual printed text.

MISCUE ANALYSIS- the teacher keeps a detailed recording of the errors or inaccurate attempts of a child reader during a reading assessment. These are recorded within a running record. This helps the teacher see whether the cues-syntactic, semantic, or graphophonemic-the child is using are accurate.

MONITORING READING- various strategies that children use to monitor their readings. A sample are maintaining fluency by bringing prior knowledge to the story to make predictions, using these predictions to do further checking, searching, and self-correcting as the story progresses, and using problem-solving word study skills to make links from known words to unknown words.

MORPHEMES- the smallest units of meaning in words. There are two types of morphemes; free morphemes, which can stand alone such as *love,* and bound morphemes, which must be attached to another morpheme to carry meaning such as *ed* in *loved.*

NARRATIVE TEXT- one of the two basic text structures. The narrative text tells or communicates a story. Narrative texts are novels, short stories and plays. Some poems are narratives as well. The narrative text needs to be taught differently than the expository text because of its structure.

ONE TO ONE MATCHING- matching one spoken word with one written word.

ONSET-RIME BLENDING –ONSET-Everything before the vowel and RIME (the vowel and everything after it). For example, the word "sleep" can be broken into /sl/ and /eep/. Word families are build using rimes. The /eep/ word family would include *jeep, keep* and *weep.*

ORTHOGRAPHY- a method of representing spoken language through letters and diacritics.

PERCENTILE- if a child scores at the 56th percentile for his/grade level, his/her score is equal to or above that of 56 percent of the children taking that standardized test and below that of 46 percent of the children on whose scores the test was normed.

PERFORMANCE ASSESSMENT- having children do a task that demonstrates their knowledge, skills and competency. Having children author their own alphabet book on a particular topic would be a performance assessment for knowledge of the alphabet.

PHONEME- The speech sound units that make a difference in meaning. The word "rope" has three phonemes /r/, /o/, and /p/. Change one phoneme, say /r/ to /n/, and you have a different word *nope.*

PHONEMIC AWARENESS- the understanding that words are composed of sounds. Phonemic awareness is a specific type of phonological awareness dealing only with phonemes in a spoken word.

PHONICS- the study of relationships between phonemes (speech sounds) and graphemes (letters) that represent the phonemes. It is also decoding or the sounding out of unknown words. that are written.

PHONOLOGICAL AWARENESS- the ability to recognize the sounds of spoken language and how they can be blended together, segmented, and switched/manipulated to form new combinations and words.

PHONOLOGICAL CUES- readers use their knowledge of letter/sound and sound/letter relationships to predict and confirm reading.

PHONOLOGY- the study of speech structure in language that includes both the patterns of basic speech units (phonemes) and the tacit rules of pronunciation.

PORTFOLIOS- collections of a child's work over time. They include a cover letter, reflections from the child and teacher, and other supportive documents including standards, performance task examples, prompts and sometimes peer comments.

PRIMARY LANGUAGE- (ELL term)- the language an individual is the most fluent in and at ease with. This is usually, but not always the individual's first language.

PROMPTS- when the teacher intervenes in the child's independent reading to help the child pronounce or comprehend a specific word or prompt. On a reading record, the teacher notes the prompt. When the teacher wants to match a child with a particular book or determine the child's stage of reading/level, the teacher does not use prompts.

QUESTION GENERATING STRATEGY FOR AN EXPOSITORY TEXT- first the child previews the text by reading titles, subheads, looking at pictures or illustrations, and reading the first paragraph. Next the child asks a "think" question which he or she records. Then the child reads to find information that might answer the "think" question. The child may write down the information found or think about another question that is answered by what the child is reading. The child continues to read using this strategy.

READING FOR INFORMATION- Reading with the purpose of extracting facts and expert opinion from the text. Children should be introduced to the following information reading resources: web resources that are age and grade appropriate for children, the concept of the table of contents, chapter headings, glossaries, pictures, maps, charts, diagrams and text structures in an information text. They should be taught to use notes, graphs, organizers, and mind maps to share information extracted from a text.

RECODE- To change information from one code into another, as recoding writing into oral speech.

RECOGNITION VOCABULARY- the group of words which children are able to correctly pronounce, read orally and understand on sight.

RECORD OF READING BEHAVIOR – (running record) an objective observation during which the teacher records, using a standard set of symbols, everything the child reader says as the child reads a book selected by the teacher.

REFLECTION- to analyze, discuss, and react to one's learning on any grade or age level.

RETELLING- retelling can be written or oral. Children are expected and encouraged to tell as much of a story as they can remember. Re-telling is far more extensive than just summarizing. Children should include the beginning, middle and end plot lines and should be able to tell about the book's characters.

RUBRIC- a set of guidelines or acceptable responses for the completion of any task. Usually a rubric ranges from 0 to 4 with 4 being the most detailed response and 0 indicating a response to the task which lacked detail or was in other ways insufficient.

SCAFFOLDING- refers to the teacher support necessary for the child to accomplish a task or to achieve a goal which the child could not accomplish on his/her own. Vygotsky termed this window of opportunity the "zone of proximal development." Ultimately as the child becomes more proficient or capable, the scaffold is withdrawn. The goal of scaffolding is to help the child to perform the reading task independently and internalize the behavior. During SHARED READING, the task is scaffolded by the teacher's reading to the children aloud. As the teacher reads, the teacher scaffolds the initial decoding and helps with the meaning making/construction.

SEARCHING- children pause to search in the picture, print, or their memory for known information. This can happen as the child tackles an unknown word or after an error.

SECOND LANGUAGE-(ELL term)-A language acquired or learned simultaneously with or after a child's acquisition of a first language.

SEGMENTING- the process of hearing a spoken word and identifying its separate phonemes or syllables.

SELF-CORRECTION- children begin to correct some of their own reading errors. Generally this behavior is accompanied by the re-reading of the previous phrase or sentence.

SEMANTIC CUES- children use their prior knowledge, sense of the story, and pictures to support their predicting and confirming the meaning of the text.

SEMANTIC WEB- a visual graphic organizer that the teacher can use to introduce a reading on a specific topic. It visually represents many other words associated with a target word. The web can help activate the children's prior knowledge and extend or clarify it. It can also serve to check new learning after guided or independent reading.

SPATIAL LEARNING- Using images, color, or layout to help readers whose learning style is spatial.

STANDARD SCORE- how far a child's grade on a standardized test is from the average score (mean) on the test in terms of the standard deviation. If a child scores 70 on a standardized test and the standard deviation is 5 and the average (mean) score is 65, the child is one standard deviation above the average.

STANDARDIZED TEST- a test given under specified conditions allowing comparisons to be made. A set of norms or average scores on this test will be used for comparisons.

STOP AND THINK STRATEGY- a balanced literacy strategy for constructing meaning. As the text is being read, the child asks himself or herself, does this make sense to me? If it does not make sense to me, I should then try to re-read it or read ahead. I can also look up words that I don't know or ask for help. Generally the teacher models this strategy with the whole class as a mini lesson and then it is posted prominently in the classroom for continued reference by the children.

STRATEGIC READERS- as defined by researchers Marie Clay and Sharon Taberski, strategic readers are self improving and do the following as they read: (A lengthy glossary explanation of this term has been provided because it can appear in a variety of multiple choice questions on the examination as well as part of a constructed response question).

- Monitor their reading to see if it makes sense semantically, syntactically, and visually.
- Look for and use semantic, syntactic, and visual clues.
- Uncover and identify new things about the text.
  Cross check and use one cueing system against another.
- Self-correct their reading when what they first read does not match the semantic, syntactic and visual clues
- Solve for and identify new words using multiple cueing systems

Beyond these behaviors, a strategic or self-improving reader uses many strategies to construct meaning. When their reading experience is going well- they know the words and understand the text or story-they are working continuously (even if they are not conscious of it) at maintaining meaning. If and when the strategic or self-improving reader runs into an unfamiliar word, then the reader has many strategies to identify that word. Becoming a successful strategic reader is a goal that can and should be shared with children as early as the middle of the first grade, although the term "self-improving reader" might be used at that point.

TEXT FEATURES- children need to be alerted to the following text features which may initially appear strange to them. The features of text include: a period which marks the end of a "telling sentence;" a question mark that is at the end of a sentence that asks a question, an exclamation mark used to express surprise or excitement at the end of a sentence, capital letters which begin a sentence, and the names of persons, places, and things; bold italicized or underlined text to highlight key ideas; quotation marks which show dialogue, a hyphen used to break a long word up into its syllables, a dash used to show a break in an idea, or to indicate a parenthetical element or an omission; an ellipse, which shows an omission or break in the text; and a paragraph in nonfiction which shows a new point being made.

TRANSITIONAL READERS- recognize an increasing number of "hard" words that are content related. They can provide summaries of the stories that they read. They are more at ease with handling longer, more complex, connected text with short chapters. Transitional readers can read independent level texts with correct phrasing, expression, and fluency. When they encounter unfamiliar words, they have a variety of strategies to figure out the unfamiliar words. Their reading demonstrates that they are able to integrate meaning, syntax and phonics in a consistent manner so that they can understand the texts they are reading.

VENN DIAGRAM- a diagram consisting of two or three intersecting circles to visually represent similarities and differences for texts, characters and topics. No author study is complete without VENN DIAGRAMS comparing different author's works. This is the most commonly used graphic organizer in elementary schools today. It can be used effectively as part of an answer to a constructed response question.

VISUAL CUES- readers use their knowledge of graphemes to predict and confirm text. The graphemes may be words, syllables or letters.

WORD ANALYSIS- the analysis of words employing letters, phonic structures, contextual clues, or dictionary skills.

WORD IDENTIFICATION- how the reader determines the pronunciation, and the meaning of an unknown word.

WORD RECOGNITION- The process of determining the pronunciation and some degree of the meaning of an unknown word.

WORD WORK- the term that the balanced literacy approach uses for the study of vocabulary.

Directory of Theorists and Researchers

Introduction

Many questions on the teacher certification examinations can only be correctly answered if you know the theorist or the research that is referenced. The teaching of reading owes much to the work, principles and guidelines of teacher educators and university field researchers who have changed the style, methods and practice of teaching reading. While those listed in this directory are by no means all the major researchers (page constraints would make a complete listing impossible), the individuals listed below are those whose contributions are frequently referenced on the certification tests and whose work is evident in today's elementary classroom teaching and learning of reading.

PHONICS CENTERED APPROACH

In 1955 Rudolph Flesch gained national prominence when he publishedx *Why Johnny Can't Read*. This book went on to become a best seller and has now become a classic which is readable and speaks to current concerns. Flesch became the spokesperson for a war that periodically resurfaces in the reading world.

Flesch, Chall (1967) Stahl (1992), Adams (1990), and Johnson and Bauman (1984) believe that a phonics-based approach is crucial for reading success. Flesch and others feel that the balanced literacy advocates are seriously undermining the crucial role that phonics plays in the children's development as successful decoding readers. However, it must be noted that while balanced literacy does emphasize the use of literature based reading programs, it in no way dismisses phonics from its reading program; indeed phonics is included in the crucial "word work" component of the reading and writing workshop.

The phonics advocates point to the fact that most research shows that early and systematic instruction in phonics skills results in superior reading achievement in elementary school and beyond.

Adams (1990) detailed what type of phonics instruction is needed.

To learn to read skillfully, children need practice in seeing and understanding decodable words in real reading situations and with connected text.... phonics instruction {needs to be} part of a reading program that provides ample practice in reading and writing. Encouraging children with connected text can also show them the importance of what they are learning and make the lessons in phonics relevant and sensible. Phonics centered advocates believe that children should begin to learn letter associations in kindergarten with most useful phonics skills being taught by first grade. These basic skills should then be reviewed in second grade and beyond.

Consonant sounds should be taught first, since they are more reliable in their letter-sound associations.

Short vowel sounds appear more frequently in beginning reading materials, so they should be introduced before long vowels. Phonics advocates believe that most beginning readers need to be taught letter sound associations explicitly. Phonics advocates also believe that beginning readers need to read stories that have words to which phonics skills apply. This allows them to practice their phonics skills as they write and spell words. They should also play lots of letter-sound association games.

Phonics advocates claim that when phonics is abandoned reading scores drop and balanced literacy advocates counter with the fact that they have never advocated abandoning the teaching of phonics.

As Jeanne Chall, a professor at Harvard's Graduate School of Education notes: "a beginning reading program that does not give children knowledge and skill in recognizing and decoding words will have poor results."

Theorists and Researchers:

Adams, Marilyn Jager

Noted for her research on early reading, Adams lists five basic types of phonemic awareness tasks which should be covered by the end of first grade. These include: ability to hear rhymes and alliterations, ability to do oddity tasks, ability to orally blend words, ability to orally segment words, ability to do phonemic manipulation tasks.

Clay, Marie M. Marie

A New Zealand born researcher, in the field of special needs emergent literacy and in the development of assessment tools for these children. Her research in this field is felt throughout the Reading Recovery movement and involves the use of her, *Reading Recovery: A Guidebook for Teachers in Training,* in the majority of graduate emergent literacy courses and in many classrooms in the US including those that do not have a Reading Recovery teacher.

Her doctoral thesis focused on what was to become her life's work, emergent reading behavior. At the crux of her research for the dissertation, Clay reviewed and detailed the progress week by week of one hundred children during their first year of school (1966). An important outcome of the dissertation was her development of reliable observation tools for the assessment and analysis of changes over time in children's literacy learning. These assessments are the crux of *An Observation Survey of Early Literacy Achievement* (1993) which is an essential work for the primary school educator. The assessments have been validated and reconstructed for learners from the Spanish, Maori and French languages. A special appendix in this guide includes the *Record of Reading Behavior* tool she created with Kenneth Goodman.

Reading Recovery is a key Clay contribution to the field of foundations of reading teaching. The movement, which is discussed in detail in this section, was born out of the concerns of classroom educators who were upset that even with excellent programs and expert teaching, they were not able to positively influence the literacy progress of some of their young children. Clay posed the question of investigating what would happen if the design and delivery of traditional reading education were changed for these struggling young learners.

The whole thrust of the Reading Recovery movement has been to improve the early identification and instructional delivery for these struggling young readers. Her goal was to develop a system which would bring those children scoring the lowest in assessment measures to the level of the average readers within their classes.

With the support of Barbara Watson and others, the program was developed in three years. The first field tests of the program took place in the late 1970's in Auckland schools. To date, circa 2005, the program is operating in most English speaking countries and has been reconstructed for use in Spanish and French.

Janet S. Gaffey and Billie Askew have said of Marie Clay (l991) that her contribution "has been to change what is possible for individual learners when teaching permits different routes to be taken for desired outcomes."

Reading Recovery has been identified by the International Reading Association as a program that not only teaches children how to read, but also reduces the number of children who are labeled as "learning disabled." It further lowers the number of children who are placed in remedial reading programs and classes.

Clay Reading Recovery lessons are designed to promote accelerated learning so that children can catch up to their peers and continue to learn independently.

The hallmark of the Reading Recovery program is that the Reading Recovery teacher works with one student at a time over a 12 to 20 week period. Each daily 30 minute lesson is tailored to address the needs of the individual student. Therefore Reading Recovery teachers generally teach no more than four or five students per day in individual lessons.

The Clay Observation of Early Childhood Achievement (l993) is used to assess children's strengths and weaknesses. Reading Recovery teachers devote the first ten minutes of their sessions with individual children to assessment as the children engage in reading and writing. A running record of the child's progress is taken every day and is used to plan future lessons.

The lessons themselves include the use of familiar stories. Children engage in assembling and in sequencing cut up stories. They work with letters or write a story. Teaching style involves the teacher demonstrating strategies and the child then developing effective strategies to continue reading independently. Key components of each lesson include: phonemic awareness, phonics, spelling, and comprehension study. Much time is devoted to problem solving so that the children's decoding is purposeful. Children are given time to practice and demonstrate fluency skills.

Ultimately what sets Reading Recovery aside is the fact that it is one-to-one tutoring. This is also what makes it effective for children, and of course, what raises issues about it are costs for the school systems which may want to adopt it. Obviously the districts and education systems have to decide whether they want to pay the costs of this and other individualized tutoring systems now in the primary school years or pay later as these children become adults whose literacy skills are not sufficient for proactive citizenship.

Fountas, Irene C and Gay Su Pinnell

These two researchers have developed a leveling system for reading texts, which arranges them by level of difficulty. Beyond a specific analysis of set titles, the theorists have explained in several published works how to use their leveling system to meet and assess the progress of various readers. They also provide detailed explanations and support for reading teachers of young children K-3 in using reading records and benchmark texts.

They are the key articulators of the balanced literacy model that includes reading and writing workshop. Among their other contributions to the field are: guidelines for creating sets of leveled books, assessment rubrics, strategies for fostering "word solver" skills in child readers, and methods for teaching phonics and spelling in the literacy classroom.

Routman, Regie

Routman's contributions to Reading Foundations are the result of over three decades of experience as an elementary school teacher, a reading specialist, a learning disabilities tutor, a Reading Recovery teacher, a language arts and mentor teacher and a staff developer. Due to these various experiences, her insights into reading resonate with a broad spectrum of school community members.

Routman's works are conversational, teacher to teacher sharings of her daily experiences in classrooms. In her published books on the teaching of reading (i.e. *Reading Essentials*-Heinemann, 2002), Regie shows teachers how to teach consistent with the findings in reading research, yet also with highly practical "scripted lessons" and teaching tips which make the classroom come alive. She advocates literature based teaching and meaning centered approaches for learning.

In addition, she is a strong advocate of using poetry from grades one and beyond as an integral thread for a reading program. She is the author of *Kids' Poems: Teaching Children to Love Writing Poetry* (Scholastic, 2000) which includes separate volumes of poetry for grades K-4.

Routman believes in teaching reading to meet specific children's needs regardless of the particular reading program in place. She is a strong advocate for the use of small guided reading groups and reading for understanding. Phonics and other word analysis strategies are part of her reading framework, but not at its core. Her focus for the reading classroom is on the development and the use of the classroom library as the center for an independent reading program, shared reading and reading aloud.

Routman has designed informal reading evaluations on books/texts her students are reading (her published works are known for their appendices replete with templates for evaluations, projects, reports, book lists, suggested texts by topics etc.). Her classroom model includes matching children with specific library books as well as linking assessment with instruction. Finally she is a researcher who sees reading as intimately linked to writing.

Routman is also involved with the politics of literacy. This vision of literacy involves the image of the teacher, as an informed professional, who regularly reads the latest professional books, collaborates with colleagues in school and beyond, and deals with the most recent research developments. Interestingly, Routman is one researcher who also feels that an informed professional can and should know when to question research. Other aspects of the politics of literacy as Routman conceptualizes them are: communicating effectively with parents and dealing with testing and standards mandates.

Two of her published works, *Conversations: Strategies for Teaching, Learning, and Evaluating* (Heinemann, 2000) and *Invitations: Changing as Teachers and Learners k-12* (Heinemann, l991 and l994) are essential for the elementary reading teacher's bookshelf and can take the teacher through several years of work.

Taberski, Sharon

Taberski is an experienced elementary teacher educator who is also a member of the Primary Literacy Standards Committee run by the National Center on Education and the Economy and the University of Pittsburgh. Her works in the field are served up as wonderfully accessible and necessary advice from "the veteran teacher across the hall" who loves her students and is delighted to help a new colleague.

Unlike many theorists in the field of reading, Taberski's work is not focused around a prescribed set of skills, but rather around a series of interconnected interactions with the learner.

Among these interactions which are detailed and clearly communicated in her book *On Solid Ground* (2000-Heinemann) are:

- Assessment- Procedures for assessing children's reading, and to inform teaching, scheduling and managing reading conferences, taking oral reading records, and using retellings as discussion tools.
- Demonstration- Taberski developed and field tested strategies for using shared reading and read aloud as platforms for figuring out words and comprehending texts. She is a strong advocate of small group work-guided reading, word-study groups and teaching children one on one.
- Practice- In the Taberski framework, independent reading is used as a time for practice. Students play key roles in this practice and Sharon has a set of detailed and easily adaptable guidelines for matching children with books for independent reading. Her work includes booklists and ready to use information that is available for reproduction.
- Response- It's important for students to know that they are doing well and where they must focus their efforts to improve skills. Taberski explains how her students use writing and dialogue as tools for independent reading.

Vail, Priscilla

Noted for her research in the study of dyslexia and its myths, Vail has articulated ways in which children can develop their reading skills as they cope with this disorder and techniques parents and educators can use to support reading development. She has also worked on specific test taking skills for children coping with dyslexia and other special needs. Her strategies can be infused in the regular education program to enhance all students' reading achievement schools. She is a proponent of phonics instruction and skills within the context of an integrated whole language approach (once called integrated language arts).

Another focus of Vail's research is the link between language and thinking. She is concerned with how a child's receptive language, expressive language and metacognition can be fostered. She has developed assessment methods for each of these capacities and activities to help strengthen them in children grades k-4.

BIBLIOGRAPHY OF PRINT RESOURCES

PROFESSIONAL BOOKS:

Adams, M. (1990). *Beginning to read: Thinking and Learning about Print.* Cambridge, MA: MIT Press.

Anders, P., & Bos, C. (l986). Semantic Feature Analysis: An Interactive Strategy for Vocabulary Development and Reading Comprehension, *Journal of Reading,* 29, 610-616.

Blevins, W. (l997). *Phonemic Awareness Activities for Early Reading Success.* New York: Scholastic.

Boyd-Bastone, P. (2004). Focused Anecdotal Record Assessment (ARA): A Tool for Standards Based Authentic Assessment. *Reading Teacher, 58* (3), pp. 230-239.

Calkins, Lucy McCormick. (2001). *The Art of Teaching Reading.* New York: Longman.
> This is the woman who beautifully explains the reading workshop and its relationship to the writing workshop as she shares wonderful snapshots of mini lessons, conferring, conferencing, independent reading, guided reading, book talks, prompts, coaching, and classroom library use. Exceedingly readable and direct.

Campbell, Robin. (2004). *Reading and Writing for Real Purposes.* Portsmouth, NH: Heinemann.
> This work focuses on how children who deftly absorb and interconnect symbols and sounds of their universes can be supported in K-1 classes to extend this ability into phonics learning. Campbell demonstrates how immersion in a highly literate classroom filled with print and language stimuli allows kids to build accurate letter-sound relationships. The book provides a framework for teaching phonics using proven field-tested Campbell strategies.
>
> Among these strategies are: early mark making, read-alouds, playing with language in rhyme and song, writing and reading in a variety of genres, exploring environmental and classroom print, and using students' own names. Samples of student work are included.

Chancey, C. (l994). Language development, metalinguistic awareness, and emergent literacy skills of 3 year old children in relation to social class. *Applied Psycholinguistics*, 15, 371-394.

Clay, Marie M. (1993). *An Observation Survey of Early Literacy Achievement.* Portsmouth, NH: Heinemann.

Clay, Marie M. (1993). *Reading Recovery: A Guidebook for Teachers in Training.* Portsmouth, NH: Heinemann.

Cooper, J. David. (2004). *Literacy-Helping Children Construct Meaning.* Boston, MA: Houghton Mifflin. (5th Edition).
   This book explains with numerous charts, tables, templates, and excerpts form actual texts, what the balanced literacy approach to the teaching of reading and writing is. It offers the new teacher: exact schedules, strategies, guidelines, assessment tools, bibliographies, research, and even scripts for conferring with children.

   Cooper is a clear and crisp writer who does not overwhelm the reader, but rather engages the reader. Even veteran teachers would return again and again to this text for support and refreshing insights.

Cox, Carole. (2005). *Teaching Language Arts.* Boston, MA: Pearson.
   A compendium of state of the art lesson plans, web resources, online case studies, teaching ideas and extensive templates. All of these materials are aligned to the balanced literacy reading and writing workshop model.

   The book also includes teaching ideas for the ELL reader, children with learning disabilities, and speakers of non- standard dialects. The book also features snapshots of second language learners as well as bi-literacy web resources.

Cullinan, Bernice E. (1998). *Three Voices-An Invitation to Poetry Across the Curriculum.* New York: Stenhouse. K-6 and beyond.
   Two classroom educators and a noted researcher in children's literature demonstrate how poetry can be used in the classroom to teach various aspects of reading and to nurture lifelong literacy. Thirty-three grade and age appropriate strategies are included which have been field tested in classrooms across the country.

Ezell, H. K., & Justice, L. M. (2000). Increasing the Print Focus of Adult -Child Shared Book Reading through Observational Learning. *American journal of Speech Pathology*, 9, 36-37.

Flesch, Rudolf. (1985). *Why Johnny Can't Read* New York: Harper and Row.

Fountas, Irene C., & Gay Su Pinnell. (2001). *Guiding Readers and Writers 3-6.* Portsmouth, NH: Heinemann.
   This work includes 1000 leveled books with guidelines for using them as part of a reading and writing workshop. The book explains how to use various genres in the classroom and how to use visual graphic organizers for the teaching of reading and writing.

Fountas, Irene. C., & Gay Su Pinnell. (l999). *Matching Books to Readers Using Leveled Books in Guided Reading K-3.* Portsmouth, NH: Heinemann.
    This major contribution to the field has a list of 7, 500 grade and age appropriate books. In addition the authors include word counts to be used for keeping running records, text characteristics, guidelines for leveling of additional books and suggestions for developing classroom library collections.

    Other works by these researchers also published by Heinemann include: *Voices on Word matters: Learning about Phonics and Spelling in the Literacy Classroom* (l999) and *Word Matters-Teaching Phonics and Spelling in the Reading/Writing Classroom* (1998).

Fry, Edward Bernard, Kress, Jacqueline, Fountakidis, Dona Lee. (2000). *The Reading Teacher's Book of Lists.* San Francisco, CA: Wiley Press.
    This book is an invaluable one for the working classroom educator. It includes ready to use lists that cover a multiplicity of teacher needs. Among them are: spelling demons, readability graphs, phonics, useful words, reading math, vowel lists, anagrams, portmanteaus (do you know what they are and how well they can work in word study?), web sites, classic children's literature, etc. Even a veteran teacher educator will find useful and new resources. Also wonderful for developing independent word study investigations and literature explorations.

Ganske, Kathy. (2000). *Word Journeys-Assessment-Guided Phonics, Spelling, and Vocabulary Instruction.* New York, NY: Guilford Press.
    This book offers a practical approach for assessing children's spelling. The author has created a DSA (Development Spelling Analysis) tool which teachers can use to evaluate individual children's spelling progress and to differentiate instruction. The book includes snapshots of children at different levels of spelling development.

Hall, Susan. (l994). *Using Picture Books to Teach Literary Devices.* Westport, CT: Oryx Press.

How to Help Every Child Become a Reader. Just Publishing. K-6 and beyond.
    This accessible text draws on materials developed by the US Department of Education to share research, resources, referrals and suggestions for supporting all children to become lifelong and engaged readers. It offers specific suggestions and resources for assisting struggling readers including those with special needs and those from ELL backgrounds.

Labov, L. (2003). When Ordinary Children Fail to Read. *Reading Research Quarterly*, 38, 128-31.

Macmillan, B. M. (2002). Rhyme and Reading. A Critical Review of the Research Methodology. *Journal of Research in Reading,* 25(1), 4-42.

Makor, Barbara. *Primary Phonics Readers.*
Short storybooks that K-2 can own and read independently.
> They feature phonetically controlled texts, sounds and spellings that are grade and age appropriate and high interest child-centered themes. As children progress through the series of twenty titles, they review and enhance their mastery of phonetic elements, sight words, and sequences at a more rapid pace. This material is compatible with the majority of phonics programs.

Munro, J. (1998). Phonological and Phonemic Awareness: Their Impact on Learning to Read Prose and Spell. *Australian Journal of Learning Disabilities*, 3, 2, 15-21.
> Paperback Nursery Rhyme Sampler-Whispering Coyote Press- Essential for a Prek-1 classroom and useful even in grades 1 and 2; these classic nursery rhymes promote phonemic and phonological awareness and children's ownership of their reading through song and movement.

Routman, Regie. (2000). *Conversations: Strategies for Teaching, Learning, and Evaluating.* Portsmouth, NH: Heinemann.

Routman, Regie. (1994). *Invitations: Changing as Teachers and Learners K-12.* Portsmouth, NH. Heinemann.
Routman, Regie. (1996). *Literacy at the Crossroads: Crucial Talk About Reading, Writing, and Other Teaching Dilemmas.* Portsmouth, NH: Heinemann.

Routman, Regie. (2002). *Reading Essentials.* Portsmouth, NH: Heinemann.

Statman, Ann. *Handprints-Leveled Storybooks for Early Readers Educators Publishing Service-*Grades K-2.
> These fifty titles which come with five teacher's guides were leveled using the Fountas and Pinnell Guided Reading Leveling System. The stories reflect real world situations and people young readers know. They include: sentence structure, pictures and cues that focus strategic reading. Print size, sentence positioning, and word spacing is appropriate for the level of the particular storybook. The titles build a strong sight vocabulary through the use of high frequency words. Language used within the series progresses from natural to formal book language.

Schumm, Heanne Shay. *The Reading Tutor's Handbook.* Free Spirit. K-6 and beyond.
> This guide offers step by step instructions, templates and handouts for providing children with differentiated reading support. It is not only helpful for teachers, but also can be shared with paraprofessionals, teachers, interns, and parents as a support framework for the classroom reading program.

Taberski, Sharon. (2000). *On Solid Ground: Creating a Literacy Environment in Your K-3 Classroom.* Portsmouth, NH: Heinemann.

Terban, Marvin. *Time to Rhyme-A Rhyming Dictionary*. Boyd Mills Press. Grades 1-3.

> This book is easily enough formatted so that it can be used to introduce children in the early elementary grades to the use of a rhyming dictionary as a reference tool. Its simple word groupings encourage writing which can also reinforce and reciprocally enhance reading skills through the reading and writing workshop.

Vail, Patricia. *Reading Comprehension-Students Needs and Teacher's Tools.* Educators Publishers Service K-6 and beyond.

> This is a compendium of explanations of specific instructional practices, terms, student projects, learning games and resources which are critical for successfully teaching reading.

ALPHABET BOOKS

A major genre of fiction and non-fiction for the teacher of reading is the alphabet book. These books' appeal, concepts, and efficiency as models for reading and writing merit them a special section in this bibliography. Even those whose text is simple enough for Prek-2, can serve as anchor books and models for writing workshop in grades 3-6.

Aigner-Clark, Julie. (2002). *Baby Einstein- The ABCs of Art*. Illustrations by Nadeen Zaidi. New York: Hyperion Books.

Beaton, Clare. *Zoe and Her Zebra*. Barefoot Books. Prek-1.

> This board book features a character young children can identify with named Zoe. Her adventures are told in a simple, repetitive text with a soft literally "touchy" felt art.

Bunting, Eve. *Girls A to Z*. Boyd Mills Press. PreK-1.

> This book uses the alphabetic format to promote the opportunity for girls to select various professions and careers ranging from astronaut to zookeeper. Bunting's text is breezy and rhymes.

Cheney, Lynne. (2002). *America- A Patriotic Primer.* New York: Simon and Schuster Books. Illustrated by Robin Priess Glasser.

Cheney, Lynne. *A Is For Abigail: An Almanac of Amazing American Women.* New York: Simon and Schuster Books. Ages 4-8.

Glaser, Milton. (2003). *The Alphazeds*. Miramax. Ages 4-8.

Grimes, Nikki. *C is for City*. Illustrated by: Pat Cummings. Boyd Mill Press. K-3.

> This alphabet rhyme book doubles as a guide to city activities. With its built in invitations to readers to search for alphabetical items, it is perfect for use as an informal assessment tool or an interactive/paired reading anchor text.

Inkpen, Mick. (2000). *Kipper's A to Z*. San Diego: Harcourt. Ages 3-7.

Isadora, Rachel. (1999). *ABC Pops! (Picture Books)*. Disney Press. Ages 4-8.

Johnson, Stephen. (1995). *Alphabet City*. Penguin Books. All ages.

Kelley, Marty. *Summer Stinks*. Zino Press. Prek-1.
  This work describes the summer season in terms of things which "stink" about it, including ants, bugs, and sweat. Fun to read and add to as the alphabet letters are learned and vocabulary is built up.

Martin, Mary Jane. *From Anne to Zach*. Boyd Mills Press.
  In this captivating book which can serve as a touchstone text for model collaborative authoring, children learn the letters of the alphabet through other children's names.
Melmed, Laura Krauss and Frane Lesser. (2003) *Capital! Washington DC from A to Z*. New York: Harper Collins.

Musgrove, Margaret. (1976). Illustrated by Leo and Diane Dillon. *Ashanti to Zulu. African Traditions.* New York: Dial Books for Young Readers.
  This is a Caldecott-winning book which uses the alphabetic format for a richly detailed and researched study of 26 African Peoples. It includes a map and pronunciation guide and illustrations that were researched in the Schomberg Center and the American Museum of Natural History. Even the frame design for each illustration reflects the African Kano knot which signifies endless searching.

Paratore, Colleen. *26 Big Things Hands Do*. Minneapolis, MN: Free Spirit.
  What is delightful about this alphabet book is that it presents the alphabet letters as positive actions children can perform with their own small hands to help others. These actions include: applauding, giving gifts, planting, and volunteering. Of course, alphabet study can continue with adding other "helping actions" to the word wall or substituting them in the text.

Pelham, David, (1991). *A is for Animals*. New York: Simon and Schuster

Seeley, Lorna. *The Book of Shadow Boxes*. Peachtree.
  Within the shadow of each letter's shadow box lies a hidden treasure for the young reader to find. The book is intricately and exquisitely designed and conceptualized by Ms. Seeley. Its visual fascination extends well beyond the elementary grades as it of course fosters not only the alphabetic principle, but also reading comprehension and literacy response.
Sneed, Brad. (2002). *Picture a Letter*. New York: Penguin Books.

Seuss. *ABC*. Random House. Ages 2-up.

Thornhill, Jim. *The Wildlife ABC and 123: A Nature Alphabet and Counting Book.* Maple Tree Press. K-1 with additional nature notes on the species for the teacher/parent.

> In addition to fostering the alphabetic principle, the book nicely mixes geographic, multicultural, and scientific knowledge into a beautifully designed text. It uses children's fascination with nature to foster reading and math literacy.

Zschock, Martha and Heather. (2002). *Journey Around New York from A to Z. Beverly.* Mass: Commonwealth Editions

Zschock, Martha. (2001). *Journey Around Boston from A to Z.* Beverly Mass: Commonwealth Editions.

TRADE BOOKS

These books foster particular aspects of reading skills, fluencies and competencies.

Blackstone, Stella. *Where's the Cat?* Barefoot Books. Prek-k.

> This book which focuses its primary school readers on searching for a lost cat provides excellent use of repetitive language and encourages interactive reading.

Campbell, Bebe Moore. (2003). Sometimes *My Mommy Gets Angry. New York, New York: G. P. Putnam's Sons.*

> This is a moving story about a young girl whose mother suffers from mental illness. It is told in a way that is easy to read, along with beautiful illustrations. The main character is Annie. Sometimes her mother is very happy and other times very angry and sad. Annie has learned what to do when her mom is having a bad episode. She has books to read, a special stuffed animal and some secret snacks. Annie also has a strong support system in place with friends, neighbors, her teacher and grandmother. This book is a good introduction to the issue of mental illness. It is especially important in that students see how this young girl is able to cope with this difficult part of her life. "Sometimes by mommy has a dark cloud inside of her. I can't stop the rain from falling, but I can find sunshine in my mind."
>
> Teachers can introduce students to this issue with this poignant book. Students can brainstorm different scenarios and discuss how they can be resolved. They can discuss who their support network includes and what it takes for a person to be strong enough to weather such a storm.

The book is a much needed resource for children in times where Annie's situation is far more common than is generally known. Annie's capacity to make effective, affirming social decisions makes the work an inspirational touchstone for other peers who need to confront their parents' emotional crises. Children might be inspired to author poetry or create deliberately fictionalized narrative accounts about how they have confronted various crises.

In offering an upper elementary grade and age appropriate narrative of a peer dealing with an emotionally ill parent, this book provides readers confronting similar family and caregiver issues with an opening for discussion and for hopeful outreach. Just reading this account may well be the first step necessary to assist a youngster in acknowledging a "hidden problem" and getting crucial adult assistance in dealing with the crisis.

Garza, Carmen Lomas. (1990). *Family Pictures Cuadros de familia*. Children's Book Press.

This book tells the story of the author's childhood growing up in a Hispanic community in Texas. The book is written in both Spanish and English, accompanied by the author's most incredible paintings. The paintings are unique, somewhat folksy, colorful, and totally entrancing. They bring you into Carmen's world. Once inside it, you don't want to leave.

There is so much to explore in this book; it works well with the study of "myself and family", community, communities around the world, Mexico, family traditions and customs. It emphasizes social and emotional learning and how a young girl can find her way in the world. The traditions followed by her community and family were not necessarily accepted or understood by white America. Yet these values gave her the strength to be her own person and to rely on both her relationships and rich inner life to express herself.

There are so many activities that this book inspires. Children can study the origins of the piñata, and make one. They can make a cookbook of recipes from Mexico or from their own homes. Children can also be encouraged to design their own book of family pictures. They can emphasize special occasions that they celebrate or focus on family traditions which reflect their cultural backgrounds. The richness and lushness of the paintings invites the readers to construct meaning and to create their own narratives, procedural accounts, poetry, and dialogues inspired by one or more of the paintings.

Picture walk through the illustrations. Given the Spanish/English text, this strategy can be an engaging spatial entry point for descriptive and narrative spoken and written presentations. The lushly detailed illustrations of family rites and celebrations can be springboards for children's literary and artistic renditions of equivalent family pictures and events which are prompted by Carmen's selections.

Use of dual language text for the book validates children's and family member's responses in languages other than English. Obviously, this book and its format are inspirational for ELL/Bilingual learners and for special needs learners who can be captivated by the paintings.

The power of this book lies in its accessing and modeling the magic of family rites and rituals for a broad spectrum of linguistics, intrapersonal, spatial, and kinesthetic learners from monolingual, bilingual and special needs backgrounds. Common to all of its audience members are the social and emotionally celebratory components of Family Pictures.

Glaser, Shirley, & Glaser, Milton. (2003). *The Alphazeds Words*. Hyperion Books. This book is incredible in so many ways! It is an alphabet book that can be read by or to little ones and not so little ones. It starts with an empty room. One by one, each letter of the alphabet enters the room, each with its own distinct look, fantastic illustrations and typography by the designer Milton Glaser. Each of these letters also has its own distinct personality. A is angry, B is bashful, J is jealous, and so on. The room gets quite crowded. How do all of these different personalities manage to get along and coexist? Not too well apparently, as there is shouting, pushing, hitting and kicking. In the midst of all the chaos, the light in the room goes out and there is silence.

> "When the light came back on, something
> extraordinary had happened. Four letters
> had gotten together to comfort one another.
> Together they had managed to create something
> larger and more important than themselves.
> *"They had made the first word."*

This is a great lesson on how each of us can be an individual, yet when we work together, something wonderful can happen. This book illustrates an incredible lesson in social and emotional maturity, and helps the child realize that it isn't just about "me."

There are many different activities that a teacher can use with this book. The children can work in groups to make their own alphabet book of emotions. They can then present the book as a group, discussing the roles each of them played, and how they each used their unique talents to make the book.

Older children grades 3 and up, can research and present as a group some important discoveries that were made more special because they involved people working together. They can also work on a project about cooperative learning, perhaps surveying class and schoolmates on how they feel they learn the best.

Hest, Amy. (1985). *The Purple Coat.* New York: Macmillan Publishing Co.
In the autumn of every year, Gabrielle travels with her mother to New York City to visit her Grandpa who owns a tailor shop. Once there, he always makes her a new coat, but this year Gabrielle decides the usual navy blue coat won't do. The Purple Coat follows Gabrielle in her attempt to establish her own identity.

Lionni, Leo. (1980). *Inch by Inch.* Astor-Honor Publishing Co. Inc.
In *Inch by Inch*, an inchworm (which is a caterpillar, or larval stage, of the fall cankerworm, which becomes a moth) keeps itself from being eaten by various birds by proving its worth as a measuring device.

Lupton, Hugh. *The Story Tree- Tales to Read Aloud.* Barefoot Books. K-3
These seven multicultural stories are accessible enough to children to encourage their eventually taking over the read aloud sharing on their own. This book is also a good one for family literacy sessions and for parent volunteers to read aloud in the classroom.

Martin Jr., Bill, & John Archambault. (1966). *Knots on a Counting Rope.* New York, New York: Henry Holt and Company.
This beautifully illustrated book reaches out in so many different directions, and we can all learn so much from it. Knots on a Counting Rope is the story of a Native-American boy who is blind and is learning from his grandfather how to survive in this world. Boy-Strength-of-Blue-Horses insists on hearing the story of his birth over and over again.

Every time his grandfather retells the story of the boy's birth, he adds a knot to his counting rope. Each time he hears the story, Boy- Strength-of-Blue-Horses gains more confidence in himself. The story emphasizes the Native-American tradition of storytelling, and there are numerous art, math and social studies lessons that offshoot from this book.

Of course, the telling and retelling of the story celebrate the young blind hero's strengths and weaknesses and ability to set goals with optimism. Stories of one's birth related by others are powerful demonstrations of social skills of the highest order.

This book also deals extensively with social and emotional learning. Children learn that those with disabilities need to be treated with sensitivity while learning to find their place in the world. One way in which children's social and emotional learning is strengthened is by understanding themselves and those around them. In order to facilitate this, each child will interview at least one family member about when he/she was born. The accounts collected with appropriate photos or memorabilia can then be shared in class and perhaps even authored into a *Knots on a Counting Rope* style book format.

Children can also retell the story of the boy using the counting system of cultures other than Native American. This literary response will incorporate cultural study, respect and empathy into ongoing reading and writing workshop efforts.

McCully, Emily Arnold. (1992). *Mirette on the High Wire*. G.P. Putnam's & Sons.
Mirette helps her mother run a boardinghouse for acrobats, jugglers, actors and mimes. Her life changes when she discovers a boarder crossing the courtyard on air. She begs him to teach her how he does it. He refuses to teach her, but she begins practicing on her own. As she improves, he begins to help her. In the end she helps him overcome his fear of the high wire.

Rabe, Bernice. (1981). *The Balancing Girl*. E.P. Dutton.
Margaret, a girl in a wheel chair is excellent at balancing all kinds of objects. Margaret shows her friend Tommy how good she is at balancing at the school carnival.

Ringgold, Faith. (1991). *Tar Beach*. New York, New York: Crown Publishers.
This book is one of my favorites, and it is moving in its words, art, and the beautiful story it tells. This is an effective book to use for younger grades to connect with myself, my family and my community. It can also be used in connection with a mapmaking unit. The children can be encouraged to make a map of their neighborhood from an aerial view.

A starting point for a discussion would be why the author portrayed New York from such a vantage point. In this beautiful book, the narrator, Cassie Louise Lightfoot, lets her dreams and ambitions take her to places in New York City that she ordinarily would not be able to be part of because of her circumstances. As a result of her self-motivation and self-awareness, Cassie is able to go as far as her dreams will let her. In this book Cassie also shows strengths in the areas of emotional sensitivity, as well as inter and intra-personal relationships.

Children can author their own Tar Beach equivalent night fantasies and then share them with one another through an exhibit or big books. Although Cassie's family is obviously poor since they have to picnic on their roof, Cassie's dreamlike lushly illustrated flight over Harlem validates the beauty of their family life and of the city landscape which is accessible to all. This is an invaluable lesson in the importance of the wealth inherent in the appreciation of family connections and the beauty of nature and public architectural designs! A song of family and of the city!

Schories, Pat. *Breakfast for Jack/Jack and the Missing Piece*. Front Street.
These wordless stories help pre-literate children, ELL learners new to this country and special needs children explore the basic elements of story-character, setting and plot. The lack of words allows the children to "construct their own meaning," and create their own different stories which "fit" the illustrations.

Steinberg, Laya. *Thesaurus Rex*. Barefoot Books.
This book introduces a dinosaur with an interest in words whose story is told through a wonderful rhyming text which can be used for fostering phonemic awareness and for choral readings.

Uhlberg, Myron. *The Printer*. Peachtree.
This story celebrates the conventions of print in that the boy narrator's father is a deaf man who speaks with his hands and as a job chooses to turn lead type letters into words and sentences. An excellent book to support family literacy and an appreciation for the conventions of print.

Van Allsburg, Chris. (1988). *Two Bad Ants*. Houghton Mifflin Co.
In *Two Baxd Ants*, news comes to the ant world of a great discovery in a far away place. A delicious crystal has been found. A group of ants set out to bring back this crystal to their queen. Two ants are overwhelmed by the treasure and stay behind in this dangerous alien world. It is a tale of choices, consequences and the discovery of life's real treasures.

Walter, Mildred Pitts. (2004). Illustrated by Larry Johnson. *Alec's primer*.
Lebanon, NH: University Press of New England.
This is the true account of a Virginian slave who was taught to read by his owner's daughter. He later fought in the Civil War on the Union side and became a landowner himself in Vermont. The beautifully written narrative is complemented by the vibrant paintings of Larry Johnson which include authentic period details.

Webliography

Reading Online
http://www.readingonline.org
This online web resource which is sponsored by the International Reading Association is full of specific reading teaching ideas, lessons and new research. It includes summaries of conference presentations and even tips on how to use technology to teach reading.

Balanced Literacy
http://www.thekcrew.net/balancedliteracy.html
Established in 1996, this site is organized according to the components of the balanced literacy approach. It also has an excellent listing of professional books that can assist with various aspects of teaching reading.

Carol Hurst
http://www.carolhurst.com/index.html
This is a terrific resource for exploring the children's literature works which are at the crux of author and genre study. It can be used for material to supplement period studies and discussions of authors' lives. Older children will be able to explore it on their own.

Read, Write, Think
http://www.readwritethink.org/lessons/
This resource maintained by the NCTE, National Council of Teachers of English, has a growing database of age and grade specific literacy lesson plans. It also includes all the graphic organizers cited in this book and many more, ready to download.

Inspiration Software
http://www.inspiration.com
http://www.inspiration.com/freetrial/index.cfm
This is the home site for the Inspiration and Kidspiration mind mapping software. These online templates and capacities assist the reading teacher with customizing the various graphic organizers discussed throughout the book, and with gaining the ability to design customized graphic organizers for a particular theme, study or student group. A free trial version of this resource which is child friendly can be downloaded.

Visual Thesaurus
http://www.visualthesaurus.com/online/
This is really both an online dictionary and a thesaurus.

Resources for Read Aloud, Shared Reading, and Independent Reading available on the Internet include the following:

http:// www.mightybook.com/library_4to6.htm.
This is a library of books read aloud by the computer. Children can listen to these books or practice reading with a buddy as the computer broadcasts the text. Of course, this type of read aloud would only be used IN ADDITION to the vibrant read-aloud of the teacher.

http://www.enchantedlearning.com/Rhymes.html
These are online nursery rhymes ready for reading to the children and posting throughout for room or for literacy center display.

SEDL-RCI Framework of Reading
http://www.sedl.org/reading/framework/assessment.html
This is an excellent resource for readings in the theories and methods of foundations. There are topic aligned links to specific theorists which can be included at the close of your lesson planning and may be reviewed before certification tests.

TOOLS TO HELP YOU TEACH THE FOUNDATIONS OF READING AND SUCCEEDING IN CONSTRUCTED RESPONSE CERTIFICATION EXAMINATIONS

Appendix 1- The Record of Reading Behavior- A close up look at a key assessment tool.

Often in the constructed response question on a foundations of education certification test or on a general elementary certification test; the educator is asked to analyze a record of reading behavior or to construct an appropriate one from data given in an anecdote. Furthermore with the current climate of accountability, it is a good idea for new teachers and for career changers to examine closely the basic elements of recording reading behavior.

While there are various acceptable formats for emergent literacy assessment used throughout the country, the one selected for use here is based on the work of Marie Clay and Kenneth Goodman. These two are key researchers in the close observation and documentations of children's early reading miscues (reading mistakes).

It is important to emphasize that the teacher should not just "take the Record of Reading Behavior " and begin filling it out as the child reads from a random book prior to beginning of the observation. There are specific steps for taking the record and analyzing its results.

1. Select a text
If you want to see if the child is reading on instructional level, choose a book that the child has already read. If the purpose of the test is to see whether the child is ready to advance to the next level, choose a book from that level which the child has not yet seen.

2. Introduce the text
If the book is one that has been read, you do not need to introduce the text, other than by saying the title. But if the book is new to the child, you should briefly share the title and tell the child a bit about the plot and style of the book.

3. Take the record
Generally with emergent readers' grades 1-2, there are only 100-150 words in a passage used to take a record. Make certain that the child is seated beside you, so that you can see the text as the child reads it.

If desired, you may want to photocopy the text in advance for yourself, so you can make direct notations on your text while the child reads from the book. After you introduce the text make certain that the child has the chance to read the text independently. Be certain that you do not "teach" or help the child with the text, other than to supply an unknown word that the child requests you supply. The purpose of the record is to see what the child does on his or her own.

As the child reads the text, you must be certain to record the reading behaviors the child exhibits using the following notations.

In taking the record, keep in mind the following: Allow enough time for the child to work independently on a problem before telling or supplying the word. If you wait too long, you could run the risk of having the child lose the meaning and his/her interest in the story as he or she tries to identify the unknown word.

It is recommended that when a child is way off track, you tell him or her to "Try that again" (TTA). If a whole phrase is troubling, put it into square brackets and score it as only one error.

The notation for filling out the Record of Reading behavior involves noting the child's response on the top with the actual text below it.

Comprehension Check

This can and should be done by inviting the child to retell the story. This retelling can then be used to ask further questions about characters, plot, setting and purpose which allow you to observe and to record the child's level of comprehension.

Calculating the Reading Level and the Self-correction Rate

Calculating the reading level lets you know if the book is at the level on which the child can read it independently or comfortably with guidance or if the book is at a level where reading it frustrates the child.

Generally, an accuracy score of 95-100% suggests that the child can read the text and other books or texts on the same level.

An accuracy score of 90-94% indicates that the text and texts likely will present challenges to the child, but with guidance from you, a tutor or parent, the child will be able to master these texts and enjoy them. This is instructional level.

However, an accuracy score of less than 89% tells you that the material you have selected for the child is too hard for the child to control alone. Such material needs to be shared with the child in a shared reading situation or read to the child.

KEEPING SCORE ON THE RECORD

Insertions, omissions, substitutions, and teacher told responses, all count as errors. Repetitions are not scored as errors. Corrected responses are scored as self corrections.

No penalty is given for a child's attempts at self correction that results in a finally incorrect response but the attempts should be noted. Multiple unsuccessful attempts at a word score as one error only.

The lowest score for any page is zero.
If a child omits a line or lines, each word omitted is counted as an error. If the child omits a page, deduct the number of words omitted from the total number of words which you have used for the record.

Calculating the Reading Level

Note the number of errors made on each line on the Record of Reading Behavior in the column marked E (for Error).

Total the number of errors in the text and divide this number into the number of words that the child has read. This will give you the error rate.

If a child read a passage of 100 words and made 10 errors, the error rate would be 1 in 10. Convert this to an accuracy percentage, or 90%.

Calculating the Self Correction Rate

Total all the self-corrections.
Next, add the number of errors to the number of self-corrections and divide by the number of self-corrections.

A self correction rate of 1 in 3 to 1 in 5 is considered good. This rate indicates that the child is able to help himself or herself as problems are encountered in reading.

Analyzing the record

This record should assist the educator in developing a detailed date specific picture of the child's progress in reading behavior. It should be used to help the educator individualize instruction for the specific child.

As the errors are reviewed, consider whether the child made the error because of semantics (cues from meaning), syntactic (language structure), or visual information difficulties.

As self-corrections are analyzed, consider what led the child to make that self-correction. Check out and consider what cues the child does use effectively and which the child does not use well.

Consider the ways in which the child tackles a word which is unknown. Characterize that behavior and consider how the teacher can assist the child with this issue.

If a child can retell at least three quarters of a story, this is considered adequate for retelling.

Analysis of reading behavior records can and should support the educator in designing appropriate mini lessons and strategies to help the child with his or her recorded errors and miscues.

Sample Test

1) The major difference between phonemic and phonological awareness is:

A) One deals with a series of discrete sounds and the other with sound-spelling relationships.

B) One is involved with teaching and learning alliteration and rhymes.

C) Phonemic awareness is a specific type of phonological awareness that deals with separate phonemes within a given word.

D) Phonological awareness is associated with printed words.

2) The theorist in early reading (emergent reading) who has identified five tasks for phonemic awareness is:

A) John Munro

B) Brian Cambourne

C) Marilyn Jager Adams

D) Lucy Calkins

3) An oddity task is one in which children:

A) Identify the odd number in a mathematical series and talk about how they did it.

B) Perform a creative exercise designed for differentiated learning styles.

C) Recognize which sound is odd in a series of like sounds.

D) Design a different activity for themselves.

4) All of the following are true about phonological awareness EXCEPT:

A) It may involve print.

B) It is a prerequisite for spelling and phonics.

C) Activities can be done by the children with their eyes closed.

D) It starts before letter recognition is taught.

5) Ms. James is seated with a child by her side. The child is reading aloud from an open book. Ms. James is teaching in a school that has embraced the Balanced Literacy Approach. Therefore it is most likely that Ms. James is writing and recording:

A) The child's use of expression in reading aloud.

B) The child's errors and miscues.

C) Her observations of the child's attitude toward reading.

D) The child's feelings about the particular passage being read.

6) Most of the children in first-year teacher Ms. James's class are really doing well in their phonemic awareness assessments. However, Ms. James is very concerned about three children who do not seem to be able to distinguish between spoken words that "sound alike," but are different. Since she is a first year teacher, she feels her inexperience may be to blame. In truth, the reason these three children have not yet demonstrated phonemic awareness is most likely that:

A) They are not capable of becoming good readers.

B) They are bored in class.

C) They may be from an ELL background.

D) Ms. James does not pronounce the different phonemes clearly enough.

7) **Ms. Ramsey has forgotten her credit cards and has limited cash in her wallet. She is buying supplies for her reading classroom that she wants to have annotated with the children's names by the first day of school. She should buy all of the following with her cash except:**

A) Folders.

B) Markers.

C) Rulers.

D) Index cards.

8) **Ms. Rivers is preparing for a parent teacher conference. She does all of the following EXCEPT:**

A) Collects individual child running records.

B) Puts away all the book bags and leveled pots so the classroom will be more spacious.

C) Puts out by each child's seat the child's weekly log and spelling folder.

D) Sets up work samples by each child's place.

9) **In terms of a balanced literacy classroom, a "leveled bin" indicates:**

A) A plant set at child's eye level for descriptive writing purposes.

B) A bin with books the child has selected.

C) A bin with books leveled by the teacher.

D) A bin with all kinds of reading materials including magazines and packaging on a child's level.

10) **Mark Garner has been told that he will have to support some special needs readers in his classroom in addition to the rest of the students. He can expect to have:**

A) Gifted children who are accelerated in reading skills for their grade and age.

B) Children who have disabilities and will need special support in accessing the content and methods he uses with the rest of the class.

C) Children who come from native language backgrounds other than English.

D) Children who display the capacities and needs detailed in a and b.

11) Julia has been hired to work in a school that serves a local public housing project. She is working with kindergarten children and has been asked to focus on shared reading. She selects:

A) Chapter books.

B) Riddle books.

C) Alphabet books.

D) Wordless picture books.

12) It is 4 PM, yet Francine is still in her classroom. The seats in her classroom are filled with adults of various ages who are holding books. They are seated two by two with both holding copies of the same book. Francine probably is:

A) Explaining to parents how she will teach a particular story.

B) Demonstrating shared reading with a buddy for volunteer parents.

C) Hosting a parents organization meeting for her grade level.

D) Distributing old books from the class library to parents.

13) The work of Chard and Osborn (1999) in establishing guidelines for children with reading disabilities has shown that it is essential for them to:

A) Read wordless picture books.

B) Learn at least 10 sight words.

C) Work intensely on the alphabetic principle.

D) Focus on using syntactic clues.

14) A key theorist whose work has helped teacher's document children's oral reading progress throughout the school year is:

A) Jerome Bruner.

B) Daniel J. Chard.

C) J. David Cooper.

D) Marie Clay.

15) The first grade class is on a neighborhood walk. As the children approach the neighborhood Kentucky Fried Chicken chain, Danny reads from the store window "Kentucky Fried Chicken Hot and Crunchy." Danny has never read or been taught to read this before. The most likely explanation for Danny's being able to read this is that he is:

A) An advanced reader who is self improving.

B) His parents have taught him to read the signs and materials at the Kentucky Fried Chicken store.

C) He is in the logographic phrase of phonics learning.

D) This was just a lucky guess on his part.

16) An observer enters Julia's first grade classroom. Children are working with oaktag strips and placing the word letters on these strips on a sentence strip holder. Then they seem to be involved in some kind of counting. The observer is confused. This activity is taking place during the reading block. Julia explains:

A) The children are counting letters.

B) This is word sorting and the children are grouping words by length, common letters and sound.

C) The children are combining mathematics counting and word study.

D) The children are doing a strategy sheet based on a particular word family.

17) As he walks up and down the hallway, Mr. Adams, the new Assistant Principal, continually hears Ms. Brown telling her children to go to the wall. Mr. Adams looks briefly at the literacy block schedule and continues on his walk through the building. He realizes that Ms. Brown's children are at work on:

A) A new hall display.

B) Taking down an old display and then redoing it for a new theme.

C) Adding words to their spelling word wall.

D) Measuring the height of plants for a mathematics lesson.

18) Randy is proud of how many new vocabulary words he has learned. He enjoys playing with a device his teacher has, since it helps him to show all the words he can create from various letters. The device is a:

A) Word strip.

B) Letter holder for making words.

C) Word mask.

D) None of the above.

19) Ability grouping means:

A) Grouping of children according to the results of an IQ test.

B) Grouping of children with similar test results for instructional purposes.

C) Grouping of children according to their oral reading accuracy rate.

D) Grouping of children wit similar needs for instructional purposes.

20) Tim is not in the same ability group as his best friend Alex. He starts to cry even though he is a second grader. The teacher comforts him by telling him the truth that:

A) He is just as smart as Alex.

B) He can play with Alex during recess.

C) Ability groups change as the children's needs in them change during the year.

D) Tim is smarter than his best friend Alex.

21) "Beautiful Beth is the Best Girl in the Bradley Bay area." This sentence could be used to help children learn about:

    A) Assonance.

    B) Alliteration.

    C) Rhyming pairs.

    D) None of the above.

22) Greg Ball went to an author signing where Faith Ringgold gave a talk about one of her many books. He was so inspired by her presence and by his reading of her book *TAR BEACH,* that he used the book for his reading and writing workshop activities. His supervisor wrote in his plan book, that he was pleased that Greg had used the book as an/a _____ book.

    A) Basic book.

    B) Feature book.

    C) Anchor book.

    D) Focus book.

23) A delegation from the United Kingdom has come to the United States and since they are considering adapting the balanced literacy approach, they are very interested in seeing the small group demonstrated. Mr. Adams knows that he should bring them into Greg's room when Greg is doing which activity?

    A) A mini lesson.

    B) A conference with individual students.

    C) A time when children are divided into small and independent study groups.

    D) A read-aloud.

24) As the visitors from the United Kingdom tour the school, they are pleased to hear a sing-song chant "Don't fall asleep at the page, don't forget the _____ " Mr. Adams explains to them that the first graders are learning about pointing at words and moving from the left to the right, this is called:

    A) Directionality

    B) Return sweep

    C) Top to bottom

    D) Line for line reading

25) **Andrew is just starting school, but it looks like he will be successful in reading because:**

    A) He comes from a family which cares about his progress.

    B) He is phonemically aware and knows his alphabet.

    C) He has been in pre-school.

    D) He is well behaved.

26) **Gracie seems to be struggling with her reading, even in first grade, although her mother works at a publishing firm and her dad is an editor. Her speech is also full of mispronunciations, although her parents were born in the school neighborhood. Gracie should be checked by:**

    A) A reading specialist.

    B) A speech therapist or an audiologist

    C) A pediatrician.

    D) A psychologist.

27) **Ronald's parents are hearing impaired. He probably will need:**

    A) Extensive work with the use of picture cues

    B) Work with songs, rhymes and read alouds to promote phonemic awareness.

    C) No extra work or support.

    D) None of the above.

28) **Maria was an outstanding student in her elementary school in Brazil. Now she is nervous about starting fourth grade in the US, although she learned English as a second language in Brazil. She and her parents should be relieved to know that:**

    A) She will get extra help in the United States with her English.

    B) There is a positive and strong correlation between a child's native language and his/her learning of English.

    C) Her classmates will help her.

    D) She will have a few months to study for the reading test.

29) Paul is a new teacher. He has just started his logs and assessments for his children's phonemic awareness. He asks a reading teacher to look over his log, but the log is returned to him:

A) Paul gave the log to the wrong colleague.

B) The colleague would not help him out by reviewing it.

C) The log did not have the dates the child's behavior was observed and had no stated performance standards.

D) The log didn't have a cover letter from Paul.

30) The term graphophonemic awareness refers to:

A) Handwriting skills.

B) Letter to sound recognition.

C) Alphabetic principle.

D) Phonemic awareness.

31) A stationery store owner in the neighborhood of the school is amused by the fact that the children on a school walk, are rushing up to various store signs and street signs. The children are probably exploring:

A) The alphabetic principle.

B) The principle that print carries meaning.

C) Letter sound recognition.

D) Phonemic awareness.

32) As Ms. Maxwell enters a first grade class, the teacher is busily writing down what the children are saying. The teacher is probably doing this to:

A) Demonstrate how to copy down speech.

B) Make a connection and promote awareness of the relationship between spoken and written language.

C) Authenticate the children's comments.

D) Raise the children's self esteem.

33) **A district observer notes that fifth graders are showing younger peers in the third grade how to hold a book and walk around with it, they assume:**

A) That the fifth graders are particularly theatrical.

B) That the fifth graders are proud of how they read stories aloud.

C) That the fifth graders are training the younger children in book holding.

D) That this has nothing to do with instruction.

34) **Environmental print is available at all of the following except:**

A) Within a newspaper.

B) On the page of a library book.

C) On a supermarket circular.

D) In a commercial flyer.

35) **Book handling skills include ALL of the following except:**

A) Putting a cellophane or plastic cover on a book.

B) Identifying the back cover of the book.

C) Reading the book jacket.

D) Reading dedication page and the title page of the book.

36) **The best way for a primary grade teacher to model directionality and one to one word matching would be:**

A) Using a regular library or classroom text book.

B) Using her own person reading book.

C) Using a big book.

D) Using a book dummy.

37) **As far as the balanced literacy movement is concerned the "WHOLE" is:**

A) All the reading themes to be covered that day.

B) The whole class meeting for the mini lesson.

C) The complete unit to be covered over the month.

D) All of the reading and writing work to be done in connection with one book.

38) The "TO, WITH, BY" continuum means:

A) The teacher works with the children.

B) The children work Independently.

C) Everything is led by the teacher and taught to the children.

D) The teacher first teachers to the children, then works with them and ultimately the children learn by themselves.

39) Factual book features children should learn include:

A) Captions.

B) Glossaries.

C) Diagrams.

D) All of the above.

40) When they are in 6th grade, children should be able to independently go through an unfamiliar collection and:

A) Use only the table of contents.

B) Use the first line indices, and find a poem by author and subject.

C) Use only the glossary.

D) None of the above.

41) At a faculty meeting Ms. Riley found out that she might have crisscrossers in her class and that Mr. Brown had them and he was happy about it:

A) Crisscrossers are students who have skipped a grade.

B) Crisscrossers are students with excellent skills in reading and in Math.

C) Crisscrossers are second language learners who have a positive attitude toward first and second language learning.

D) Crisscrossers are second language learners who are only positive about English Language Learning.

42) Cues in reading are:

A) Vowel sounds.

B) Digraphs.

C) Sources of information used by readers to help them construct meaning.

D) None of the above.

43) As part of a study for a unit on the history of Massachusetts, Mr. Gentry is using the early childhood book *26 Letters and 99 Cents* by Tina Hoban. He wants his readers to study it and create a more detailed guide to their state using its concept. This is a technique frequently used in:

   A) Reading and writing workshop.

   B) Writing process instruction.

   C) Readers workshop.

   D) Technical writing.

44) A key theorist who supports a phonics centered approach is:

   A) Marie Clay.

   B) Sharon Taberski.

   C) Shelley Harwayne.

   D) Rudolf Flesch.

45) To decode is to:

   A) Construct meaning.

   B) Sound out a printed sequence of letters.

   C) Use a special code to decipher a message.

   D) None of the above.

46) To encode means that you:

   A) Decode a second time.

   B) Construct meaning from a code.

   C) Tell someone a message.

   D) None of the above.

47) There are two basic types of text structure:

   A) Fiction and non-fiction.

   B) Primary and pre-k.

   C) Expository and narrative.

   D) Wordless and text rich.

48) While the supervisor is pleased overall with Barbara's first year of teaching, he feels that given the fact that two of her students are transfers from Mexico and one student has a hearing impairment, she has to plan for:

   A) Extra homework for all of them.

   B) Extra time for the hearing impaired child.

   C) A buddy to work with the two students from Mexico.

   D) Differentiated instruction to meet these students varied special needs.

49) The district is emphasizing that all students in grades 3-6 must focus this month on the reading of functional documents. Ms. Ramirez just smiles and scoops up a handful of free newspapers which she gets on subscription. This is Wednesday and there is a food section. She plans to use:

A) The main news stories.

B) The sports pages.

C) The recipe pages.

D) The comics.

50) Ms. Ramirez also wants the children to share their functional reading skills with their families, so she asks that they take the newspapers home to focus on the:

A) Advice columns.

B) Fill in coupons.

C) Metropolitan news briefs.

D) Weather section.

51) Mr. Adams was pleased with Ms. Ramirez's reading lesson, but he realized that she would have visually represented the comparisons she was trying to get the children to make better, if she had used:

A) a big book.

B) More expressive language.

C) A better literary example.

D) A graphic organizer.

52) Margaret is the winning Ps 123 orator. She loves reciting poetry by Shel Silverstein. Who would guess that she is also a poet in her first language? Margaret's first language is definitely:

A) English.

B) French.

C) Spanish.

D) NOT English.

53) A teacher is asking children to look at the beginning letters of words. She then asks the child to connect the beginning letter to the text and story and to think about what word would make sense there. This is an example of:

A) A balanced literacy approach.

B) A phonemic approach.

C) A phonic approach.

D) AN ELL differentiated approach.

54) The teacher is watching the children go from oral speech into writing. The teacher says, "Great job:"

A) A good decoding.

B) A good recoding.

C) A good encoding.

D) All of the above.

55) By November the first graders have a vocabulary of words which they can correctly pronounce and read aloud. These words are their:

A) Sight vocabulary.

B) Recognition vocabulary.

C) Personal vocabulary.

D) Working vocabulary.

56) As the child is reading and has made an incorrect attempt, the teacher prompts:

A) That is a mistake, do it again.

B) No, you are stupid. .. why can't you get it?

C) Does that make sense to you?

D) Forget it, this is too hard for you.

57) Asking a child if what he or she has read makes sense to him or her, is prompting the child to use:

A) Phonics cues.

B) Syntactic cues.

C) Semantic cues.

D) Prior knowledge.

58) When you ask a child, if what he or she has just read "sounds right" to him or her, you are trying to get that child to use:

A) Phonics cues.

B) Syntactic cues.

C) Semantic cues.

D) Prior knowledge.

59) By definition, which children in a classroom will have trouble with syntactic cues?

    A) Those from families who do not have household libraries.

    B) Those not in a top reading group.

    C) Those from ELL backgrounds.

    D) All of the above.

60) "Self correct" in reading means:

    A) The teacher corrects on the record the errors the child makes.

    B) The child goes back and corrects errors made in a running record.

    C) The reading specialist teaches this to the child.

    D) a and b.

61) A natural role for a highly proficient reader would be:

    A) To assist the teacher with cleaning the classroom and organizing the student folders.

    B) To develop charts for the teacher by copying needed poems for full class study.

    C) Tutor and support struggling readers.

    D) Work on his/her own interests while the teacher works with the rest of the class.

62) A theorist who believes that there is a finite body of approved literature children should be taught on various grade levels and has produced books about what everyone needs to know to be literate on various grade levels is:

    A) Rudolf Flesch

    B) J. David Cooper

    C) John Dewey

    D) E. D. Hirsch

63) **Children "own" words when all of the following happen except:**

A) They find these words on their own.

B) The teacher provides a mandated word list.

C) They use the words in their own writings.

D) The words appear in literature that interests them.

64) **A discussion circle can convene:**

A) After the children have finished reading a text as a group.

B) Before the children read a text as a group.

C) While the reading of the text is going on.

D) All of the above.

65) **To promote word study, children can:**

A) Be required to go to the dictionary at least once or twice a day.

B) Collect and share words of interest they find in their readings.

C) Do vocabulary work sheets from a basal reader or commercial vocabulary book.

D) Do all of the above.

66) **In order to get children to compile specialized vocabulary, they can use:**

A) Newspapers.

B) Internet resources and approved web-sites that focus on the special interest.

C) Experts they can interview.

D) All of the above.

67) **If children are engaged in creating a museum within classroom project to exhibit their work, they are:**

A) Not doing any reading or writing.

B) Doing many authentic reading, writing, and researching tasks.

C) Not likely to visit a real museum.

D) All of the above.

68) **Teachers should select at least ___words for pre-reading vocabulary discussion:**

A) 12.

B) 15.

C) 2-3.

D) 8-10.

69) **The teacher should choose words for pre-story discussion and exploration based on:**

A) The teacher's interest.

B) Whether the teacher feels the children have prior knowledge of or experience with the words.

C) A pre-existing grade level required vocabulary list.

D) Words that will impress his or her supervisor.

70) **Two steps a teacher might take before selecting words for study are:**

A) Reading the story and story mapping.

B) Asking advice from a veteran teacher and the grade leader.

C) Looking in a teacher's guide and copying out the words listed there.

D) All of the above are correct

71) **A teacher discovers after considering his class's prior knowledge of the story material that he would need to teach 12 words at least before he starts teaching the story to the whole group. This indicates:**

A) The children will need a read-aloud.

B) The children will need independent reading.

C) The children will need guided reading.

D) The children will need shared reading.

72) The teacher is very concerned about identifying a book that is "just right" for Jay to read independently. This means that Jay should be able to read this book with:

A) Below 92% accuracy

B) 100% accuracy

C) 95-100% accuracy

D) 92-97% accuracy

73) Jay really wants to read a book that he can only read with 94% accuracy. He could get to read this book as:

A) An independent reading.

B) A guided reading.

C) A shared reading.

D) All of the above.

74) When taking a child's running record, the kinds of self corrections the child makes:

A) Are not important, but the percentage of accuracy is important.

B) May show something about which cueing systems the child relies on.

C) Can be meaningful if analyzed over several records.

D) Both b and c

75) A "decodable text" is:

A) A text that a child can read aloud with correct pronunciations.

B) A text that a child can answer comprehension questions about with a high percentage of accuracy.

C) Text written to match the sequence of letter-sound relationships that have been taught.

D) None of the above.

76) Once a teacher has carefully recorded and documented a running record:

A) There is nothing further to do as long as the teacher keeps the running record for conferences and documentation of grades.

B) The teacher should review the running record and other subsequent ones taken for growth over time.

C) The teacher should differentiate instruction for that particular student as indicated by growth over time and evidence of other needs.

D) Both b and c

77) The reliability of a test is measured by:

A) The number of children who can pass it.

B) The number of children who fail it.

C) The degree to which it measures what it is supposed to measure over time.

D) None of the above

78) A quartile on a test is:

A) A quarter of the grades grouped.

B) The division of the percentiles into four segments each of which is called a quartile.

C) 25 of the tests scored.

D) b and c

79) Validity in assessment means:

A) The test went off without any previewing of the questions or leaks on its contents.

B) The majority of test takers passed.

C) The correct time was allowed for the children to complete the test.

D) The test assessed what it was supposed to assess and measure.

80) Vocabulary should be introduced after reading if:

A) The children have identified words from their reading which were difficult and which they need explained.

B) The text is appropriate for vocabulary building.

C) The teacher would like to teach vocabulary after the reading.

D) a and b

81) The teacher is working on a life science unit in grade five and using many print and electronic sources for information. Some of these words have a linear and some of them a hierarchical relationship to one another. The teacher has spent much time explaining how the words connect with one another. At this point, it would be a good idea to:

A) Use a root family diagram or tree.

B) Work with the base words.

C) Use hierarchical and linear arrays.

D) Start semantic mapping for a particular concept.

82) Direct teaching of a concept or strategy means:

A) The teacher teaches the concept or strategy as part of a genre lesson.

B) The teacher teaches the concept as part of the writing workshop.

C) The teacher explicitly announces to the class that this strategy will be taught.

D) The teacher teaches the strategy to a small group of children or to an individual child.

83) The word "bat" is a ___word for "batter-up":

A) Suffix.

B) Prefix.

C) Root word.

D) Inflectional ending.

84) "Ballgame" is a _____word. Its meaning is derived from the combination of "Ball" and "Game":

A) Contraction.

B) Compound.

C) Portmanteau.

D) Palindrome.

85) In a balanced literacy classroom, new vocabulary would most likely appear on:

A) An experiential chart.

B) A class newspaper.

C) The word wall.

D) Outside the room on a bulletin board.

86) An effective way to build vocabulary and to make connections with mandated science and mathematics material is to teach Greek and Latin roots using:

A) Semantic maps.

B) Hierarchical arrays.

C) Linear arrays.

D) Word webs.

87) As a parent walked through the first grade floor of her school, she kept hearing repeated clapping. Most likely the children were:

A) Clapping to show respect for one another.

B) Rehearsing for how they would clap at a play.

C) Clapping out syllables of multi-syllabic words.

D) All of the above.

88) As part of study about the agricultural products of their state, children have identified 22 different types of apples produced in the state. They can use a _____ to compare and contrast these different types of apples:

   A) Word web.

   B) Semantic map.

   C) Semantic features analysis grid.

   D) All of the above.

89) Based on individual conferences with many children, the teacher realizes that although they are all self-improving readers, they need help in better use of the context to define words. The teacher decided to try the use of:

   A) A dictionary to look up words.

   B) A thesaurus to use with the dictionary.

   C) Contextual redefinition training.

   D) Instruction in how to effectively use a dictionary.

90) The parents of Ramon, a child who has grown up in Puerto Rico and studied English there as a second language, ask that the teacher provide him with individual support in context redefinition. Ramon is scoring above grade level in reading. His mother, who is also a teacher of reading, argues that:

   A) He should get extra help because he has just transferred from another country.

   B) Being walked through the process of using contexts is helpful for an ELL student.

   C) He needs to work with a peer on this skill.

   D) None of the above.

91) A bound morpheme is:

   A) A prefix.

   B) A contraction.

   C) An inflectional ending that can be added to a base word to change its case, gender, number, tense or form.

   D) A root word.

92) **A second grader is writing his first book review. He has conferred with his teacher several times while he was writing the book review. Now he is rehearsing it with the teacher before he reads it aloud to the class. The child's learning of how to compose and deliver a book review has been:**

A) Done independently.

B) Assisted by family support.

C) Done in a cooperative group setting.

D) Scaffolded by the teacher.

93) **One of the many ways in which a child can demonstrate comprehension of a story is by:**

A) Filling in a strategy sheet.

B) Retelling the story orally.

C) Retelling the story in writing.

D) All of the above.

94) **A strategy is:**

A) A practice or routine the teacher can continually refer to.

B) A practice or routine a child can continually refer to or use.

C) A sheet or template for a practice the child can continually fill out.

D) All of the above.

95) **The Stop and Think Strategy means that the child reader will:**

A) Read through until the end of the story or text.

B) Ask himself or herself if what he or she has read makes sense to him or her.

C) Stop after reading some text and write down his/her concerns.

D) All of the above.

96) **Taking responsibility for a child's own learning, will usually involve the child in:**

A) Reading and writing on his/her own.

B) Developing a personal literacy project which will later be shared with the teacher and peers and family.

C) Putting away books and materials when directed.

D) a and b.

97) **"Sounds right" can sound wrong to:**

A) Any reader who is not a fluent or early reader.

B) AN ELL reader.

C) A struggling reader.

D) None of the above.

98) **"Bias" in testing occurs when:**

A) The assessment instrument is not an objective, fair and impartial one for a given cultural, ethnic, or special needs participant.

B) The testing administrator is biased.

C) The same test is given with no time considerations or provisions for those in need of more time or those who have handicapping conditions.

D) All of the above.

99) **Norm-referenced tests:**

A) Give information only about the local samples results.

B) Provide information about the local test takers did compared to a representative sampling of national test takers.

C) Make no comparisons to national test takers.

D) None of the above.

100) If you get your raw score on a test, you will get:

A) The actual number of points you scored on the test.

B) The percentage score of the number of questions you answered correctly.

C) A letter grade for your work on the test.

D) An aggregated score for your performance on the text.

101) The data coordinator of the district who is concerned with federal funding for reading will probably want to start aggregating scores immediately because:

A) It is interesting to crunch more data.

B) By aggregating, the individual scores can be combined to view performance trends across groups.

C) This will help the district determine which groups need more remedial instruction.

D) b and c

102) A standardized test will be:

A) Given out with the same predetermined questions and format to all.

B) Not be given to certain children.

C) If given out in exactly the same format with the same content, may be taken over a lengthier test period (i.e. 4 hours instead of three or two).

D) All of the above.

103) Mr. Mandrake is subbing for Ms. Matley. He sees by the schedule that he is supposed to start the day after the morning meeting with a Read-Aloud. He notes a large picture on the easel and grabs the book just two minutes before the Read-Aloud is to start. He shouldn't heave a sigh of relief because:

A) He needs to be familiar with the book so that he can plan the read-aloud.

B) He does not know if the class has already heard this book.

C) He has not planned vocabulary, themes, or activities to go with the book.

D) All of the above.

104) The science fair is coming up and Ms. Gardner is trying to find time in her busy schedule to work on her class's earth worm diary project. With all of the mandated tests and assemblies, she has not found time to start her students on their earth worm research. Within the context of reading instruction, she can:

A) Begin a thematic study unit.

B) Start with a read aloud of the *Diary of an Earth Worm* by Doreen Cronin.

C) Scaffold the research process by going online with her children using an approved search engine to find matches for earthworm sites.

D) All of the above.

105) Annie's mother has been invited to class to serve as a guest reader. She scoops up her favorite books from her family bookshelf and rushes off to school. When she gets to Annie's classroom, she is greeted and ushered into a rocking chair and given a special hat to wear. The explanation is:

A) The children are excited to have a volunteer and are bored with their teacher day in and day out.

B) This is a class designated author's chair and an author's hat has been worked on by the whole class for anyone who comes to read to them or who reads his/her own writings.

C) Both a and b

D) None of the above.

106) Four of Ms. Wolmark's students have lived in other countries. She is particularly pleased to be studying Sumerian proverbs with them as part of the sixth grade unit in analyzing the sayings of other cultures because:

A) This gives her a break from teaching and the children can share sayings from other cultures they and their families have experienced.

B) This validates the experiences and expertise of ELL learners in her classroom.

C) This provides her children from the US with a lens on other cultural values.

D) All of the above.

107) As Ms. Wolmark looks at the mandated vocabulary curriculum for the 6th grade, she notes that she can opt to teach foreign words and abbreviations which have become part of the English language. She decides:

A) To forego that since she is not a teacher of foreign language.

B) To teach only foreign words from the native language of her four ELL students.

C) To use the ELL students' native languages as a start for an extensive study of foreign language words.

D) To teach 2-3 foreign I language words that are now in English and let it go at that.

108) As Mr. Adams exits his school building, he notices that Mr. Mark, a new teacher, is leading a group of happy looking fifth graders back into the building. They are carrying all kinds of free pamphlets and circulars from a local coffee house. Mr. Adams immediately asks Mr. Mark why the class went to that coffee house during the lunch break. When he hears Mr. Mark's answer, he is delighted:

A) Mr. Mark says they went looking for environmental print and words with a café and latte root.

B) Mr. Mark says they didn't spend any money and got free hot chocolate.

C) The children will have to summarize a pamphlet as homework.

D) All of the above.

109) Mr. Adams has complained to Mr. Mark that there are too many newspapers piled up in his classroom. Mr. Mark has responded that he does not want to throw away these piled up newspapers because:

A) They can be used for letter–sound correspondence.

B) They represent environmental print.

C) They can be used to create print-meaning signs.

D) All of the above.

110) In Ms. Francine's class, dictionary use is a punishment. Mr. Adams is:

A) Pleased with the way that Ms. Francine approaches dictionary use

B) Unconcerned with this approach to the use of the dictionary

C) Convinced that the teacher should model her own fascination and pleasure in using the dictionary for the children.

D) Delighted by the fact that children are being forced to use the dictionary.

111) Dictionary study:

A) can begin in grades 1 or 2.

B) can begin in pre-K using the lush picture dictionaries.

C) should start on grade three level.

D) a and b.

112) An excellent research project that can combine dictionary study with science research would be:

A) A student authored dictionary terms and phrases about earthworms.

B) A teacher developed specialized dictionary of words and phrases about. earthworms.

C) A collection of articles on earthworms put together by the school librarian.

D) b and c.

113) A veteran teacher waited for her adult daughter outside of her daughter's first class in the Teaching of Reading. As she and her daughter talked about the first session of the course, the teacher never heard an explicit mention of the teaching of reading. All she heard about was:

A) Learning about narratives.

B) Dealing with text structures.

C) Constructing meaning.

D) All of the above.

114) Making inferences from the text means that the reader:

A) Is making informed judgments based on available evidence.

B) Is making a guess based on prior experiences.

C) Is making a guess based on what the reader would like to be true of the text.

D) All of the above.

115) Sometimes children can be asked to demonstrate their understanding of a text in a non-written format. This might include all of the following except:

A) A story map.

B) A Venn diagram.

C) Storyboarding a part of the story with dialogue bubbles.

D) Retelling or paraphrasing.

116) A very bright child in a grade one class came from a family which did not a have a strong oral story telling or story reading tradition in its native language. This child would need support in developing:

A) Letter-sound correspondence skills.

B) Schemata for generic concepts most children have in their memories and experiences based on family oral traditions and read a loud.

C) Oral expressiveness.

D) b and c.

117) The concerned parent whose child had a visual impairment wanted as much help for him as the teacher and the school district could give her. She begged: "Please, he didn't attend pre-school, he has no prior knowledge." Strictly speaking this is:

A) Correct, since he didn't get pre-school experiences.

B) Incorrect, since prior knowledge covers everyone's experiences.

C) Incorrect, since he did have prior knowledge experiences but these didn't match those of many of his peers, so he would need to enhance his prior knowledge.

D) b and c

118) Mr. Mark is a brand new teacher who is not from the neighborhood where his school is located. He is a bit nervous as this is his first teaching assignment. He does not yet know how to relax enough to get his students to activate prior experience. He should:

A) Try a free recall question: Tell us what you know about...

B) Try an unstructured Question: Let's talk About...

C) Use word association: What do you associate X with?

D) All of the above.

119) Among the literary strategies that teachers can use to activate prior knowledge are:

A) Predicting and previewing a story.

B) Story mapping.

C) Venn diagramming.

D) Linear arrays.

120) Ms. Angel has to be certain that her fourth graders know the characteristics of the historical fiction genre. She can best support them in becoming comfortable with this genre by:

A) Providing sequel and prequel writing opportunities using that genre.

B) Reading them many different works from that genre.

C) a and b.

D) Having them look up the definition of that genre in a literary encyclopedia.

121) Author's viewpoint questions stump Gary. His teacher can help him by asking him during their reading conferences:

A) If Gary feels the book he is reading, is it just right for him.

B) What the author would say about what the character is doing in the story.

C) How the story can be changed to another genre.

D) If Gary wants to read more books by this author.

122) Ms. Clark-is seen by outside observers from her district, seated in front of her class of sixth graders with a notebook in her lap and an easel. She reads aloud from a book and then writes down a series of questions. As she reads along, she sometimes writes down the answers to her own questions. This is most likely:

A) A sign that Ms. Clark is uncertain of her own comprehension capacity.

B) She is modeling self questioning for the children.

C) She is aware that she is being watched and wants to make a good impression.

D) All of the above.

123) Bill has been called up to the teacher for an individual conference. She asks him to retell one of the books he has listed on his weekly log. He begins and is still talking 7 minutes later. Most probably, Bill:

A) Told the entire story with all its details and minor characters.

B) May or may not have really gotten the main points and perspectives of the story.

C) May have really liked the Story.

D) None of the above.

124) **Ms. Ancess used to take time to have her children memorize major poems and even had an assembly for parents and school staff where the children dramatically recited various poems. Now that she is worried about the children's reading scores, she doesn't want to waste time with this memorization. Actually if she still includes this high interest, child-centered experience:**

A) The children can use their oral fluency and her modeling as a bridge for enhanced comprehension.

B) The children can get a sense of "ownership" of the words.

C) Children and parents will have a "break" from worrying about the test.

D) None of the above.

125) **To help children with "main idea" questions, the teacher should:**

A) Give out a strategy sheet on the main idea for children to place in their reader's notebooks.

B) Model responding to such a question as part of guided reading.

C) Have children create "main idea questions" to go with their writings.

D) All of the above.

Answer Key

1. C	47. C	93. D
2. C	48. D	94. D
3. C	49. C	95. B
4. A	50. B	96. D
5. B	51. A	97. B
6. C	52. D	98. D
7. B	53. C	99. B
8. B	54. B	100. A
9. C	55. B	101. D
10. D	56. C	102. D
11. D	57. C	103. D
12. B	58. B	104. D
13. C	59. C	105. B
14. D	60. B	106. D
15. C	61. C	107. C
16. B	62. D	108. D
17. C	63. B	109. D
18. B	64. A	110. C
19. D	65. D	111. D
20. C	66. D	112. A
21. B	67. B	113. C
22. C	68. C	114. A
23. C	69. B	115. D
24. B	70. D	116. B
25. B	71. C	117. D
26. B	72. D	118. D
27. B	73. A	119. A
28. B	74. D	120. C
29. C	75. A	121. B
30. C	76. C	122. B
31. B	77. C	123. A
32. B	78. B	124. A
33. C	79. D	125. D
34. B	80. D	
35. A	81. C	
36. C	82. C	
37. B	83. C	
38. D	84. B	
39. D	85. C	
40. B	86. D	
41. C	87. C	
42. C	88. D	
43. A	89. C	
44. D	90. B	
45. B	91. C	
46. B	92. D	

Rationales for Sample Questions

1. The correct answer is C. This is a sheer memorization question. By definition, phonemic awareness falls under the phonological awareness umbrella. All of the other choices do not deal with the DIFFERENCE between the two types of awareness.

2. The correct answer is C. Another memorization question which can only be answered by either knowing Adams's theory or by knowing that the other theorists listed did not present that theory. Anywhere from 10-15% of the questions on the certification tests are based on knowledge of the theorists and key terms associated with their theories.

3. The correct answer is C. This question involves the test taker's knowing that in reading the term "oddity task" involves identification of an odd sound within a series of like sounds. Choice A dealing with mathematics plays on that discipline's definition of odd which would not be tested on a foundations of reading exam. The other choices are "common sense definitions" of oddity which are not appropriate answers for a test in reading.

4. The correct answer is A. The key word here is EXCEPT which will be highlighted in upper case on the test as well. All of the options are correct aspects of phonological awareness except the first one, A, because phonological awareness DOES NOT involve print.

5. The correct answer is B. This question requires knowledge of running records and familiarity with error recording and miscues. The test taker has to know that this is the standard format for a running record of reading behaviors and that choices "C" and "D" deal with attitudes and feelings which are not part of the running records used as part of the balanced literacy approach.

6. Choice A is not correct. All children are capable of becoming good readers and the other choices, given Ms. James's dedication, are not the most likely reason these three children (a minority of the class) are struggling. The correct answer is C.

7. The answer is "B" because all of the other options are essential for record keeping. The key word here is "EXCEPT."

8. The answer is "B" because the teacher does not want the room to appear more spacious, but wants parents to have a feel for the book bags which indicate the primacy of reading.

9. The answer is "C" and this is a memorization question.

10. All the answers are correct.

11. Given the fact this is a kindergarten in a public housing project, she will be most successful with wordless picture books, since there is no guarantee the children have had prior exposure to the other types of books listed. The answer "D" will allow them to construct a story from the pictures.

12. The answer is "B" because the question details that the adults are seated two by two holding copies of the same book. This is the buddy reading style.

13. The answer is "C" and this is a memorization question.

14. The answer is "D", Marie Clay, and this is a name you "have to know" from this guide or your courses.

15. This is a classic manifestation of "C", the logographic phrase of phonics learning.

16. The answer is "B", and again this answer would grow out of teaching experience and familiarity with manipulatives or reading this guide.

17. The answer is "C" because in today's balanced literacy classroom, a wall is a word wall.

18. The answer is "B" and this is a familiar device in today's reading classroom.

19. The answer is "D" and this is a key definition which should be memorized.

20. The answer is "C" by definition; also a teacher would never get into the other personal comments which are offered as choices with a second grader.

21. This is a question that any English literature or Reading major can answer. The answer is "B."

22. This is another question using current terminology. While all the other choices make sense, "C" is correct because a book that is used to teach reading and writing is called an Anchor book.

23. "C" is the only correct answer choice because small refers to group size.

24. The answer is "B" and this term is in the Glossary.

25. This IS a deliberately tricky question. Each of the choices has merit. The best choice is "B" because that one is confirmed by current research.

26. This one is "B" because Gracie is a neighborhood child and shouldn't be having these difficulties with pronunciation.

27. This is one you can work out. The answer is "B" because obviously Ronald's parents will not be singing with him and doing lots of read alouds.

28. All of these choices have an element of truth in them, but go with "B" which reflects research results.

29. The answer is "C" because all logs need to have dates and standards.

30. The answer is "C" and it is a definition question.
If you missed it, re-read through the Glossary.

31. The behavior described here only matches one reading activity, "B."

32. This is another deliberately tricky question. All of the answers may appeal to you, but, choice "B" is the theoretical way to describe what the teacher is doing when he or she writes down what the children are saying.

33. This is a standard part of "book holding", so that the answer is "C."

34. The key word here is "EXCEPT" and environmental print is not defined as print in a library book, so choice "B" is the right one.

35. Ironically "A" is correct because book handling as defined in reading, does not include putting covers on books.

36. Key word in this question is "best" and the answer is "C" because this type of a book is best for teaching and display.

37. This is another deliberately tricky question, since all of the answers make sense, but only "B" is correct because that is the definition of "WHOLE" in balanced literacy.

38. The answer is "D" and is another definition question.

39. The answer is "D." All of the above is the correct answer because captions, glossaries and diagrams are but three of the text features that students need to be able to identify in a text. Other text features include headings, charts, maps, indexes, and tables

40. This is a question, you can reason out. The most complex task described here is "B.".

41. This is a definition question and the answer is "C."

42. This too is a definition question and the answer is "C."

43. The answer is "A." The fact that Mr. Gentry wants his class to use this for both reading and writing , should help you pick the right choice even if you don't know the answer.

44. The answer is "D." Flesch was a proponent of the phonics approach to reading in his book "Why Johnny Can't Read" which was essentially a critique of the American educational system. Neither of the other three choices propose explicit teaching of phonics to help children master reading.

45. The answer is "B" and a definition question.

46. The answer is "B" and is a definition question. If you are missing many definitions, perhaps make flash cards of the Glossary words and study them intensively.

47. The answer is "C," Expository and Narrative. Fiction and non-fiction are genres, Primary and pre-K are grade levels, and Wordless and text rich are types of books for young children.

48. This is a tricky question because all of the choices have an element of truth in them. But the best choice is "D" because it includes the special approaches Barbara will have to take with her ELL and special needs students.

49. Functional literacy refers to knowing things that students have to do on a day to day basis. Reading a recipe is classified as functional literacy because students learn how to read directions to perform a task. The answer is "C."

50. Coupons, like want ads are functional the families can fill in or act on. The answer is "B."

51. The answer is "A" because the BIG BOOK is a good visual display tool, ' .

52. This is a deliberately misleading question; all the test taker can know for certain is that Margaret's first language is NOT English. You know she is an ELL student because the question talks about her "first language." The answer is "D."

53. The focus on letters and sounds is "C" a phonics approach.

54. This is another definition question; read the definition section carefully before the exam. The answer has to be "B."

55. The term is "B" recognition vocabulary. This is a definition you have to know.

56. Obviously, "B" can not be right. Generally, a caring teacher would not say "D," but "C" is the preferred wording in use now in reading classrooms.

57. Semantic cues are the hints that students can discern from the reading to help them make sense of the text. In some cases, the message of the text depends on the other words around them, so students learn how to determine the meaning from context clues. The answer must be "C."

58. This is another one of those answers using the language of linguistics in reading. The answer has to be "B," syntactic clues.

59. This question can actually only have a single correct answer. It is "C" because by definition a child from an ELL background does not have a strong accurate sense of what "sounds right" in English.

60. There is only one correct answer here and it is "B." This is a key principle of the running record.

61. While all of the choices are possibilities, the concept of the highly proficient reader tutoring leads to answer "C."

62. The answer is "D" and this has to be memorized and known.

63. Again the test taker has to find the choice which is incorrect and it is choice "B" when the teacher puts up a mandated word list.

64. By definition, a discussion group can convene only "A" after the children have read a work.

65. All of the answers will promote vocabulary, so the answer is "D."

66. The answer is "D" because all of the responses are correct.

67. There is only one correct answer here and it is logical, "B."

68. The correct answer is "C," 2-3 words. Teachers should select a small number of words for pre-teaching to allow the students time to comprehend the text and achieve the objectives related to the reading. For example, in a non-fiction text, these words could be key terms related to the main topic. Even students with an extensive oral vocabulary may not be able to recognize words in print because they are not words that they normally encounter in their reading. The activities the teacher plans in relation to the words will help the students internalize the strategies more readily when only a few words are selected each time.

69. This is another one where the correct answer is "B" and only "D" is an unlikely choice.

70. This is one you can reason through and choose "D" easily.

71. This is one you can reason through, if you know that generally during READ ALOUD you do not stop to explain many words. You would not want to give material for independent or shared reading where so many words had to be explained. Hence the correct choice is "C," guided reading.

72. The answer is "D" because those are the "just right percentages."

73. The answer by definition is "A" because if "just right." is synonymous with the independent reading level.

74. The answer is "D" and related to taking a child's running record.

75. This is choice "A" which is the definition of decodable.

76. Students learn at different rates, therefore students in any class will be at varying levels of learning. By differentiating instruction and incorporating assessment **for** learning rather than assessment **of** learning, teachers can help students succeed. When teachers assess student growth over time and monitor the areas in which they are experiencing difficulty, they can alter the instruction and the activities to match student needs. The answer is "C."

77. This is a definition question and the answer is "C."

78. While this is also a definition question, choice "B" is one that a linguist would choose.

79. "D" is the answer here and it also makes good sense to the test taker.

80. This is a question the literate test taker should be able to "reason" through. Vocabulary introduced by children and a good text with opportunities to expand vocabulary are needed. Answer "D" which includes both "A" and "B" is the right choice.

81. The astute test taker should get this right whether he or she actually knows these materials or not. "Hierarchical" appears in both the question and in the correct choice "C."

82. The answer is "C" and this is a definition question.

83. The answer is "C."

84. Answer "B."

85. The answer can only be "C" and should be part of the test taker's theoretical background.

86. The answer is "D" and historically these have been used to teach Greek and Latin roots.

87. This is related to phonics and the answer is "C."

88. The answer here is "D" and all of these graphic organizers would work with the topic of apples.

89. The answer is "C" and the trick is to notice the "better use of context" in the question and match it up with "C," contextual redefinition training.

90. The answer is "B" and it is one that is confirmed in theory and is referenced in this guide.

91. The answer is "C," a definition question.

92. This is easy to see that it is "D", scaffolded by the teacher. The child has been assisted by the teacher as he prepared the book review.

93. The answer is "D" since all the options are good ones.

94. The answer is again "D" since all the options work.

95. This is a tricky question and requires that the test taker know the very specific definition of the STOP and THINK strategy to know that the only correct answer is "B."

96. Again this has to do with the way "responsibility for your own learning" is now defined and the answer is "D."

97. This is a truism of ELL education and the answer is "B."

98. This is one where the correct answer of "D" is also the commonsense response that a literate test taker would select.

99. There is only a correct answer here by definition and "B" is it.

100. Again these are all definitions which the test taker should memorize before the test (see the Glossary in this guide). The correct answer is "A."

101. Again this is a definition answer and the correct choice is "D."

102. This is all about what a standardized test means and answer is "D."

103. The answer is "D," but this is a question anyone who has gotten through the coursework or taught, should have no problem with.

104. This is a question someone who has taught or gone through course work should ace to get "D." Remember going online with children and using approved search engines is fine.

105. The best answer is "B" and involves knowing about the "author's chair" concept.

106. This a question where the correct answer "D" makes good common and educational sense.

107. This is a question where you can reason your way to the correct answer, "C." "A" sounds chauvinistic and unrealistic and "B" is limiting and teaching only 2-3 words is not a good use of instructional time.

108. This is a question where the correct choice is "D" and makes good teaching and learning sense.

109. This is a question where choice "D" makes good sense to a teacher who knows the value of having newspapers for class projects.

110. The word "punishment" in the question should alert the test taker to the answer that the only choice "C" can be right.

111. This is a question that any literate test taker who has been in a children's book section recently can answer. Choice "D" is correct.

112. This question is tricky in that only choice "A", which deals with a student product, is correct. The others are all adult centered.

113. The only answer here is "C" which emphasizes "constructing meaning," the current phrase for "reading."

114. This is a definition question that a literate test taker can answer based on the general definition of inferences. The answer is "A."

115. Answer "D" is correct. Retelling and paraphrasing can be in oral form whereas the other choices all involve writing or the use of pencil and paper. By asking students to retell a story, the teacher can determine the level of comprehension. Of course, this has to be modeled for the student, especially paraphrasing, so that the student relates the important facts or events and does not include any information that is not necessary.

116. Although the question appears to be a very technical one, it actually can be easily and correctly answered by seeing how choice "B" echoes the fact that most children would have schemata based on family oral traditions.

117. This is a question which a caring and literate test taker could correctly answer and get "D" as a response. Everyone has prior knowledge of some sort.

118. Again this is a common sense question and "D" is the correct choice.

119. This is a question that a literate test taker could answer and the best choice is "A" because in their predictions, children evidence prior knowledge.

120. The answer is "C. "Online encyclopedias meet the information technology outcomes that align with language arts outcomes. When students are taught to avail of the online encyclopedias, it can save enormous amounts of space in the classroom as well as trips to the library. Students can complete all their work on the computer without having to stop and thumb through a regular encyclopedia to find the information they need.

121. This is a question where the correct choice "B" is the only one that mentions an author.

122. The only answer here is "B" because this is a technique children are taught and Ms. Clark is modeling it. "C" is insulting to Ms. Clark and "A" is insulting as well.

123. The only obvious choice after 7 minutes of talk is "A."

124. Choice "A" is the best theory answer here.

125. This is one where all the options are right. The answer is "D."

Constructed Response Questions

Constructed Response Question One
Jean is a first year teacher who is taking over the classroom of a thirty-year veteran teacher who is retiring. Jean goes in to meet with the teacher. The teacher, Ms. Banks, talks about the importance of teaching the young first graders the concepts of print.

She gives Jean a list of these concepts and suggests that Jean create some assessment format so that she can be certain that all of her first graders learn these concepts. She also tells Jean that she will be volunteering her time in a neighborhood preschool program close to her home and so she will be taking her private books and materials with her. She suggests that Jean go over the list of concepts of print and consider the needs of her class as she prepares for teaching this crucial set of skills. Before Jean leaves the classroom, Ms. Banks tells her that the kindergarten teacher has let her know that three children who will be in her class next year are from ELL backgrounds where their families are not involved in oral story telling or reading from native language texts.

Ms. Banks' concepts of print list:

- STARTS ON LEFT

- GOES FROM LEFT TO RIGHT

- RETURN SWEEP

- MATCHES WORDS BY POINTING

- POINTS TO JUST ONE WORD

- POINTS TO FIRST AND LAST WORD

- POINTS TO 1 LETTER

- POINTS TO FIRST AND LAST LETTER

- PARTS of the BOOK: Cover, Title Page, Dedication page, Author and Illustrator

Jean thanks Ms. Banks for all of this help and asks if she can send Ms. Banks some of her teaching ideas for Concepts of Print and the ways she plans to differentiate instruction for her ELL students before the end of the year. Ms. Banks smiles and says she feels good to know that her classroom will be taken over by Jean. She promises to review Jean's response.

Constructed Response Answer One

First, as far as assessment for the key skills of concepts of print, I have decided that it is very important that I have a record of when and how well each of my students masters these concepts. After much thought, I realized that I will be keeping assessment notebooks for all of my students as part of my general reading and teaching. Therefore, I plan to print out all the key concepts of print on an 8" x 11" piece of paper in a grid format. This sheet will be included with other assessment grids for each individual child.

After conferencing with the child and I determine the child has demonstrated mastery of a particular concept, I will check it off on the grid and date that mastery. If I have other comments to make about the child's level of mastery or fluency, I will make an anecdotal notation about the child as well. I think that this will guarantee that I have a detailed checklist record and anecdotal record of all my children's individual progress on concepts of print.

I plan to use big books and many of the latest picture books, including Caldecott award winners in demonstrating and sharing with children many of the concepts of print. I will do much of my instruction mini-lessons. In fact I intend to use some of my own favorite alphabet books to introduce these conventions. With a book like Clare Beaton's, *Zoe and her Zebra*, I can easily and naturally cover the title page, cover, illustrator, and also manage to engage the children in the use of repetitive language.

Once I have shared that delightful book with the children as a read-aloud, we will be able to return to it again and use the repetitive language of it in its big book format to demonstrate for the children how they can point under each word as if there is a button to push. I can also demonstrate for the children how they should start at the top of the text and move from left to right. I will model going back to the left and under the previous line in a return weep.

After modeling this as part of the mini-lesson, the children can be divided in small groups or pairs and take other big book and practice the "point under each word" and the "return sweep" as part of "shared reading" or buddy reading. I should be able to identify some highly proficient readers who will be happy to serve as 'buddy" reader/tutors for the ELL children. I will ask that these "buddies" take time in small groups to work on another book from the alphabet book collection to share with the class as a whole. The use of the alphabet books also helps me to get some time in on the alphabetic principle.

I will also do a classroom writing workshop using the original alphabet book I use for the read-aloud, say *Zoe and Her Zebra* as a model for creating our own story. Perhaps we will call it *Barry and his Boxer*. In this way we will have a concrete literary product that demonstrates the children's mastery of and fluency in the concepts of print as they create an "in style of" story about a peer using illustrations, title page, dedication page, numbering of pages, back and front cover and other concepts of print.

I think that using individualized assessments, a group/class collaborative writing project, and an anchor alphabet book will help me successfully teach the concepts of print and address the needs of my ELL learners as well.

Constructed Response Question Two

Marianne has been selected as one of a team of teachers who will start teaching in a brand new school building that has been under construction for several years. While Marianne, a grade three teacher , is thrilled to be moving into new facilities, she is a bit overwhelmed to have to "set up her room" all over again at the new site. Her administrator, Mr. Adams, tells her that there are five new teachers with no previous experience teaching primary school age children who will be on staff. He tells her that these educators could really use help setting up their classrooms.

Marianne smiles and decides that she would very much like to use her set-up of her own grade three classroom as a workshop and demonstration for setting up a literacy teaching environment for these new staff members. Mr. Adams thinks that is a great idea and asks Marianne for an agenda and for a general description of what she will cover in her three hour workshop so that he can give it to the district office.

Marianne is happy to comply because she realizes that she will be assisting new colleagues and getting ten helping hands to help her set up all the materials she has accumulated over a twenty-year career.

Constructed Response Answer Two

The concept of sharing with new colleagues how to set up a classroom is very exciting to me. I know, based on my experiences, how crucial a well-planned and conceptualized space is for young learners' literacy learning. Therefore this is an agenda for what I will cover in my three hour in service session for my new colleagues.

First, I will discuss how whatever the size of the classroom space, it must be sectioned off into the following areas: a meeting area, with a sofa or "soft" setting; a chair, easel and basket to store book bags; a conference table; children's tables; and bin/basket main area for trade books; and another space for computers.

I may even give out a diagram of my classroom from my old school and some pictures. We will discuss collaboratively how I will set up my own new space as well as how they will want to set up their own spaces to allow for different uses of space within their own classrooms.

I will get into the issue of whether or not they want to have a traditional desk or use smaller tables for everyone. I think that they will need time to consider their own teaching styles in this regard. All teachers need to set up a space where they can easily confer with children and have access to individual assessment notebooks, reading folders (plus poetry/spelling, reading response, and handwriting notebooks) for all their students. I intend to show them how to prepare these folders for each child and how to store them so they can get to them when they need to make additional annotations for each child. Given the fact that I am working with new colleagues, I suspect that this will take at least an hour and a half of our time. I am also going to model for them a weekly reading log.

Most important of all, I am going to spend the major amount of time talking to them about the book bins as I place mine around the classroom. I will show them how to label the books using the Fountas and Pinnell levels and how to arrange the book bins with the spines out so that the children can see the books. Together we will examine how the bookcases should be close to the walls and the expository books should be separated from the narrative texts. I will also get together my audio-cassettes and book sets so that they can see how I set up my read-along center for all my children. I will share some dual language tapes I use with ELL students as well. I have some extra "author's hats" and author's chair slipcovers I will share with them.

I also intend to show them how to select big books for the easel display and anchor books to be shown there as well. By the way, I will also coach them how to write away for supplies and how to store supplies in common areas so that some children are not missing necessary materials for class activities.

Even though we are focusing on literacy, I am going to show them where to store mathematics materials, other texts, and art supplies. I will end the session by making sure that they know where to place their chart wall and the word wall. If I have time, I will sit down with each of them and start them on the word wall and some key charts for their first day. They will leave my room with an actual experience of setting up a literacy environment, plus viable teaching and reading suggestions for the first day. Most importantly, I will be available for an in-school classroom consultation, if necessary.

Tips and Reflections for tackling the Constructed Response Questions:

- Use as many phrases and words from the question as possible in your response.

- Be specific. Mention specific books, authors, theorists, and strategies you have studied. Even though this is a test about the teaching of reading, make specific use of children's trade books and literature if appropriate.

- Use as many details as you are given in the question to make your response. Write no more than 5-7 moderately brief paragraphs. The more you write, the larger the margin for error. Check your spelling, grammar and check to see that you answered everything that was asked, but no more than what was asked. Be positive and proactive about your ability to respond to whichever situation is presented.

- Stick with strategies, teaching ideas, and methods that are tried and true.

- Reread your writing at least twice for spelling and grammatical errors.

Additional Professional Citations

Block, Cathy Collins. (2002). *Comprehension Instruction: Research Based Practices.* New York: The Guilford Press.

Calkins, Lucy McCormick. (2001). *The Art of Teaching Reading.* New York: Longman.

Cambourne, Briane. (2002). "Conditions for Literacy Learning." *The Reading Teacher,* 55, (8): 758-62.

Cambourne, Briane. (1993). *The Whole Story: Natural Learning and the Acquisition of Literacy in the Classroom.* Auckland, NZ: Ashton, Scholastic.

Cunningham, Patricia M. (2000). *Phonics They Use: Words for Reading and Writing.* 3rd Edition. New York: Addison Wesley Longman.

Evidence Based Reading Instruction. (2002) Articles from International Reading Association. Newark, Delaware: *International Reading Association.*

Hoyt, Linda. (2002). *Make it Real-Strategies for Success with Informational Texts.* Portsmouth, NH: Heinemann.

Kimball-Lopez, Kimberley. (1999). *Connecting with Traditional Literature.* Boston: Allyn and Bacon.

Moustafa, Margaret. (1997). *Beyond Traditional Phonics.* Portsmouth, NH: Heinemann.

Owocki, Gretchen. (2003). *Strategic Instructions for K-3 Students.* Portsmouth, NH: Heinemann.

Owacki, G, and Y. Goodman. (2002). *Kidwatching-Documenting Children's Literacy Development.* Portsmouth, NH: Heinemann.

Quindlen, Anna. (1998). *How Reading Changed My Life.* New York: Ballantine Books, 1998.

Routman, Regie. (2000). *Conversations.* Portsmouth, NH: Heinemann.

Schultz, C. (2000). *How Partner Reading Fosters Literacy Development in First Grade Students.* Action Research project, Saginaw Valley State University, University Center, Michigan.

Short, K., J. Harste and C. Burke. (1996). *Creating Classrooms for Authors and Inquirers.* Portsmouth, NH: Heinemann.

Trelease, Jim. (2001). *The Read-Aloud Handbook*. 4th Ed. New York: Penguin.
Wilde, Sandra. (2000). *Miscue Analysis Made Easy: Building on Student Strengths*. Portsmouth, NH: Heinemann.

Wilde, Sandra. (2000). *Reading Made Easy*. Portsmouth, NH: Heinemann.

XAMonline, INC. 21 Orient Ave. Melrose, MA 02176

Toll Free number 800-509-4128

TO ORDER Fax 781-662-9268 OR www.XAMonline.com

TEXAS EXAMINATION OF EDUCATOR STANDARDS- EXAMINATION FOR THE CERTIFICATION OF EDUCATORS - TEXES/EXCET - 2007

PO#   Store/School:

Address 1:

Address 2 (Ship to other):

City, State Zip

Credit card number_____-_____-_____-_____   expiration_____

EMAIL _____

PHONE   **FAX**

13# ISBN 2007	TITLE	Qty	Retail	Total
978-1-58197-925-1	ExCET ART SAMPLE TEST (ALL-LEVEL-SECONDARY) 005 006			
978-1-58197-949-7	TExES CHEMISTRY 8-12 140			
978-1-58197-938-1	TExES COMPUTER SCIENCE 141			
978-1-58197-933-6	TExES ENGLISH LANG-ARTS AND READING 4-8 117			
978-1-58197-935-0	TExES ENGLISH LANG-ARTS AND READING 8-12 131			
978-1-58197-926-8	ExCET FRENCH SAMPLE TEST (SECONDARY) 048			
978-1-58197-930-5	TExES GENERALIST 4-8 111			
978-1-58197-945-9	TExES GENERALIST EC-4 101			
978-1-58197-946-6	TExES SCIENCE 4-8 116			
978-1-58197-931-2	TExES SCIENCE 8-12 136			
978-1-58197-604-5	TExES LIFE SCIENCE 8-12 138			
978-1-58197-932-9	TExES MATHEMATICS 4-8 114-115			
978-1-58197-937-4	TExES MATHEMATICS 8-12 135			
978-1-58197-939-8	TExES MATHEMATICS-PHYSICS 8-12 143			
978-1-58197-948-0	TExES MATHEMATICS-SCIENCE 4-8 114			
978-1-58197-929-9	TExES PEDAGOGY AND PROFESSIONAL RESPONSIBILITIES 4-8 110			
978-1-58197-899-5	TExES PEDAGOGY AND PROFESSIONAL RESPONSIBILITIES 8-12 130			
978-1-58197-943-5	TExES PHYSICAL EDUCATON EC-12 158			
978-1-58197-928-2	TExES PRINCIPAL 068			
978-1-58197-941-1	TExES READING SPECIALIST 151			
978-1-58197-942-8	TExES SCHOOL COUNSELOR 152			
978-1-58197-940-4	TExES SCHOOL LIBRARIAN 150			
978-1-58197-934-3	TExES SOCIAL STUDIES 4-8 118			
978-1-58197-936-7	TExES SOCIAL STUDIES 8-12 132			
978-1-58197-927-5	ExCET SPANISH (SECONDARY) 047			
978-1-58197-944-2	TExES SPECIAL EDUCATION EC-12 161			

	SUBTOTAL
FOR PRODUCT PRICES GO TO WWW.XAMONLINE.COM	Ship $8.25
	TOTAL